STUDIES IN GDR CULTURE AND SOCIETY 8

Selected Papers from the Thirteenth New Hampshire Symposium on the German Democratic Republic

Editorial Board:

Margy Gerber, Chief Editor
Christine Cosentino
Volker Gransow
Nancy A. Lauckner
Christiane Lemke
Arthur A. Stahnke
Alexander Stephan
W. Christoph Schmauch

UNIVERSITY PRESS OF AMERICA

Lanham • New York • London

Copyright © 1988 by

University Press of America,® Inc.

4720 Boston Way
Lanham, MD 20706

3 Henrietta Street
London WC2E 8LU England

Printed in the United States of America

British Cataloging in Publication Information Available

Co-published by arrangement with the
International Symposium of the German Democratic Republic

"Rock Music and Everyday Culture in the GDR"
© 1988 by Peter Wicke

ISBN 0–8191–7047–X (pbk. : alk. paper)
ISBN 0–8191–7046–1 (alk. paper)

Table of Contents

iii

Contributors to the Volume   205

Acknowledgments

The editors wish to express their thanks to the publishing house Der Morgen in Berlin for granting them permission to print an English translation of Heinz Knobloch's "Der Max-Herrmann-Preis" from his *Berliner Grabsteine.* (1987).

Preface

With the exception of the prose text by Heinz Knobloch, the articles collected here are revised versions of papers presented at the Thirteenth New Hampshire Symposium on the German Democratic Republic, which took place at the World Fellowship Center near Conway, N.H. from June 19-26, 1987.

The general theme of the Symposium, which was attended by GDR specialists from the United States, Canada, the Federal Republic, and the GDR, was *Alltag* in the GDR. A special section was devoted to Berlin in commemoration of the 750th anniversary of the city's founding. Other seminar topics included regional differences in the GDR, quality of life, film and popular culture, the GDR and its international environment, methodology, and literature and aesthetics. Some thirty papers were given by sociologists, political scientists, Germanists, film critics, and others in combined sections.

The Symposium is pluralistic in its philosophy. It has no particular political stance and welcomes well-argued and well-documented views from all sides. With the increased participation of specialists and authors from the GDR in recent years — seven attended in 1987 — the Symposium has become a meeting place between East and West.

This present volume includes contributions from four GDR participants: Heinz Knobloch, author and columnist for the Berlin *Wochenpost,*; Lothar Bisky, cultural sociologist and *Rektor* of the Hochschule für Film und Fernsehen of the GDR, Manfred Lötsch, sociologist at the Akademie für Gesellschaftswissenschaften beim ZK der SED, and Peter Wicke, director of the Forschungszentrum populäre Musik at the Humboldt Universität in Berlin. While not necessarily in agreement with all views presented, the members of the Editorial Board consider it important that GDR scholars have the opportunity to participate in Western discussion of the

GDR, and that Western GDR specialists be familiar with GDR positions and research.

With this volume, as with the seven that have preceded it, we would make research results presented at the Symposium available to a wider audience and thus promote both research and teaching about the GDR.

Margy Gerber
Chief Editor

The Max Herrmann Prize

Heinz Knobloch

Every year in May, during Book Week, one of the librarians at the German National Library in Berlin is awarded the Max Herrmann Prize. The prize was instituted in 1979. Of our libraries only the National Library presents a prize of its own. To qualify for it one must have attended to the readers' needs in an exemplary fashion.

The bestowal ceremony, quite an informal affair, is held in the conference room hung with oil paintings of men who have administered the library and added to its treasures since 1661. It must be an odd feeling for Professor Dr. Friedhilde Krause to know that one day in the distant future her portrait will be added to this gallery. And that, later still, no-one will be surprised to see a woman as director of the library.

Anyone looking for Max Herrmann (1865-1942) among those portrayed looks in vain. Max Herrmann was never on the staff of the library, he was just a reader. But what a reader! A friend of many years' standing, an insatiable library user, a giver and taker, one of those readers who are the delight of librarians, since their queries make the latter take no end of pains, which in turn pleases librarians, as they are there to be consulted — and that is the way they like it, to be smart and resourceful and considerate.

Max Herrmann was a university professor in Berlin, where he founded a department concerned with the science of dramatic arts. He was a stimulator, collector and editor, a humanist and passionate seeker of truth who, ten days before the Book Burning in 1933, came out against the attempts to stifle freedom of thought. And he was dismissed from the university where he had taught for forty-five years. Because his father had been a Jew.

At first Herrmann, who continued to work untiringly, was still allowed to use the university library; then only the National Library (in which an entire department owes its existence to his industry). Then he was denied permission to enter the reading room; then he could no longer borrow books; and, finally, he could only look at the books on the circulation desk, and that while standing. Then this privilege too was withdrawn.

We know these details through Dr. Ruth Möwius, his student, to whom he entrusted his last manuscript (*The Rise of Professional Acting*) in a hallway on August 29, 1942. Some 600 closely written, exercise-book pages composed in circumstances so difficult as to be hardly conceivable. Eleven days after that, Max Herrmann was deported to Theresienstadt, where he died shortly thereafter.

Ruth Möwius has described the scholar's route to the National Library, on foot, since, being a Jew, he was not allowed to use public conveyances, nor set foot in a park, nor rest on a park bench. He had to make a detour, certain streets in the city center being out of bounds to Jews. Arriving at the National Library after a two-hour trudge he sat down exhausted on a sofa there; "a few seconds later an official approached him, telling the seventy-five-year-old to get up, because as a Jew he had no right to sit anywhere in the building of the National Library."

Every year in May our National Library gives the Max Herrmann Prize for courteous treatment of its users.

(Translation of "Der Max-Herrmann-Preis" from Heinz Knobloch's *Berliner Bausteine* [Berlin: Buchverlag Der Morgen, 1987])

East Berlin as a Metropolis

Richard L. Merritt

In its four decades of existence East Berlin has by and large failed to attract the attention of Western scholars and writers. More fascinating have been the broader Berlin *problématique* in global politics, spectacular events such as the Blockade in 1948-49 and the wall's construction in 1961, West Berlin's security needs, its subsidized economy, and student unrest. East Berlin suffers by comparison. The result is that, although many of us Westerners have passed through the city, we know precious little about East Berlin *qua* city.

This lack of attention is unfortunate. First of all, East Berlin is a major world municipality of some interest. Then, too, its history has much to say about processes of political development. Transforming its 700-year integration with the city's western region into a model communist city that now has its focus toward the east has been a major task. Ultimately, however, it is not international crisis management but "normal" policymaking that shapes a municipality's future — decisions to build or not to build a new sewage treatment plant, to direct potential students toward one rather than another course of study, to find the appropriate mix of strategies that can boost production without damaging the quality of the water or air, in short, to deal effectively with the host of events that make up the political environment of a city.

This article explores the question, How can we understand East Berlin as a metropolis *in its own right*? In other words, what do we need to find out before we can see East Berlin in its proper comparative perspective as one of the major capital cities of the world? I shall illustrate dimensions of this question by looking at two areas of middle-level politics in East Berlin. One, city planning, focuses on public policymaking and management, that is, how the governmental system decides what is to be done and undertakes the necessary steps to implement its decisions. The other, relations between church and state, involves social as well as governmental agencies. In this case, the government may set parameters for outcomes but is unable to control completely the behavior of other significant actors as it can in its planning activities.

Legal Status of East Berlin

This is not the place to recount in detail the development of Berlin's status in international law. Great Britain, the Soviet Union, and the United States, in the London Protocol of September 12, 1944, specified:

> Germany, within her frontiers as they were on the 31st December, 1937, will, for the purposes of occupation, be divided into three zones, one of which will be allotted to each of the three Powers, *and* a special Berlin area, which will be under joint occupation by the three Powers.[1]

The protocol was expanded in early 1945 to include France as a fourth occupation power. But, of course, the split among the wartime Allies and the resulting cold war ended their joint occupation in fact if not in legal principle. The Berlin Blockade that began in June 1948 ended formal ties in the city between the Soviet Union, on the one hand, and America, Britain, and France, on the other. A few weeks later unruly mobs forced representatives of Berlin's twelve boroughs under Western control to leave the city hall, located in the East Berlin borough of Mitte (or City Center), and repair to the West to create a new government. On November 30 an "Extraordinary Municipal Delegates' Assembly" met at the Admiral Palace in East Berlin to set up a new Magistrate, ostensibly to govern the whole of Berlin but in fact only the eight boroughs in the East. Thus Berlin became a divided city.

The ensuing years saw the gradual erosion of other aspects of the city's four-power status. By January 1952 there were legislative assemblies for East Berlin as a whole and for each of

---

[1] Cited in *Documents on Berlin 1943-1963*, ed. Wolfgang Heidelmeyer and Günter Hindrichs (Munich: Oldenbourg, 1963), p. 2; emphasis added.

its eight boroughs. Five years later the Magistrate was made formally responsible to the GDR's Council of Ministers, and the Municipal Delegates' Assembly (Stadtverordnetenversammlung) to the national People's Legislature (Volkskammer). Eventually East Berliners became subject to conscription into the National People's Army, the application of national legislation to East Berlin became almost automatic, and, with the building of the wall in August 1961, the eastern portion of the city was insulated from any contact with West Berlin. Slightly more than a year passed before the Soviet Union terminated the position of City Commandant and turned over to the commandant of Soviet troops in Germany the exercise of remaining four-power functions. In June 1976 the distinction was removed between East Berlin's representatives to the People's Legislature and those from the rest of the GDR; in January 1977 control stations at the boundary between East Berlin and the rest of the GDR were dismantled; and in June 1979 new legislation permitted East Berliners to elect their representatives directly to the People's Legislature. Today, East Berlin is for all practical purposes a constituent part of the German Democratic Republic.[2]

And, yet, East Berlin's special status continues to exist (and continues to rankle the GDR's leadership circles). For one thing, the Western Allies still insist on the city's *de jure* four-power status. On May 9, 1977, for instance, American, British, and French representatives stated in London:

> The three Powers recalled that the Quadripartite Agreement was based explicitly on the fact that quadripartite rights and responsibilities and the corresponding wartime and post-war four Power agreements and decisions were not affected. They reaffirmed that this status of the special area of Berlin could not be modified unilaterally. The three Powers will continue to reject all attempts to put in

---

[2] See Siegfried Mampel, *Der Sowjetsektor von Berlin: Eine Analyse seines äußeren und inneren Status* (Frankfurt am Main/Berlin: Alfred Metzner, 1963); Ernst R. Zivier, *Der Rechtsstatus des Landes Berlin: Eine Untersuchung nach dem Viermächte-Abkommen vom 3. September 1971*, 3rd ed. (Berlin: Berlin Verlag, 1977); and, for an East German view, Gerhard Keiderling and Percy Stulz, *Berlin 1945-1968: Zur Geschichte der Hauptstadt der DDR und der selbständigen politischen Einheit Westberlin* (Berlin: Dietz, 1970).

> question the rights and responsibilities
> which France, the United States, the
> United Kingdom and the Soviet Union re-
> tain relating to Germany as a whole and to
> all four sectors of Berlin.[3]

The three Western Allies continue to send military patrols into East Berlin, utilize flight paths over that portion of the city, protest perceived violations in East Berlin of quadripartite agreements,[4] and otherwise behave as though the London Protocol of 1944 still governs the entire city's status — all the while, of course, eschewing concrete steps designed to disrupt the new status quo, Berlin's *de facto* division into two separate cities. For another thing, even though both the GDR and the Soviet Union repeatedly declare "Capital Berlin" to be formally and in every other way a part of the GDR, they continue, as Erich Honecker pointed out in November 1972, to "accept certain practices that still exist."[5] The GDR has moved very carefully toward full integration of East Berlin into the German Democratic Republic.

Governance of East Berlin[6]

The governmental structure of East Berlin rests on two pillars: primacy of the communist Socialist Unity party (SED)

---

[3] *The Department of State Bulletin*, 76, No. 1980 (June 6, 1977), p. 593.

[4] A recent example is the GDR decision of May 1986 to require all diplomats crossing Checkpoint Charlie to present their passports for examination rather than simply showing their special identity cards through the automobile window. This step, had it been successful, would have lent legitimacy to the boundary between East and West Berlin as an international border. A combination of Western and, presumably, Soviet pressure forced the GDR to back down.

[5] Remark made in an interview with C. L. Sulzberger (but not appearing in the latter's column, "Through a Sieve Darkly," *New York Times*, 24 November 1972, p. 37); reported in *Neues Deutschland*, 26 November 1972, p. 1. My translation.

[6] My description of the structure of government in the GDR and East Berlin rests on Mampel, *Der Sowjetsektor von Berlin*, pp. 71-101; Siegfried Mampel, "Die politische Ordnung im Sowjetsektor und ihre Stellung zur Sowjetzone," in *Berlin Sowjetsektor: Die politische, rechtliche, wirtschaftliche, soziale und kulturelle Entwicklung in acht Berliner Verwaltungsbezirken*, ed. Liselotte Berger (Berlin: Colloquium Verlag, 1965), pp. 54-76; Joachim Nawrocki and Manfred Rexin, *East Berlin: A Portrayal of the Political and Social Structures* (Berlin: Informationszentrum Berlin, 1981); *DDR Handbuch*, 3rd ed., ed. Hartmut Zimmermann et al. (Cologne: Verlag Wissenschaft und Politik, 1985); and, for the years since 1960, my own archive of newspaper clippings, interview reports, and other material.

and democratic centralism. As one of fifteen governmental districts in the German Democratic Republic,[7] the city enjoys a middle-level position in the political hierarchy; and, yet, as capital, its position is *primus inter pares* with respect to both party and structural organization.

The development of the SED in East Berlin followed a slightly different path than it did in the other governmental districts. The city's four-power status in 1946 gave Social Democrats the opportunity to refuse their subsumption into the SED, and for the next fifteen years the two parties operated independently throughout the entire city. The SPD's refusal to play the political game demanded in the East nonetheless deprived its own functionaries in East Berlin of any chance for political effectiveness. Nor was the SED much better off in the hostile environment of West Berlin, but the possibility for political activity existed and this in turn required the party to maintain subsidiary organizations in all of the city's twenty boroughs. In August 1961, shortly after the wall went up, the SPD in East Berlin chose to dissolve itself rather than face the prospect of its takeover by communists.[8] About a year later the SED organizations in the twelve western boroughs broke off — technically, but hardly so in reality — from the mother party to form the Socialist Unity Party of West Berlin (SED-W, later SEW). The borough organizations in the remaining eight (now eleven) boroughs of East Berlin constitute the SED at the district level.

Each of the GDR's fifteen district governments is organized similarly, and so, too, are those of subsidiary governmental units. In the case of East Berlin, the main legislative bodies are the Municipal Delegates' Assembly (Stadtverordnetenversammlung) at the district level and the borough assembly (Stadtbezirksversammlung) in each of the boroughs. The executive organs are, respectively, the Magistrate and the borough councils. Besides the governing mayor and deputy mayor, the Magistrate comprises ten functional representatives, ten city councillors, and the secretary.

---

[7] Technically the GDR has 14 districts *plus* East Berlin, but increasingly East Berlin is accorded status as a 15th district.

[8] Richard L. Merritt and Ronald A. Francisco, "The SPD of East Berlin, 1945-1961," *Comparative Politics*, 5, No. 1 (1972), 1-28. On the creation of the SED, see Henry Krisch, *German Politics under Soviet Occupation* (New York: Columbia University Press, 1974), and Gregory W. Sandford, *From Hitler to Ulbricht: The Communist Reconstruction of East Germany, 1945-46* (Princeton: Princeton University Press, 1983).

Various published decisions promise to each of these subnational bodies substantial autonomy to function in its own area. The fact is that each is subsidiary to its higher-level counterpart. The integration is especially tight between the district bodies, on the one hand, and, on the other, the borough bodies, for the GDR is anxious to maximize the appearance of harmony in East Berlin, the city most frequently visited by outsiders. Coordination is achieved through oversight by the Magistrate, to which the borough councils are ultimately responsible. The Magistrate is responsible to the Council of State, of which the governing mayor is a member. Thus lying only slightly below the surface of political and administrative decision-making in the city as a whole are the Council of State and Central Committee of the SED, which play dominant roles.

Once we turn from the structure of government to political processes — the middle-level politics I mentioned earlier — we find great gaps in the amount and quality of our information. Rigorous analysis of decision-making is not a forte of East German scholarship, nor do the country's media provide us directly with views and information other than what the political leadership would have us believe. My personal experience in interviewing municipal officials and others in East Berlin suggests that the norms of secrecy and suspicion are too strong for meaningful exchanges of information to take place. One other possibility, interviewing former officials who have since moved to the Federal Republic, seems not to have caught the imagination of those interested in municipal as opposed to national politics in the GDR. In any outline of areas for further research on the GDR, that of political decision-making in its urban centers certainly deserves a prominent place. The sections that follow will look at two dimensions of this area of research.

Spatial Development in East Berlin[9]

The analytic dilemma posed by the paucity of concrete information on the GDR's political processes is nowhere clearer than with respect to city planning and urban develop-

[9] This section draws heavily on my "Infrastructural Changes in Berlin," *Annals of the Association of American Geographers,* 63, No. 1 (1973), 58-70. See also *Die unzerstörbare Stadt: Die raumpolitische Lage und Bedeutung Berlins,* ed. Institut für Raumforschung Bonn (Cologne/Berlin: Carl Heymanns, 1953); and Frank Werner, *Stadtplanung Berlin: Theorie und Realität, Teil I: 1900-1960* (Berlin: Kiepert, 1976).

ment in East Berlin. We have ample information about spatial developments before the city's division, and can observe the construction patterns of recent years. But Western city planners and scholars are inadequately informed about the considerations and costs involved in moving from what was to what is, and it is impossible to say with certainty what will be.

Berlin was not designed to be a divided city. From the original core of Berlin and Cölln, united in 1307, the city slowly expanded outwards into the Brandenburg March. The Hohenzollerns' decision to make Berlin their capital presaged a period of rapid growth in both size and importance. From an area of 5.4 square miles in 1825 and with a population of a quarter million, it grew to 25 square miles and 3.7 million inhabitants on the eve of World War I, and, after the incorporation of its suburbs into Greater Berlin (1920), to over 341 square miles and almost 4.5 million people before the great bombing raids of 1943. Evacuations during the next two years cost the city almost one and a half million citizens. The result of the wartime and postwar confusion was that, at the time of the city's division in 1948, West Berlin had about 2.1 million people living on 185 square miles of territory, and East Berlin 1.2 million people on 156 square miles.[10]

The history of city planning in Berlin reflects a pattern of growth in rings around the central core. Canalization, completed in 1868, provided a basis for major arteries radiating from the center; and it was on these arterial highways that transportation systems and subsequent housing patterns were built. By the 1870s municipal officials were beginning to build the inner and outer belts of electrified elevated railways that were completed by 1914. The integrated networks of transportation facilities, utilities such as gas and power companies, and other infrastructural aspects of a large city, in place by the end of the 1930s, survived the aerial bombardments and savage streetfighting of the war.

---

[10] West Berlin's population rose to 2.23 million in 1957 before declining slowly to 1.88 million in 1987, while that of East Berlin, which dropped to 1.06 million in 1962, is now back to 1.21 million; see Statistisches Landesamt Berlin, *Statistisches Jahrbuch 1986* (Berlin: Kulturbuch, 1987), p. 38; Statistisches Landesamt Berlin, *Berliner Statistik Monatsschrift*, 41, No. 8 (1987), Zahlenspiegel-1; and *Statistisches Jahrbuch 1986 der Deutschen Demokratischen Republik* (Berlin: Staatsverlag der Deutschen Demokratischen Republik, 1986).

Political division in 1948 led fairly rapidly to the infra-structural division of Berlin. Prewar traffic, for instance, including automobile, truck, and public transport, was heavy in the inner city and radiated toward the suburbs, and an east-west axis had begun to develop between the borough of Mitte (now in East Berlin) and the fashionable West End, which included the Zoo Quarter. After the political split and establishment of controls at the boundary between East Berlin and the western sectors, traffic on the main access routes from the West to Mitte fell off sharply. (The construction of the wall eliminated this traffic altogether.) New traffic patterns stressed linkages between the centers of East and West Berlin and their respective suburbs.

Changes came even more abruptly in other aspects of Greater Berlin's infrastructure. In 1952 officials of the GDR cut off all telephone communication (except for a very small number of official lines) between the two halves of the city; not until 1971 would any telephone contact for the general public be reestablished. Early in the Blockade period East and West Berlin began to sever the networks of electrical, gas, water, and some sewage lines that unified the city underground. In most cases this process was complete by 1952. The main sewage lines remain open today, to be sure, for both practical and political reasons; for the most part, however, the two cities have established complete independence from each other in their municipal services.[11]

Spatially, the result of these developments was that the western portion of Greater Berlin broke off to form a new political community with all the aspects of any other insular city. The process resembled the division of a cell. West Berlin has a new core area, comprising both a highly developed central business district and an adjacent belt of high administrative density; population is shifting from the center to the periphery; the lines of communication feed into and focus on the new core area; and sharply delineated boundaries mark off West Berlin from East Berlin and the German Democratic Republic.

---

[11] See Richard L. Merritt, "Political Division and Municipal Services in Postwar Berlin," in *Public Policy*, Vol. XVII, ed. John D. Montgomery and Albert O. Hirschman (Cambridge: Harvard University Press, 1968), 165-98. Since October 1985, after years of negotiation, West Berlin has purchased natural gas from the Soviet Union, shipped through GDR utility systems.

But what about East Berlin? For years the city lay in ruins while Soviet and East German officials concentrated their reconstruction efforts elsewhere. Several considerations account for this: the sheer enormity of the task of rebuilding the city, hesitancy about expropriating foreign-owned buildings and land, including the sites of former embassies, and especially the need to develop the new industrial regions that would make the East German economy viable. There was little money for new construction, even in the mid-1950s after the Soviet Union stopped ordering reparations. Finally, along with the symbolic advantages of controlling the city's old core area in the borough of Mitte came responsibility for preserving and restoring its historic landmarks. If the choice was between restoring the cathedral and constructing a new steel mill, then it was clear where East German priorities lay. The net effect was that East Berlin retained a bombed-out aspect long after West Berlin had become a sparkling "showcase of democracy."

The first major buildings to be restored or built after the war were those required for administrative and political purposes. This meant some city buildings, party offices, the Soviet embassy, and the cultural institutions (opera, theater, university, museums) by which the communists hoped to gain credit as legitimate successor to all that was good in past German culture. These buildings were concentrated around the point where the east-west axis of Unter den Linden crosses the north-south axis of Friedrich Street (See map). Almost all were within a half-mile of the Brandenburg Gate, and most were considerably closer. Meanwhile city planners began to rebuild residential areas in the other inner boroughs of Prenzlauer Berg and Friedrichshain. At the construction site of a gigantic residential and shopping complex on the latter's main artery, then Stalinallee but since 1961 Karl-Marx-Allee, increases in the workers' production norms tipped off the short-lived revolt of June 17, 1953.

In the 1960s the pattern of construction moved eastward, especially after a decision made in September 1964 by the Politburo of the SED to concentrate new construction around Alexander Square. "Alex," as Berliners have fondly termed it since 1805 when, on the occasion of a state visit by Tsar Alexander I, the square received its present name, is roughly 1.7 miles east of the Brandenburg Gate, and close to the point where the boroughs of Mitte, Prenzlauer Berg, and Friedrichshain meet. A parade ground in the eighteenth century, by the late nineteenth century it had become an important nodal point in Berlin's new elevated railway system. An extensive shopping area sprang up around the railway station, and with it a lively nightlife and underworld. Before its destruction in 1944-45 it was well on its way to becoming the focal point of Berlin's east side, just as the Zoo Quarter was becoming the center of the West End.

The planners of the 1960s merely reinstituted this trend. They closed off the square itself and built tunnels under it to facilitate the flow of motorized and pedestrian traffic. A television tower, one of the world's tallest structures (1,197 feet), was constructed near its western rim, apartment houses to the southwest, and a large hotel on the north side. Office buildings, a department store, conference center, and well-appointed shops now ring "Alex." Municipal engineers broadened the radial streets leading to Alexander Square, and began planning a set of limited-access highways that form a ring, with the square as its central node.

"Alex" has once again become to East Berlin what the Zoo Quarter is to West Berlin. Construction on Spree Island of a major entertainment and conference center, the Palace of the Republic, as well as a luxury-class hotel and shops across the street, has made the area between Alexander Square and the Palace of the Republic a focal point of East Berlin's social and cultural life and point of attraction for East German and foreign visitors. As in West Berlin, traffic patterns circle the new core area just as though the other part of the city did not exist. If East Berlin's core area is not completely encapsulated, as West Berlin's is, it is merely because the city opens out to the rest of the GDR.

Housing construction on East Berlin's periphery was also significant. For instance, a planned garden city in Marzahn was developed in the late 1970s. Until then Marzahn was one of several sleepy villages caught up in the incorporation act of 1920, a small community at the city's northeastern edge built around a village church and surrounded by farmlands and the colonies of weekend gardeners. In 1976, however, plans were announced in *Neues Deutschland* to build over the course of the next nine years 35,000 apartments to house 130,000 East Berliners, some thirty schools to accommodate their children, two medical clinics each with a staff of fifty doctors, new elevated railway stations, and a wide range of shops, pubs, and other services for the quarter's residents. (Interestingly

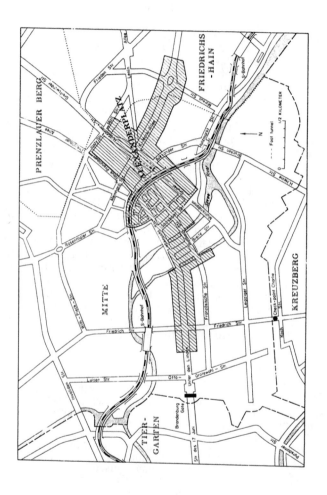

Alexander Square: East Berlin's Core Area

Source: Richard L. Merritt, "Infrastructural Changes in Berlin," *Annals of the Association of American Geographers,* 63, No. 1 (1973), 68.

enough, the planners also restored the church and other historic buildings comprised in the original village.) In 1979 GDR officials announced that Marzahn would henceforward be East Berlin's ninth borough.[12]

Even before residents had fully occupied the new garden city, however, GDR planners were having second thoughts. For one thing, they were finding the populace to be far less enchanted with the idea of planned garden cities than the planners had anticipated. Berliners wanted a home nearer the center of activity, a variety of opportunities for shopping and relaxation, and withal a measure of individualism in their own lives. Marzahn's designers had produced what one English journalist termed "a gigantic monument to misunderstood garden city housing, [a] pre-fab wasteland."[13] Meanwhile, pressure for building one-family homes grew, creating drastic shortages of building materials.[14] The lesson learned in Marzahn and elsewhere was simply that people like variety.

Furthermore, in its drive for greater international recognition and an enhanced sense of national self-awareness, the country's political leadership decided to appropriate for the GDR everything that was good in German history. This meant some bizarre twists in the Party's line, for example, embracing Frederick the Great as well as Martin Luther as heroes of the German working classes. In terms of city planning, it meant that serious attention was given to reconstructing as much of "old Berlin" as possible. Officials could be heard lamenting as unduly precipitate earlier decisions to tear down such historic buildings as the palace on Spree Island; and before long messages coming from government offices were rife with plans to build some of them anew.

12 See Werner Thies, "100 000 Mieter rund um das Dorf Marzahn," *Der Tagesspiegel* (West Berlin), 17 June 1978, p. 16. The Western Allies were initially inclined to protest the decision to turn Marzahn into a separate borough but decided against such a move because its boundaries did not extend beyond Berlin into the GDR; see "Alliierte Stellungnahme zum neuen Stadtbezirk Ost-Berlins," *Der Tagesspiegel*, 3 April 1979, p. 2, and "Westmächte nahmen Stellung zu neuem Bezirk in Ost-Berlin," *Der Tagesspiegel*, 7 April 1979, p. 1. In 1985 the Municipal Delegates' Assembly ratified a plan to turn part of Weißensee into a tenth borough of Hohenschönhausen, and a year later turned part of Marzahn into an eleventh borough of Hellersdorf.

13 Leslie Colitt, "East Berlin: Comecon's Showcase," *Financial Times*, 30 March 1987, p. 15.

14 Michael Mara, "Baulust und Bau-Frust in der DDR: Förderung des Eigenheimbaus wird durch Materialmangel gebremst," *Der Tagesspiegel*, 9 December 1984, p. 33.

Berlin's 750th anniversary (commemorated in 1987) provided an excellent opportunity to consolidate this physical refurbishing of the past. Among other things, intense work began on both the historic Gendarmerie Market (today's Academy Square), with its National Theatre as well as French and German cathedrals, and, at a cost of nearly $150 million, the medieval Nikolai Quarter. The latter case is particularly interesting.[15] Only the barest shell of the Nikolai Church itself, Berlin's oldest, had survived wartime destruction; and postwar construction had in part destroyed the zigzag course of ancient streets in the immediate neighborhood. A competition, for which some twenty-six architects submitted plans, yielded a design that combined the desire to rebuild the nub of old Cölln as it once had been with the economic realities and living conditions of today. For example, the architects designed and installed prefabricated exteriors, some complete with gables and other medieval features, but ensured that interiors contained the latest comforts.

Celebratory construction had purposes other than politically motivated nostalgia. Into flattened areas between Friedrich Street and the wall (especially along the former Wilhelm, now Otto Grotewohl, Street) went new apartment houses, a luxury-class hotel, and still other buildings. Given new construction, East Berlin may well reach its goal of a home for each household. Organized crews of workers went through some of the older parts of the inner city, such as Prenzlauer Berg, repairing dilapidated façades and updating kitchen and bathroom facilities. The authorities have also announced plans for a complete renovation of Friedrich Straße in the next years. And the forestry department has planted an extensive green belt along Berlin's northern rim.

Careful attention to published reports, close observation of actual construction, and analysis of comments made by municipal officials enable us to say a great deal about what has happened by way of spatial development in East Berlin. From these bits of evidence we may also infer the nature of the planning that went on and perhaps even possible trends in the future. Such inferences, however, are subject to well-known fallacies, the most important of which may be the

---

[15] See Ekkehard Schwerk, "Endspurt der Bauarbeiter im Nikolaiviertel," *Der Tagesspiegel*, 10 April 1987, p. 13. More generally: *Die Bau- und Kunstdenkmale in der DDR: Hauptstadt Berlin*, 2 vols., ed. Heinrich Trost (Berlin: Henschelverlag, 1983-87).

temptation to see ordered planning where none in fact existed. Without corroborating evidence about the various pressures being applied on planning officials by factory managers interested in having workers live close at hand, budget officers trying to keep public expenditures at manageable levels, the public at large which wants better housing or privately owned shops, and still others, and without indications of how planning officials made up their own minds and tried to convince others of the wisdom of their plans, our inferences remain unsubstantiated. Nor do they provide a sound basis for projecting further spatial developments in the years to come.

The Church in East Berlin

A somewhat different problem arises when we turn to phenomena in the public arena deriving less directly from governmental decision-making. An interesting example here is the path of organized religion in East Berlin. In discussing this topic, I shall concentrate on developments in the Evangelical Church, since it encompasses by far the largest number of Berliners on both sides of the wall.[16] The Catholic Church has approached somewhat differently its dilemma of how best to serve Christ in a socialist land; and the plight of the small number of Jews remaining in East Berlin, although intrinsically interesting, is too special a case to warrant attention here.

Protestantism in Germany has long faced a degree of organizational ambivalence. The fact that it found its main strength in the provincial churches did not keep some leaders from seeking nationwide coordination and even integration. Nazi subversion destroyed the first national body (the League of German Evangelical Churches created in 1922). Anti-Nazi church leaders nevertheless moved quickly after the war to create a new one, the Evangelical Church in Germany (EKD), which came into being in 1948.

---

16 See Richard L. Merritt, "The Protestant Church in Divided Berlin," in *Federal Republic of Germany at Forty*, ed. Peter H. Merkl (Boulder: Westview Press, 1988). See, more generally, *Die evangelische Kirche in der DDR: Beiträge zu einer Bestandsaufnahme*, ed. Reinhard Henkys (Munich: Chr. Kaiser, 1982); Hellmuth Nitsche, *Zwischen Kreuz und Sowjetstern: Zeugnisse des Kirchenkampfes in der DDR (1945-1981)* (Aschaffenburg: Paul Pattloch, 1983); *Kirchliches Jahrbuch für die Evangelische Kirche in Deutschland*, ed. Johannes Schneider, Joachim Beckmann et al. (Gütersloh: Gütersloher Verlagshaus/Gerd Mohn), yearly issues since 1950; and various articles in *Deutschland Archiv*.

Conflict soon broke out between the EKD and the new East German government. The issues were manifest: control of church-state relations, financial obligations and currency systems, ties between the EKD and the West German government, and control of family life.[17] More trouble erupted in 1957 when the EKD Council agreed to offer pastoral services to the newly established West German Bundeswehr. From then on East German officials, in no uncertain terms, made it clear that cooperation with the church in the GDR would rest upon its separation from the EKD. In 1968 the eight provincial churches in East Germany formed the Federation of Evangelical Churches in the GDR (BEK), which was to be separate from but would cooperate with the EKD.

Berlin was caught in the middle of this controversy. In 1949 the provincial Evangelical Church in Berlin-Brandenburg (EKiBB), long a pillar of German Protestantism, included in its domain not only all of Greater Berlin but also three dioceses that were now part of the German Democratic Republic. Separating the loosely federated provincial churches of the EKD along east-west lines was one thing, but breaking up the long-standing organic unity of the EKiBB was something else again. Church leaders throughout the province at first rejected even the thought of division. Each dispute between the GDR and EKD played a major role in the EKiBB's four dioceses, where senior church leaders worked against the state. By 1959 the EKiBB's bishop, Otto Dibelius, who simultaneously chaired the EKD Council, fiercely opposed the GDR's efforts to restrict the churches' political autonomy and even denied the legitimacy of the entire régime.[18] The EKiBB was thus at loggerheads with the East German state.

The wall built by the GDR in August 1961 gave some church officials on both sides a new image of political reality.

---

[17] A particularly touchy problem put families and especially young people on the firing line in the cold war. When the state added an atheistic vow to membership in the virtually obligatory Free German Youth (FDJ), the bishops in the GDR forbade confirmation to any child who took the oath. Children who did not join the FDJ were likely to face severe restrictions in the schools, and their parents might find their chances curtailed in the workplace and elsewhere. See Nitsche, *Zwischen Kreuz und Sowjetstern;* and Richard W. Solberg, *God and Caesar in East Germany: The Conflicts of the Church and State in East Germany since 1945* (New York: The Macmillan Company, 1961).

[18] See, for example, Otto Dibelius, *Obrigkeit: Eine Frage an den 60jährigen Landesbischof* (Berlin: n.p., 1959).

The idea of resisting totalitarianism continued to motivate many EKiBB leaders, especially those living in West Berlin. But an increasing number — members of the liberal Weißenseer Arbeitskreis in East Berlin,[19] Bishop Kurt Scharf, who eventually replaced Dibelius,[20] and participants in synods on both sides of the city — felt that the church should rather address the central Christian mission: to bring Christianity to the individual. This meant comforting families rather than forcing them to confront the state, and accepting some state demands as a means of helping communities carry on religious activities.

What ensued throughout most of the 1960s was a not-so-genteel battle within the EKiBB itself.[21] Some on both sides of the wall held tenaciously to the position that acceding to the GDR's demand to break up the unified EKD would be unconscionable. It would, in this view, betray those Christians in the GDR who had resisted the totalitarian claims of a régime unalterably opposed to Christianity. Others in both the eastern and western dioceses argued that political opposition to the régime merely hampered the church in fulfilling its fundamental tasks. Besides, they pointed out, implacable opposition in the past had not moved the state to modify its position: state officials, when they were not harassing the church, simply ignored it. Still another, numerically smaller, group in the East wanted actively to help the state build socialism in the GDR, since they perceived socialism as a more promising system within which to achieve the goals of Christianity. (In addition, we cannot discount the possible presence of some SED party hacks who played at being Christians as a means to further the Party's political goals.)

Mutual accommodation was nonetheless in the offing. During the late 1960s Church leaders on both sides of the wall, each fighting off challenges from their own hardline "conservatives" and "liberals," moved toward a *modus vivendi*. They developed a perspective that emphasized and even built on the degree of commonality between the two regions (by re-

---

[19] See Gerhard Finn, "Ergänzende Bemerkungen zum Weißenseer Arbeitskreis," *Deutschland Archiv*, 16, No. 2 (1983), 141-44.

[20] Scharf had been Dibelius' representative in East Berlin until August 1961 when the GDR cleverly expelled him; despite the GDR's strenuous opposition, the EKiBB chose him to replace Dibelius in 1966.

[21] My discussion of the EKiBB's efforts to deal with its problem stems from protocols (located at the EKiBB archive in West Berlin) of regional synod meetings in both East and West Berlin.

quiring mutual agreement for structural change, for example), denied that recent events had damaged the capacity of the regions to function as an organizational unity, and declared that, even if they were forced to go their own ways in an organizational sense, it would not mean the end of their unity in fulfilling the Christian mission. By 1973 they had created separate bishoprics, without, however, dissolving the formal juridical ties on which the EKiBB as a whole rests.

The modality has worked well in practice. East German officials, who had already permitted the provisional bishopric in the eastern region to join the Federation of Evangelical Churches in the GDR (BEK), chose to interpret the existence of the two offices as evidence of separate organizations; officials in the West persist in stressing the continuation of formal unity. Meanwhile, especially after the Quadripartite and Inter-German Treaties of the early 1970s reopened the gates to East Berlin and the GDR, church leaders in both regions found that the new arrangement provided them with extensive opportunities for interaction and even coordination in fulfilling their worldly as well as spiritual tasks.[22]

The position of the Catholics has been even more complicated. The territorial structure of their provincial churches, for instance, cut across the postwar German-Polish boundary as well as the border between East and West Germany. What later became the GDR had only one self-contained bishopric of its own, Dresden/Meißen, while the bishopric of Berlin spread over both halves of the divided city, a goodly portion of the GDR, and, until partial accommodation was reached on the territories east of the Oder and Neiße rivers, a chunk of Poland as well. Then, too, Catholic bishops in Germany enjoy less individual and collective autonomy than their Protestant brethren, for each is ultimately responsible to the Holy See in Rome. The Vatican, for its part, has had a broad palette of policy goals and options focusing on Catholics not only in Germany but in the whole of Eastern and Western Europe. Even if Catholic leaders in the GDR were prepared to accommodate their government's wishes, the Vatican most certainly was not, and was still less inclined to act precipitately.

---

[22] This is also the case at the national level. In March 1985, for example, preparing for the 40th anniversary of Nazism's defeat, the EKD and BEK issued a joint statement in which among other things they pledged to work together to prevent war from ever again erupting on German soil; see "Deutsch-deutsches Kirchenwort zum 40. Jahrestag des Kriegsendes," *Der Tagesspiegel*, 19 March 1985, p. 1.

The bishopric of Berlin posed a special problem. It was actually fairly new, having been detached from the Breslau archbishopric as late as 1930. In its original form it stretched from the Elbe River in the west (now the GDR's western border) all the way eastward to Farther Pomerania (now Polish territory), and from Jüterbog, about 35 miles south of Berlin, all the way north to the Baltic Sea and the island of Rügen. Even after the loss in 1945 of Stettin and Pomerania it remained territorially the GDR's largest Catholic church province. In 1982 it numbered 432,000 members, almost two-thirds of them (268,000) in West Berlin.

Despite sometimes heavy pressure from GDR officials, the Berlin bishopric has retained its structural unity since 1945. In part this is doubtless because the Catholic hierarchy avoided unnecessary confrontations with the state. In contrast to the EKiBB's bishop, who lived and worked in West Berlin during the years before the separate bishopric was created, the Catholic bishop-elect at the time the wall was built lived in East Berlin. So, too, have all of his successors. In the two and a half decades and more since August 1961, every one of them has regularly been permitted to spend a certain number of days each month tending to the flock in West Berlin. The Vatican also decreed in 1976 that the Berlin Bishops' Conference, which comprises all bishops in the GDR and is chaired by the bishop of Berlin, would henceforward be independent of the (West) German Bishops' Conference — although, it must be added, the decree specified that the organizational basis of these two bodies was territorial rather than national. Even so, the bishop of Berlin, because part of his domain lies in the West, retains his membership in the German Bishops' Conference, where he is represented by a deputy from the West Berlin diocese.

For all practical purposes the Catholic Churches in East and West Germany have gone their own ways, but in the bishopric of Berlin Joachim Cardinal Meisner oversees the diocese in West Berlin from his seat in East Berlin.[23] The extent to which he plays an active role in ecclesiastical decision-making in West Berlin is less clear. It seems likely

---

[23] See, for example, Cardinal Meisner's emphasis in his New Year's address of 1985 on maintaining the unity of the Berlin bishopric: "Kardinal Meisner bekräftigt Festhalten an der Einheit des Bistums Berlin," *Der Tagesspiegel*, 27 January 1985, p. 2. See more generally Wolfgang Knauft, *Katholische Kirche in der DDR: Gemeinde in der Bewährung 1945-1980* (Mainz: Grünewald, 1980).

that he carefully eschews any action that would make more difficult the task of Vatican diplomats and the Berlin Bishops' Conference to improve the lot of Catholics and Catholicism in the GDR. The central issues are not the world-political ones of the East-West confrontation, but rather securing in East Germany the right to unfettered theological studies and training for priests, an end to discrimination against Catholics in the schools and workplace, and guarantees for Catholic childcare centers, hospitals, and senior citizens' homes.

Whether we consider the Protestant or Catholic church, the dilemma facing researchers is the same. As in the case of urban planning, our understanding of governmental policy-making must rely on information that only government officials have: for instance, going beyond their public pronouncements, what role do they envision for churches in a stable, socialist German Democratic Republic? But, unlike the situation with urban planning, we also require information and data from private associations. In some cases these are readily available. First, some Protestant leaders and publicists, especially in West Berlin, often write or talk about East-West religious activities and developments in East Berlin. Second, both branches of the EKiBB publish newspapers,[24] maintain archives, and permit limited public access to their synods.

In another respect, however, church officials of both major religions are very closed-mouthed. An issue directly linked to its organizational structure in the GDR — not, I quickly add, general political matters, such as military training required in the schools, or the citizen's right to refuse military service — results in reports and statements that are very fuzzy indeed. One can quickly ascertain that the Protestant churches in the West provide substantial financial assistance to those in the East, but a thorough search of publicly available records will turn up no data on the basis of which to make a serious evaluation of the nature or scope of this assistance. Church officials note quite simply that any publicity about such sensitive matters could force the East German government, which frequently closes an eye to the activities of the church, to take action. The consequence, understandable though it may be in organizational terms, is that researchers find it difficult to

---

[24] For example, in West Berlin, the *Evangelische Pressedienst-Landesdienst Berlin*, *Kirche im Sozialismus*, *Evangelische Kommentare*, and the *Evangelische Informationsdienst Berlin*.

bridge some particular gaps regarding church-state relations in East Berlin.

East Berlin: A Permanent Identity Crisis?

An interesting fact emerging from analyses of urban planning, church-state relations, and still other aspects of the divided city of Berlin is the extent to which East Berlin has defined its identity in terms of West Berlin.[25] This observation is not an artifact of the paucity of research on East Berlin *qua* urban center, although it is certainly true that the main thrust of most Western studies of the Berlin question centers on the legal status and tenuous position of West Berlin, and tends to view East Berlin as the misbegotten and probably illegitimate offspring of "high politics" at the international level rather than as a city in its own right. The point is that East Germans seem to have adopted this jaundiced viewpoint as well.

In the case of urban planning, it was possible to separate East Berlin physically from West Berlin but more difficult to terminate a kind of thinking that envisioned Greater Berlin as a whole. In the 1950s planners on both sides of the city developed their ideas with the thought in mind that the occupying powers would eventually reunify Germany and, with it, Berlin. The years after 1958 found East Berliners stuck with their government's argument that West Berlin existed on the territory and at the sufferance of the GDR — which implied that any viable long-term solution to the German problem would reunify Berlin under the GDR's aegis. Even before the mid-1960s, to be sure, practical planning rested on the expectation that Berlin would remain divided for the foreseeable future and that, hence, at least in the meanwhile it would be wise to concentrate on the spatial development of East Berlin alone. But not until the Quadripartite and Inter-German Treaties of the early 1970s could these planners in the East formally express such a view.

Concrete steps, beginning in August 1961 with the building of the wall, were aimed at isolating East Berlin and its

---

[25] Another area in which this characteristic is especially apparent is in the electronic media, where the West's ability to penetrate the living rooms of East Berliners is virtually complete. To be heard, the Eastern media must in effect work around the schedule of popular programs beamed from the West. See Richard L. Merritt, "Divided Airwaves: The Electronic Media and Political Community in Divided Berlin," *International Political Science Review*, 7, No. 4 (1986), 369-99.

citizens from the "corrupting" influences of West Berlin. The idea was not merely to place barriers along the sectoral boundary but to create a "modern state border" — an imposing and presumably impermeable wall, on the eastern side of which buildings were demolished and the land on which they had stood ploughed and mined. The expense of the wall in terms of both financial outlays and credibility for the socialist system should not be underestimated, but Walter Ulbricht and his associates clearly considered the insulation provided by the wall worth these costs. Concurrent steps pushed the functioning center of the city eastwards toward Alexander Square and residential dwellings still further eastwards to the city's eastern border. If at all possible, the operational code of East Berlin's planners seemed to say, the very existence of West Berlin should be blotted from view.

With respect to the provincial Evangelical and Catholic churches, too, the GDR government's goal has been to sever the bonds linking East and West Berlin. That church leaders were reluctant to do so is clear, but so is the fact that they would have paid a political price for refusing to follow the government's dictates.[26] This battle over the churches' jurisdiction ended with major concessions on their part. Even today, however, any suspicion on the part of the East German government that churches in its domain are overly attentive to policies set in the West is cause to bring out heavy artillery. An example is the difficulty that both major churches had recently in trying to persuade the government that their campaigns for nuclear disarmament were not inspired by alien forces in West Berlin, Bonn, or the Vatican.

More generally, the views circulated until very recently by East German publicists bore a strong element of ambivalence toward their capital city. East Berlin was described on the one hand as a kind of anti-West Berlin. Whatever East Berlin was, it was certainly not West Berlin — that anomaly where unrepentant Nazis and unreconstructed capitalists oppressed the working class and sowed the seeds of dissent in the GDR. Our Berlin, they seemed to be saying, had better sense than to waste its time and money on glittering boulevards and the

---

[26] It is tempting to think that the EKiBB and Catholic Bishopric of Berlin paid a price for their self-assertiveness that was disproportionately large compared to that paid by the other provincial churches in the GDR, but there is little evidence to support such an hypothesis. Indeed, given the glare of publicity in Berlin, the GDR may even have treated the churches in the city more gently than it did churches elsewhere.

excesses of a consumer society. On the other hand, the same sources sometimes seemed to be saying that East Berlin outdid the western half of the city in terms of taller structures, more modern buildings, more congenial entertainment facilities, and all the rest. So overwhelming was the presence of West Berlin in these (one might say, provincial) views that East Berlin all but faded from sight.

At the risk of overgeneralizing I would argue that, in a collective sense, East Berlin has been undergoing a crisis of identity. Despite the presence of national ministries and foreign embassies — accredited, significantly enough, "to" rather than "in" the GDR — the government has not really succeeded in generating in the minds of either East Berliners or other East Germans the idea that East Berlin is truly the capital city of the German Democratic Republic, the center of their political life. A journalist in West Berlin, Jürgen Engert, has expressed this idea well. After pointing out that East Berliners receive certain government-provided benefits not enjoyed in the rest of the country and that their living standard is considerably higher than elsewhere in the GDR, he cited examples of East Berliners' disrespect of the system. "Walter Ulbricht would have had an easier task of creating a national identity for the GDR," Engert concludes,[27] "had he moved the capital to Leipzig or Dresden instead of leaving it in East Berlin."

The extent to which East Berlin enjoys an image that does not include the counter-example of West Berlin is an interesting question deserving further study. Certainly, the presence or absence of such an image makes a difference for the GDR's future, as does the question of how the rest of the country views its capital city. Patterns of identification and self-identification provide us with clues about the degree of political community shared within a population, and hence the constraints on governmental behavior. Like policymaking and other aspects of middle-level politics, such questions point to a vast and unexplored territory for researchers interested in the GDR.

---

27 Comment in *Living with the Wall: West Berlin, 1961-1985*, ed. Richard L. Merritt and Anna J. Merritt (Durham, N.C.: Duke University Press, 1985), pp. 112-13.

East Berlin as a Theater Metropolis:
Ernst Schumacher's *Berliner Kritiken*

Margaret E. Ward

When we regard Berlin as a theater metropolis we are most likely to think of the 1920s. By the middle of that decade

> . . . Berlin had thirty-two legitimate thea-
> ters. It had Max Reinhardt, Leopold Jess-
> ner, and Erwin Piscator — stage directors
> with a zest for experiment, who considered
> the theater not mere entertainment, not
> even just art, but an essential force in hu-
> man life. In their time, perhaps in this cen-
> tury, Berlin's theater was unrivaled any-
> where in the world.[1]

Although it is practically impossible to talk about theater in Berlin today without recalling that era, I will focus here only on Berlin's recent history as a city which has fostered the theatrical arts, and, even more specifically, on East Berlin. The 750th anniversary celebration in 1987 demonstrated the importance attached to theater in East Berlin. The fifteen major East Berlin theaters feature prominently in the *Buch zum Fest*,[2] and a national theater festival and an exhibition on Berlin's theater history are listed as high points of the jubilee.

My topic will be the theater of East Berlin as seen through the eyes of the well-known Brecht scholar and GDR theater

---

[1] Wolf von Eckardt and Sander L. Gilman, *Bertolt Brecht's Berlin: A Scrapbook of the Twenties* (Garden City, N.Y.: Anchor/Doubleday, 1975), p. 77.

[2] *750 Jahre Berlin. Das Buch zum Fest*, ed. Komitee der Deutschen Demokratischen Republik zum 750jährigen Bestehen von Berlin (Berlin: VEB Tourist Verlag, 1986).

critic Ernst Schumacher, who has closely followed the theater scene there since the 1960s. The basis for the paper is the four-volume collection of his theater reviews written for the *Berliner Zeitung* between 1964 and 1984;[3] this will be complemented by some of his more recent writing, to cover the period from 1984 to the present. Looking at Schumacher's writings, we will consider such questions as: How does the socialist state view Berlin's role as a theater metropolis? How have the legitimate theaters of the capital contributed over the last quarter century to the cultural/political life of the GDR and enhanced its international stature? How does this theater history relate to everyday life?

Relying on Schumacher for answers to these questions is justified, I would argue, because the consistency of viewpoint enables one to trace more easily developments and trends over this fairly long time span, and because Schumacher's view from within, while a critical one, reflects the aims of the socialist state. A close reading of his reviews can help us to understand better the special role which the theater has been assigned in the cultural/political life of this city as we try to assess what impact it may have on everyday life. In the theory of socialist theater criticism which he outlines at the beginning of the first volume, Schumacher is careful to explain that these reviews are not intended as "culinary" criticism (I, p. 12). He hopes instead that his praise and blame will activate not only the producers of theater, but the audience as well.

Can theater in the GDR context still be considered an essential force in human life? Schumacher would like to think so. In his view the theater arts should still be considered "essentielle Bestandteile des gesellschaftlichen wie des individuellen Lebens" (I, p. 273). He is painfully aware, however, of the direct challenge which the mass media, television in particular, have posed to the legitimate theater since the 1960s. Schumacher argues that theaters can only survive if they provide a special locus for communication unlike any other cultural institution. They need to help their audiences face both the really big questions of our day — like the threat of nuclear war — and also everyday problems. He repeatedly states that if the theaters are to meet effectively the challenge

---

[3] Ernst Schumacher, *Berliner Kritiken*, 4 vols. (Berlin: Henschelverlag, 1975-86). Page references to this work will ordinarily be given parenthetically in the text. Unless otherwise stated, phrases printed in italics represent Schumacher's emphasis.

of the video media they must reach out to a new, more youthful public and seek new forms of interchange with them.

East Berlin's theaters do not always measure up to Schumacher's high expectations. He often compares Berlin's theatrical output unfavorably with that of the twenties, for Schumacher, who sees himself as part of a long and respected tradition of theater criticism in Germany — and Berlin in particular — going all the way back to Lessing, is always mindful of Berlin's theatrical traditions. He frequently invokes individual institutional histories. He regrets, for instance, that the over one-hundred-year-old Deutsches Theater has not done as much as it could in cultivating the realist and naturalist plays first introduced there by Otto Brahm. He suggests at one point that the Volksbühne, whose organization goes back to the 1880s, should perform more plays from the proletarian revolution of the 1920s and 1930s (II, p. 133). And he reminds all the Berlin theaters that when Brecht founded the Berliner Ensemble in 1949 he devised a model repertoire whose core was to be new socialist dramas (II, p. 685). His disappointment in the level of commitment in Berlin to the consistent development and performance of plays which deal with contemporary life in the GDR, the "Hier und Heute," forms a kind of "red thread" throughout these four volumes of critiques.[4]

Schumacher expects the Berlin theaters, as the most highly subsidized in the Republic,[5] to serve as a kind of flagship for the rest of the country; they are supposed to be "*künstlerische Schrittmacher*" (I, p. 277). Theater practice is seen as a constant competitive struggle in which the theaters of the metropolis are pitted not only against other theaters in the GDR, but also against those in West Berlin, the Federal Republic, other socialist countries, and theaters all over the world. Schumacher often uses imagery from the world of competitive sports to talk about Berlin's successes and failures during a given theater season. For instance he calls 1967-68 "*eine Saison großer Anläufe und mittlerer Sprünge*" (I, p. 265). He is proud whenever he can point to individual productions which represent "Spitzenleistungen" (IV, p. 247).

---

[4] See, for example, II, p. 589.

[5] In the 1982-83 season, 100 million Marks or an average of 26 Marks per seat were spent by the government on Berlin's fifteen theaters, making them among the most highly subsidized in the world (IV, pp. 51-52).

Schumacher continually emphasizes East Berlin's special place directly on the seam between two social systems. He maintains that theater in Berlin cannot help but be ideologically intensive, and therefore calls for more political education of theater staff and more communication between them and experts from political, economic, and educational institutions (III, p. 131). The contest with capitalist West Germany is viewed as particularly sharp throughout the 1960s.

After 1972-73 a new stage in this international competition was provided by the influx of tourists from East and West into East Berlin itself. Schumacher notes that one-fifth of the visitors to East Berlin theaters yearly are, in fact, foreigners, who often draw conclusions about GDR national culture on the basis of such a visit (III, p. 132). In his view it is therefore necessary for the metropolitan theaters, in particular, to consider themselves a part of a new, socialist, national theater which can be a vehicle not only for change within the GDR, but for ideological struggle with the West.

Schumacher consistently calls upon the Berlin theaters to fashion their repertoires along political lines sanctioned by the government. During the 1950s the material basis for a socialist theater had been created. Now it was up to the individual theaters to transform themselves in such a way that one could truly speak of a

> reale Sozialisierung der Berliner Sprech-
> theater, bestehend in der Gewinnung eines
> sozialistischen Bewußtseins, der Identifizie-
> rung der Schauspieler mit dem Wollen und
> Wissen der Partei der Arbeiterklasse, der
> Identifizierung des Publikums mit dieser
> (natürlich relativen) Identität von Kunst
> und Politik. . . . (I, p. 183)

Here again Berlin should be in the avant-garde: "als hauptstädtische Theater [haben sie] die Verpflichtung . . . sozialistische Leitungsmodelle zu entwerfen und anzuwenden, die für ein sozialistisches deutsches Nationaltheater von Bedeutung sind" (I, p. 408).

The Berlin theaters seem to fall short consistently. Year after year Schumacher cites productions which are either postponed or cancelled altogether. He is skeptical of the so-called Berlin Reife (I, p. 34), which makes the theaters more

28

reluctant to perform new plays or to take risks in comparison with those in the rest of the GDR. Even in the much-touted Plenzdorf season, 1972-73, when two productions of *Die neuen Leiden des jungen W.* played to sold-out houses nightly, and Volker Braun's *Kipper* was also performed in Berlin, Schumacher sees this as too little, too late (II, p. 681), for these plays did not originate in, nor were they premiered, in Berlin. He praises the 1974-75 season, on the other hand, because of the increase in the number of new productions of both classical and contemporary works, although he notes that the critical realists were slighted by comparison. Schumacher finds the virtual eclipse of a dramaturgy geared to the development of new GDR dramas, the tensions between individual theaters and their house authors, repeated management turnovers, and the increasing trend in the 1970s of key directors like Besson, Wekwerth, and the team of Karge/Langhoff to work abroad especially dismaying (III, p. 244).

Schumacher points out that Berlin theaters have been continually plagued by problems in the critical areas of management and planning. As early as 1963-64 he asks rather pointedly: "*Sind Spielplanschulden keine Staatsplanschulden?*" (I, p. 29), and sets up an industrial model of productivity. He even asks why "planmässige, proportionale Entwicklung der Volkswirtschaft" can't serve as a model for the theater (III, p. 63). He looks back to Max Reinhardt as an example of theatrical productivity and suggests that East Berlin theaters could shorten rehearsal time, indulge in less opulence, use their actors more consistently, and change their repertoires more rapidly (IV, pp. 52-53).

Schumacher blames managerial instability, in particular, for a general lack of long-range planning in Berlin theaters. In April 1969 all theaters were placed under the Berlin city magistrate in the hope that their growth and development could be better coordinated with long-range plans for the city as a whole. But by 1972 the Deutsches Theater and the Berliner Ensemble had been returned to the supervision of the Ministry of Culture. Schumacher constantly challenges the Berlin theaters to think more carefully about their special role in the cultural life of the city, especially when at the Bezirksdelegiertenkonferenz in April 1976 plans were being laid for the development of new housing and neighborhoods up to 1990 (III, p. 131). Even the relatively new theaters, like tip (Theater im Palast) and Das Ei, are located in the center of the city, and the new residential districts of Hellersdorf, Marzahn, and

Hohenschönhausen — all outlying communities — still have no theatrical institutions of their own. And despite the existence of a small studio theater, bat, Berlin continues to compare unfavorably with Warsaw, for example, in terms of experimental groups and theater labs.

On the other hand, Schumacher praises the Berlin theaters for being in the forefront of a general trend in the GDR to transform the relationship between the theater and its audience, an effort which became necessary in the 1960s when the competition from television and cinema first made itself felt with a drop in theater attendance.[6] In order to meet this competition the theaters tried to devise new ways of reaching out to their traditional audience, as well as to attract new theater-goers, especially young people. Schumacher, who urges the theaters to cultivate the collective experience which makes theater unique (I, p. 277), discusses the innovations undertaken in Berlin.

The first was the introduction of *Foyergespräche*, discussions between actors, directors, and other theater personnel, and audiences after performances. Another was the creation of audience organizations, for instance, the Gesellschaft der Freunde des Deutschen Theaters, for whom special evenings of dramatic readings were organized (I, p. 79). By the mid-1960s the theaters were beginning to contact a potentially new audience by taking entertainment into the workplace. The Berliner Ensemble, for example, organized readings at the universities and made occasional guest appearances at the Kombinat Schwarze Pumpe (I, p. 128). The Berliner Ensemble was exemplary in attracting pupils and students. It fostered special relationships with all the schools which carried Brecht's name. And in one educational effort 10,000 copies of a video program on the *Gewehre der Frau Carrar* were distributed to eighth grade classes (II, pp. 596-97).

By 1966-67 overall theater attendance in Berlin had improved, but the number of season ticket holders had dropped significantly from 22,000 to 9,000 (I, p. 195). The longer weekend had not automatically resulted in an increase in regular theater attendance as some had hoped. The public obviously preferred to pay more and choose which performances it wished to see. The demand for one play or another could be

---

[6] In the 1963-64 season, for example, the theaters were filled to only 50-70% of capacity (I, p. 29).

vastly different, even at the same theater. By the late 1960s Schumacher can, however, point to positive changes in the overall make-up of Berlin audiences, although the lack of a centralized theatrical sociology made it impossible to provide anything but a sketchy analysis. The public seems to be increasingly youthful. Statistics for the Deutsches Theater in 1967-68, for instance, reveal that 6-12% were workers, 32% members of the intelligentsia, 22% students or apprentices; 80% of the audience was under forty and showing a keen interest in plays having to do with everyday life in the GDR (I, pp. 282-83). The Gorki Theater was the only theater consistently to provide sociological studies of its audience. Changes in its audience in the early 70s could, therefore, be readily detected. Again, the public had become increasingly youthful. Between 1970 and 1972, for example, the portion of the total Gorki audience between 14 and 24 years of age rose from 25.8% to 28.7%; in 1970 only 3.4% of its public consisted of industrial workers, but this figure had increased to 7.9% by 1972 (II, p. 691).

The interest among young people continued to increase in the 1970s. One impetus may have been the popular Tenth World Festival of Youth and Students held in 1973 in East Berlin, at which theater performances played an important part (II, p. 679). A fine example of how a classical play could be used to attract young audiences was the 1970-71 Volksbühne production of Schiller's *Die Räuber* under the direction of Manfred Karge and Matthias Langhoff, in which they attempted to draw analogies with the present. The performances were nearly always sold out (II, p. 493). The same was true of the Volksbühne and Deutsches Theater productions of Plenzdorf's *Neue Leiden* two seasons later, because young people could relate to Edgar Wibeau and his idiom (II, pp. 635-40).

In May 1973 the Volksbühne began its *Autoren en suite* program, by means of which it attempted to establish new forms of communication and reach out into its heavily populated neighborhood. It was to be an evening of total theater. For two weeks three comedies were offered simultaneously on three different stages in the building, and the audience also could see two short farces performed in the lobbies. Appropriately, the program concluded with a kind of block party for the whole neighborhood. Schumacher thought that, of all the plays, *Der Abiturmann* by Arne Leonhardt was the most far-reaching in its effect; he praised the fact that the theater be-

came a public forum, an "Organ der öffentlichen Selbstverständigung über brennende Fragen der Zeit":

> In den anschließenden Diskussionen . . .
> ging es bisher immer hoch her. Schüler
> geraten sich mit ihren Lehrern in die Wol-
> le, Vertreter der Ministerien und Hoch-
> schulen müssen Rede und Antwort stehen,
> warum die Auswahl von Studienbewerbern
> jetzt sogar durch Computer erfolgen soll,
> Eltern werden "aufgeklärt", was ihre Söhne
> und Töchter so denken. . . . (II, p. 669)

In another two-week period in the fall of 1974, the Volksbühne took this experiment one step further in its *Spektakel
2 - Zeitstücke*: twelve plays, eight of them premieres, in nine
different locations. Even the children's playground behind the
building was put to use. Every evening the house was filled to
capacity, but those who could get in through a window joined
the standing-room-only crowd of 1200-1400. Only GDR
dramas were performed, thereby celebrating the 25th anniversary of the Republic. The prologue shocked many viewers
who were prepared for another evening of light entertainment. It was a performance of Heiner Müller's "Das Laken," a
scene set in Berlin in 1945, from his play *Die Schlacht*, which
premiered at the Volksbühne a year later. Plays by Volker
Braun, Christoph Hein, and Regine Weicker were also fea-
tured. But, as Ernstgeorg Hering of the Volksbühne staff observed:

> Ins Zentrum rückte die Begegnung der
> Theaterleute mit ihrem Publikum, wichtig
> war der Kontakt des Publikums unterein-
> ander. Zwischen den Stücken gab es genug
> Pausen, um miteinander zu reden. Schau-
> spieler führten ihre Gäste an die verschie-
> denen Spielorte, dann traten sie auf. An-
> schließend konnte noch bis 1.00 Uhr dis-
> kutiert, getrunken und getanzt werden.[7]

Another example of the way in which theaters reached out
to a new public, trying to get them to see theatrical arts as a
vital part of their lives rather than as an exceptional night out,

---

[7] Ernstgeorg Hering, "Zum Beispiel: SPEKTAKEL 2 - Zeitstücke: Beobachtungen zur Arbeitsweise," leaflet published by the Berlin Volksbühne, n.d., n.p.

is provided by another Volksbühne production, *Horizonte*, a play first written and performed with the help of Benno Besson by a lay theater in the petro-chemical industry (NARVA) and then adapted for the professional theater by Heiner Müller.[8] Many such specific relationships between theaters and industries came into existence during the 1970s. The Volksbühne had eighteen such contracts. Members of brigades might even be asked to participate in rehearsals. In the Volksbühne production of Heiner Müller's *Die Schlacht*, a dramaturgical assistant went to factories to have discussions with brigades of construction workers about the text and reported the results back to the director and actors.[9] Perhaps the most radical example of this kind of interchange is provided by the 1974 Maxim Gorki Theater production of Schatrow's *Wetter für morgen*, in which advice on the preparation of the play was systematically sought from Berlin autoworkers.[10]

In spite of all the efforts made, however, theater attendance has been steadily dropping since the late 1970s. As soon as the Besson era ended at the Volksbühne there was a quick drop in the attendance record there. In 1979-80 there were 100,000 fewer theater visits registered in the city than in the previous year (IV, p. 50). Some drop in attendance between 1980 and 1983 may have been due to the closing of the Kleine Komödie and the Kammerspiele stages of the Deutsches Theater for renovations. But the 1980s seem to mark a period of crisis. Schumacher complains about the inability of the theaters to even publish their repertoire plans in advance of the season. In the final season represented in Schumacher's collected reviews he has rather harsh words for the theaters' lack of preparation for the celebration of Schiller's 225th birthday commemoration; he sees this as symptomatic of the dearth of long-range planning. He suggests that the Berlin theaters may be taking their financial good fortune for granted, rather than considering themselves bound to the policy of rationalization and intensification which is in effect for every

---

[8] See "Stücke von Heiner Müller an der Volksbühne," leaflet published by the Berlin Volksbühne, n.d., n.p.

[9] Cf. Schumacher, III, p. 74.

[10] Cf. Schumacher, III, p. 74. In his story "Die Bühne" Volker Braun describes the open rehearsal of his play *Kipper Paul Bauch*: "Die Arbeiter des Kombinats waren da, zwanzig oder dreißig saßen auf den Holzstühlen, auch die Parteileitung der Stadt" (*Geschichten aus der Geschichte der DDR 1949-1979*, ed. Manfred Behn [Darmstadt: Luchterhand, 1981], p. 136).

other industry; theater is — in his view — a cultural service industry (IV, p. 249).

But what Schumacher still sees as the Berlin theaters' weakest point is their continued lack of receptivity to the newest GDR dramas. In the introduction to the final volume of reviews, written in 1985, he seems to say more in exasperation than all honesty that even the worst new play is better than none at all (IV, p. 9). Although Schumacher reiterates this point repeatedly through two decades of reviews, his disappointment during the five-year period 1979-84 seems especially profound. Although he criticizes the play itself, he welcomes the Deutsches Theater production of Christoph Hein's *Ah Q* because it brought "Punker und Popper ins Haus" (IV, p. 248). He also highlights the reprise of Volker Braun's *Tinka* at the Berliner Ensemble in 1982 because it is a play about everyday problems. But this may be just a case in point, since *Tinka* was first performed not in Berlin, but in Potsdam (1977). Schumacher sums up: "Es fehlte, es fehlt den Berliner Sprechtheatern immer mehr an wirklich 'neuen' Stücken, gegenwartsbezogen, epochenbezogen, alltagsbezogen" (IV, p. 150). And this still seems to be the case: Volker Braun's newest play *Siegfried Frauenprotokolle Deutscher Furor*, the text of which appeared in the February 1987 issue of *Theater der Zeit*, was premiered that year in Weimar, not Berlin.

However, in the *Autoren en suite* series in the Volksbühne Theater im 3. Stock in the fall of 1986, Berliners could at least hear portions of Heiner Müller's play *Verkommenes Ufer Medeamaterial Landschaft mit Argonauten*, and hear and discuss with him sections of *Wolokolamsker Chaussee*, including the third part, which has to do with the events of June 17, 1953. One GDR critic called this one of the most important theatrical events in Berlin in the 1986-87 season.[11]

Schumacher's *Berliner Kritiken* offer a fairly harsh overall assessment of Berlin as a theater metropolis for the period between 1964 and 1984. Schumacher openly doubts whether the Berlin theaters — despite their subsidies — can match the kind of innovation to be found in material production (IV, pp. 9-10). But his article on the history of Berlin theater for the 750th jubilee sounds a somewhat more hopeful, although tentative note as he looks to the future:

11 Gregor Edel, "Freundlichkeit," *Theater der Zeit*, 42, No. 2 (1987), 3-4.

Unter Berücksichtigung der Veränderung in der Lebensweise und besonders im Freizeitverhalten der Werktätigen können sich die hauptstädtischen Theater mit ihren mächtigen materiellen und künstlerischen Potenzen auf neue Weise attraktiv machen, wenn sie weiterhin "Laboratorien sozialer Phantasie" sind, den wachsenden Unterhaltungsbedürfnissen Rechnung tragen und neue Formen der Kommunikation mit dem Publikum suchen.[12]

The question remains open whether the Berlin theaters will rise to this challenge. When *Die Schlacht* premiered in 1975, Heiner Müller warned that it was all too easy for the theater to choke on naturalism, to become "a mausoleum for literature rather than a laboratory for social imagination, a preservative for superseded conditions rather than an instrument of progress."[13]

Interestingly, both Schumacher and Müller refer to Brecht's vision of the theater as a laboratory for social imagination. But there will continue to be multiple interpretations within the theatrical community of Berlin — and the GDR as a whole — as to what kind of artistic experiments are appropriate for such a laboratory. For example, the same season (1977-78) that Schumacher praised the staging of the Maxie Wander monologues, *Guten Morgen, du Schöne* (III, p. 241), he attacked Müller for advocating a "Rückgang auf die pure individuelle Erfahrung" (III, p. 243). Nevertheless, I think all those who are involved in making theater in and for the metropolis of East Berlin could agree with Schumacher that the theater needs to be a "Forum öffentlicher Selbstverständigung über alle gesellschaftlichen Probleme . . . , die einer Lösung harren. Nur so wird Theater zu einem Bedürfnis für die Dramatiker und für das Publikum" (IV, p. 53).

---

[12] Ernst Schumacher, "Das 750jährige Berlin und seine Theater," *Theater der Zeit*, 42, No. 8 (1987), 13.
[13] Heiner Müller, "A Letter to Martin Linzer," transl. Marc Silberman, *Theater*, 17, No. 2 (1986), 30. Originally published in *Theater der Zeit*, 30, No. 8 (1975), 58-59.

Trends of Film Culture in the GDR

Lothar Bisky

Reflections on GDR film and popular art are appropriate for a symposium dealing with everyday life there if one understands the concept as including everyday cultural life. My topic will be film culture in the GDR. I use this term to designate the interrelationship of production, distribution, and the social use of film. The mutual influence of these three factors can be gauged empirically. Since the early 1980s, at the latest, changes in audience reaction to cinema have been discernible in the GDR; these changes are having an influence on film distribution in the GDR and in the long run — albeit indirectly — on film production. In the following I will outline some trends of film culture in the GDR.

In medias res

To start with the situation as it is: 885 feature films were telecast on the two channels of GDR television in 1987. More could be seen on the three West German television channels that transmit into the GDR. 150 films — among them, the seventeen films that the GDR produces each year — are shown each year in the country's 5,700 movie theaters. Movie audiences numbered 70-71 million in 1987 (as opposed to about 80 million at the end of the 1970s).[1]

All in all, film has never played a greater role in the everyday cultural life of the GDR than it does today. At a colloquium at the Academy of Arts in 1983 the theater critic Ernst Schumacher put forward the following comparison: "Statistically speaking, a GDR citizen annually spends 20 to 25 minutes attending a concert, 30 to 40 minutes visiting a

---

[1] Information provided by the Programmdirektion des Fernsehens der DDR and VEB Progreß-Film-Verleih, Berlin.

museum, two hours visiting a theater, seven and a half hours going to the cinema, 120 hours reading (with only a small proportion of belles-lettres), and 750 hours watching television. . . ."[2] These figures speak for themselves. If we assume a conscious life span of sixty years, our statistical GDR citizen spends about 120 hours in the theater, and about 45,000 hours in front of his television set.

What do these figures mean for the development of culture? There is sufficient reason today to speak not only of a quantitatively, but also qualitatively, new role of the audio-visual media in our cultural development. And one must assume that this influence will not decline in the foreseeable future. Some of the reasons for assuming that the audio-visual media are influencing society in a qualitatively new way are: 1) they are playing a dominant part in satisfying people's need for information, education, entertainment, and art; 2) they are the most popular leisure time activity of people, no matter which class or walk of life; 3) they affect people's view of the world, or Weltanschauung, which comprises pictorial conceptions as well as theoretical assertions; 4) their impact on mass consciousness, on needs and expectations, is lasting.

Film and Leisure Time

Films are mainly seen on television. Not only are fewer people going to the movies these days,[3] but an ever smaller number of films are attracting large numbers of viewers. In 1980, for example, the ten most popular films (out of 140 new releases) accounted for 70% of the movie audience.[4] This tendency is continuing. Movie attendance has suffered of course with the growing availability of television — both because of the broad offerings and the fact that the first showing of some films in smaller towns takes place at nearly the same time as their TV airing. Another reason for the lower figures can be found in the present decline in the number of young people in

---

[2] Quoted from an *Arbeitsprotokoll* of the Academy of Arts. My translation here and throughout. See also Ernst Schumacher, "Probleme der Wechselwirkungen der darstellenden Künste," *Weimarer Beiträge*, 30, No. 7 (1984), 1133-51.

[3] In 1960, for example, the average per capita movie attendance was 13.8 times; in 1980, only 4.75 (*Statistisches Jahrbuch 1981 der Deutschen Demokratischen Republik* (Berlin: Staatsverlag, 1981), p. 29.

[4] Information provided by VEB Progreß-Film-Verleih, Berlin.

the GDR — young people form the bulk of the moviegoers. And people are choosing the films they see with greater care.

In addition to these factors, changes in leisure habits are making themselves felt.[5] In spite of the prolongation of leisure within the framework of the social measures of the 1970s, free time is still in short supply. Generally speaking, everyone works — the percentage of women working in the GDR is very high, compared internationally — and the demands of the household, family, social obligations, further training, etc. lead to an individual feeling of not having time. Moreover, the awareness of the importance of time has increased. Wasting time is coming increasingly under fire. Sociological studies point to a trend toward the more conscious planning of available leisure time.[6] There is also a marked tendency to spend leisure time in the country in the warmer months — the increase in the number of private cars and weekend cottages has contributed to this.

In-depth studies carried out in major Berlin *Betriebe* in 1984 showed an increased differentiation between weekend and workday leisure time.[7] Time is especially short on weekdays. Only people who are especially motivated go to the movies on workdays — for example, on the recommendation of friends. During the week, the leisure time use of television prevails; television can be viewed within the context of everyday activities. Television programming is the criterion used for deciding whether or not to go to the movies on a given evening. And in any case, most of the population is in bed by 10 p.m. since they have to get up early for work the next day.

In her cultural-sociological surveys on the social use of the arts, Ute Scheffler distinguishes between "everyday use" and

---

[5] For more information on changes in leisure activities, see Hans Koch, Helmut Hanke, Christa Ziermann, and Wilfried Barthel, *Zur Theorie der sozialistischen Kultur* (Berlin: Dietz, 1982), pp. 278ff; Helmut Hanke and Erna Schüttauf, "Freizeitverhalten - Freizeitgestaltung - Reproduktion des Arbeitsvermögens," in *Soziale Triebkräfte ökonomischen Wachstums. Materialien des 4. Kongresses der marxistisch-leninistischen Soziologie in der DDR, 26. bis 28. März 1985* (Berlin: Dietz, 1986), pp. 358ff.

[6] For more information, see *Soziale Triebkräfte ökonomischen Wachstums*, pp. 313-21, 358-62.

[7] Cf. Lothar Bisky, "Kulturbedürfnisse und Leistungsverhalten," in *Soziale Triebkräfte ökonomischen Wachstums*, pp. 215ff.

the "use of art as a special experience."[8] She shows that moviegoing today as a rule belongs to the category of special situations: cinema as a "special experience." The number of "casual moviegoers" is reduced, so that it is more and more the special film experience that lures people into the cinema. Sold-out theaters in big cities where special films are shown contrast with small audiences in local neighborhood movie houses. The family TV-room now attracts as many viewers as some cinemas. Cinemas have reacted by opening cinema cafés, cine-vision bars, etc. to heighten the moviegoing experience.

There is a certain cogency to these developments. It has been obvious for a long time that films shown in vacation centers — i.e., when people have plenty of free time — do reach the public. It seems logical that with more discretionary time there is a greater readiness to see a more diverse film program, to enjoy films not ordinarily selected under the pressured conditions of everyday life.

Film Reception in the GDR

A trend toward "functional differentiation of usage" has been observed for some time now in film-sociological surveys.[9] That is, increasingly, the same moviegoers are seeing both entertainment films and more demanding films, depending on the situation, on the film offerings, etc. The traditional social splitting of the film audience in regard to intellectual level has been largely overcome, although differences continue to exist.

On the basis of numerous empirical studies,[10] we differentiate among three levels of film reception in the GDR. On the first level, the film is understood and experienced only on the basis of what is seen and heard with no attention given to social and aesthetic factors, and without knowledge of political, economic, cultural, or historical events referred to. The film is seen merely as a sequence of various actions and events. The Soviet art scholar Mejlach calls this "elementary

[8] Ute Scheffler, "Kunst in der Lebensweise von Produktionsarbeitern - Kultursoziologische Analyse zu Interessen, Verhaltensweisen, Ansprüchen," Diss., Akademie für Gesellschaftswissenschaften, Berlin, 1985.

[9] See Lothar Bisky and Dieter Wiedemann, *Der Spielfilm - Rezeption und Wirkung* (Berlin: Henschel, 1985), pp. 147ff.

[10] For more information, see Bisky and Wiedemann, pp. 63ff.

reception."[11] Several studies show that this mode of reception is common in children.[12]

The second level differs from the first in that here the film is interpreted as a conveyor of various political, moral, or cultural messages. On this level what has been seen or heard in the film is put into a greater social context; the spectators bring their experience, knowledge, and value orientations to bear in their viewing experience.

A third level of reception is reached when the film is interpreted as belonging to a specific political, moral, aesthetic, or philosophical tradition. This presupposes knowledge and experience, as well as the ability to make abstractions, for the viewer discerns and interprets the message of the film as an example of a larger socio-cultural trend.

The same moviegoer may well use differing levels of film reception. The sophisticated film viewer may enjoy a Samurai film or a Western on the action level without perceiving the cultural codes, cultural meanings, and messages of these films. However, the trend toward a functional differentiation of film usage shows that a "mass basis" for higher levels of reception standards exists without the first steps of reception being abandoned. Summing up these tendencies, one may say that the function-oriented differentiation of use is shaping reception habits more and more. The contradictory character of these phenomena must always be taken into account.

Film reception studies have also shown that appealing films which awaken interest in the viewers can be interpreted very imaginatively.[13] The common view that watching television is a passive mode of behavior fails to take notice of these moments of productive reception, of creative interpretation and richness of thought which sometimes occur in the recep-

---

[11] Boris Mejlach, *Künstlerisches Schaffen und Rezeptionsprozeß* (Berlin/Weimar: Henschel, 1977).

[12] Uta Hallmann, "Untersuchungen zu den Spielfilminteressen der Schüler der Klassen 5 bis 7," Diss., Berlin, 1978; Karin Wadetzky, "Psychologisch-pädagogische Untersuchungen zur Aneignung von Theater durch Kinder," *Diplomarbeit*, Berlin, 1987.

[13] Dieter Wiedemann and Hans-Jörg Stiehler, "Auf der Suche nach Kommunikation," *Beiträge zur Film- und Fernsehwissenschaft*, 25, No. 4 (1984), 142ff.; Hans-Jörg Stiehler and Dieter Wiedemann, "Medienwirkungen als Analysegegenstand," *Beiträge zur Film- und Fernsehwissenschaft*, 29, No. 2 (1987), 139ff.

tion of television programs as well as films. Especially the younger generation, brought up from early youth with the media, manifest these elements of productive and imaginative viewing.

Films as Entertainment

All surveys taken on the subject in recent years indicate a growing demand for entertainment in the GDR.[14] Entertainment is defined in different ways, however, and therefore it is necessary to look more closely at what is meant by this increased need.

The survey carried out in Berlin plants in 1984 showed that the workers had well-defined entertainment concepts.[15] I will limit my comments here to their interest in entertainment films, television series, plays, and films. Generally speaking, the workers welcomed the efforts of GDR television to include more entertainment programming. But it is apparent that this statement of entertainment wishes does not do justice to the workers' expectations in regard to content and quality. More was expected than "mere amusement," particularly in regard to feature films, TV plays, and series.

The production workers interviewed made a clear distinction between "trivial, superficial" entertainment programs and "demanding" entertainment.[16] They expected moreover that the programming would have relevance for them: coping with everyday problems in an amusing or relaxing way is what was wanted — entertaining productions tackling or touching upon their own experiences, thought-provoking, heartening programming that takes the viewers seriously. This wording of a worker expresses it best: "a story we can relate to, where you can laugh here and there, encouraging us to carry on tomorrow, is really entertaining."[17] At the same time high de-

---

[14] For more information, see *Zur Unterhaltungsfunktion des Films für Kino und Fernsehen*, Arbeitshefte, No. 38, Akademie der Künste der DDR (Berlin, 1986).

[15] For more details, see Lothar Bisky, "Kulturbedürfnisse und Leistungsverhalten," pp. 218f.

[16] Lothar Bisky, "Unterhaltungsfunktion des Films und Unterhaltungsbedürfnisse," in *Zur Unterhaltungsfunktion des Films für Kino und Fernsehen*, p. 55. My translation here and throughout.

[17] Ibid.

mands were placed on artistic quality and craftsmanship. This is not least of all a result of extensive visual experience.

We can — at least hypothetically — conclude that the viewers' expectation that programming deal with everyday issues and be relevant to their own social experience, reflects their need for social and cultural identity as GDR citizens. They expect to take part in programs dealing with arguments on socialist values and way of life.

In addition, the Berlin surveys showed that the factory workers had a good remembrance of DEFA feature films and important television productions of the 1970s. This is an interesting general phenomenon in the GDR. Retrospective programs with older films and television productions are successful. People are beginning to think about how to make better use of our film heritage. The State Film Archive, one of the largest collections of international film art with more than 60,000 films, is particularly active in this regard, organizing many activities and cooperating with the film-club movement.

Film Debate: How to Reach the Public

It goes without saying that these changes in the use of film are being thought about and discussed by experts in the GDR. Questions are being raised, on the one hand, about the function, intention, and quality of films, and, on the other, about the future of film as a cultural institution in view of the decreased number of moviegoers.

The discussion of how filmmaking should react to social and cultural change in the GDR is taking place in manifold ways. Directors such as Heiner Carow, Lothar Warneke, Günther Rücker, Rainer Simon, to name only a few, have given their individual responses in recent films.[18] All are concerned about reaching the public, and try to take the social experiences of the spectators into account as well as their changed visual habits. At the CSCE cultural forum in Budapest in 1985, Lothar Warneke, concurring with sociological findings, maintained that

> the filmmaker increasingly must face the
> social experiences of the viewer. This is an

---

[18] For example, Heiner Carow, *So viele Träume* (1987); Lothar Warneke, *Blonder Tango* (1986); Günther Rücker, *Hilde, das Dienstmädchen* (1986); and Rainer Simon, *Wengler und Söhne* (1987).

element which requires truthfulness and always questions a one-sided view of reality. And here I must confess that this situation brings me in my creative activity to another dialectical contradiction, i.e., between aesthetics and morals or between aesthetics and politics.[19]

Warneke defined his position: "I cannot and do not want to stand apart as a sensitive observer and notetaker of human and social happenings. When social changes are taking place around me . . . I do not stay on the outside, I am right in the center of things and involved" (p. 99).

Of interest are the approaches of younger directors. Peter Kahane's recent film *Vorspiel* (1987) inquires into serious problems of young people, their social experiences, with a cheerful sovereignty not to be found in DEFA films up to now. The examination films of directing students at the Filmhochschule in 1987 showed a distinct trend toward powerful visual language, the deliberate use of visual experiences of the public. It is significant that documentary films made by film students consistently are received with interest and often find a remarkable echo.

Many of the young filmmakers have an unbroken faith in the future of film (including those who go into television). Generally speaking, the young generation reflects on the current trends in film culture more objectively than the older, perhaps because a nostalgic recollection of packed cinemas is not part of their social experience. This enables them to respond to trends in the development of film culture. A striving for high artistic standards is obvious. Future training programs should give more consideration to real new trends and promote the particularly gifted and their search for individual modes and style.

In the very center of the debate on film culture is the question about the essential contribution of domestic film-making to a general discussion on values and way of life in the GDR: which discoveries can it make, how can it contribute to a creative intellectual atmosphere within the process of public discussion? Although domestic films represent only a small

---

[19] *Budapester Kulturforum. Diskussionsbeiträge von Mitgliedern der DDR-Delegation* (Berlin: Dietz, 1986), p. 99.

percentage of the films seen in the GDR, they are of decisive importance for the cultural development of the GDR. Thoughts on the improvement of film production and distribution, on aesthetic education, and more productive co-operation between television and film theaters: intensive reflection on ways to reach the public has begun.

The Role of Women in GDR Films
since the Early 1970s

Heinz Kersten

Frauenschicksale (*Fates of Women*) was the title of an early DEFA film by Slatan Dudow (1952), and since then the lives of women have repeatedly played a special role in film production in Babelsberg, especially since the beginning of the 1970s. This coincides with the significance given to women's liberation in the social development of the GDR. The film medium has taken over the task of pointing out the discrepancies between the legislated equal rights of women and everyday reality, in particular in the private realm. Films reflect the situation of women in GDR society very accurately.

Some statistical background to start with: in 1974 there were approximately 1.3 million more women than men in the GDR, especially among the older generations; in the age group of 45 and older there were 10,000 unmarried women per 1,000 unmarried men. There were twice as many divorced women as men. In that year 140,000 weddings contrasted with approximately 40,000 divorces, i.e., there was more than one divorce for every four marriages. Two thirds of all divorces were filed by women.[1] In 1986 52,439 divorces were granted; there were 32 divorces per 10,000 inhabitants, the highest divorce rate since the GDR came into being.[2] Between 1971 and 1982 the number of marriages in the GDR decreased by 62,500.[3] About 50% of the GDR labor force is made up of

---

[1] Regine Sylvester, "Film und Wirklichkeit," in *Emanzipation der Frau, Information*, Nos. 6/7, 1975, published by the Hochschule für Film und Fernsehen der DDR.

[2] *Statistisches Taschenbuch der Deutschen Demokratischen Republik 1987* (Berlin: Staatsverlag, 1987), p. 147.

[3] "Scheidungsquote in der DDR 1986 auf dem höchsten Stand," *Der Tagesspiegel*, 26 July 1987, p. 2.

women. In 1985 over 81% of the female labor force had completed a program of professional or vocational training; 16.8% had a diploma from a technical college, and 5.8% an academic degree.[4]

Twenty-six films with female protagonists from the period 1971 to 1987 were analyzed for this study (the overall DEFA production for this time period averaged twelve feature films for adults per year). In the films to be treated here the following types of women and topics recurred:

- single women with children – 11 films;

- single women without children – 5 films;

- women looking for a partner (and a new beginning for their lives) – 4 films;

- women in secure or elevated professional positions – 12 films;

- women in relatively underprivileged social positions – 6 films;

- women's friendships, whereby the friend serves as a complementing or contrasting figure – women's solidarity is an accompanying motif – 7 films;

- marriage problems – 7 films;

- problems with foreigners as partners – 2 films.

The first "women's film" in the time period treated — *Der Dritte* by Egon Günther (1971) — is also one of the best known (not only in the GDR). At the same time it marks the beginning of a new phase in the development of the GDR's one film company, DEFA. The change of leadership from Walter Ulbricht to Erich Honecker — at the Eighth Party Congress in 1971 — opened up new cultural-political perspectives, which can be summed up with Honecker's frequently quoted statement that there can be no taboos in the area of art and litera-

---

[4] *Statistisches Jahrbuch 1986 der Deutschen Demokratischen Republik* (Berlin: Staatsverlag, 1986), p. 124.

ture, providing that the artist proceeds from a firm socialist position.[5]

The story of Margit Fließer, who grew up in a church-run children's home and who, after two disappointing relationships, chooses a third man herself, was first used by the writer Eberhard Panitz in his *Reportageband Der siebente Sommer* (1966) and later in his novel *Unter den Bäumen regnet es zweimal* (1969). He had come across the story in the oil *Kombinat* Schwedt. As early as 1967-68 Günther Rücker, one of the best DEFA authors, made it into a screenplay, to which Egon Günther later added the Lucie motif. The Lucie character, a common example of a single woman, complements the unusual (even if authentic) case of Margit and thereby lends the subject matter a certain general validity. What distinguished this film from most of the previous DEFA productions was the humor and imagination, poetry, and considerable irony with which Günther treated his topic. The director shattered DEFA convention by having young Margit, an overly eager member of the FDJ (Free German Youth) sleep with her anything but progressive teacher and, already unclad down to her bra, proclaim: "One has to have a goal in mind" — thus parodying a FDJ song then in vogue: "Du hast ja ein Ziel vor den Augen."

Unusually realistic for Babelsberg up until then too were scenes like an abortion attempt with hot baths and red wine, and a latently lesbian exchange of affections between Margit and her friend Lucie. The film wants to draw attention to the still existing discrepancy between reality and Bebel's postulate about woman in socialist society: "In choosing love she is as free and unimpeded as the man. She courts or lets herself be courted and makes the bond on the basis of her inclination and out of no other considerations."[6] The essence of the film's message is the monologue that Margit holds in front of her two daughters shortly before the end of the film; here she points out the contradiction between her work as a computer operator and private role expectancy: "exactly like at grandmother's time."

---

[5] See "Hauptaufgabe umfaßt auch weitere Erhöhung des kulturellen Niveaus," *Neues Deutschland*, 18 December 1971.

[6] August Bebel, *Die Frau und der Sozialismus* (Frankfurt/M.: Marxistische Blätter, 1981), p. 515. My translation here and throughout.

The motif of the single woman looking for a new partner or risking a new start in life recurs in three later films. It is used most pointedly — as a model, so to speak — in Lothar Warneke's film: *Eine sonderbare Liebe* (1984). Sybille See-wald, a professionally successful woman in her forties, head of a kitchen in a large factory, suddenly becomes aware of her private isolation; the triggering experience is the death of an unmarried neighbor, which was hardly noticed: she doesn't want to die like that.[7] Her situation becomes especially evident to her at a company party when a colleague with whom she has occasionally slept tries to conceal the relationship — he is, after all, married. She gives him his walking papers and spends the night with a widowed colleague. This spontaneous night together is followed by timid abstinence on his part, so that she once again takes the initiative, appearing one day on his doorstep with all of her belongings: "You are alone, I am alone — why don't we live together?" Such a spontaneous approach to solving their problems naturally only creates new ones, especially since they have different temperaments. She, being a very active type, tries first of all to completely redo the house; he, having a more contemplative nature, reacts by withdrawing more and more. The last scene of the film shows them sitting in bed and looking perplexedly into the camera — open end.

In addition, the film draws attention to a problem that is addressed in many films: the inability to communicate with one another, to discuss common problems and conflicts in order to possibly reach a solution. On the other hand, films in the GDR often give rise to discussions. This is one of the most positive functions which film exercises in GDR society — incomparable with the role of film in the West. Not only are so-called film forums regularly held, that is, film makers travel around the country and discuss their films with their audience; in some instances films are catalysts for deeper discussions which are carried out in the press. One example is *Eine sonderbare Liebe*: in the February 1985 issue of *Weimarer Beiträge* seven authors discuss the film thoroughly and controversially; in addition to an examination of aesthetic aspects, the article provides a critical reflection on problems of

---

[7] In the previous film by Warneke, *Die Beunruhigung*, the protagonist, after a medical diagnosis pointing to possible breast cancer, reflects on her situation: living alone with her nearly grown son, she is having an affair with a married man who has no time for her at this important moment in her life.

women's liberation and partnership problems in the GDR as a whole.[8]

In *Dach überm Kopf* (1980) by Ulrich Thein, the protagonist is a woman who, as she puts it, waited with "Nibelungian fidelity" for the return of her child's father. When her son is old enough to stand on his own feet, she ends her waiting and gives up her job as a cook in her mother's restaurant in a small village on the Isle of Rügen. She goes to Berlin and works as kitchen help in a big company where she must hold her own against an overbearing boss. In general, life in the big city represents a test of strength for her. Her uncle's small house, which she takes over, turns out to be a run-down *Wohnlaube*, which she first has to fix up, with the help of a construction crew. She eventually finds a new partner in the construction foreman, after initial quarrels and measuring of the other's strength.

The heroine of the film *Kaskade rückwärts* (1984) also leaves her secure job in the country and moves with her half-grown daughter to Berlin. She accepts a job as conductor with the Reichsbahn and privately starts her search for a man. An affair with a composer living in the same house ends in disappointment. Some comical episodes follow and a few typically male behavior patterns are depicted when she continues her search by means of a personal ad in the newspaper. Finally a rather shy colleague from the railway appears to be the "right" new partner.

Iris Gusner, the director of this film, is one of the few female filmmakers in the GDR. As such, she has repeatedly dealt with women's problems. Her first treatment of the topic was a hilarious short film for TV on the role reversal of a young married couple, *Man nennt mich jetzt Mimi* (1976). While vacationing on the Baltic Sea, she appears as the man; he, as the woman.[9]

In *Alle meine Mädchen* (1980), Iris Gusner portrays the tense relations between the world of work and the private sphere using the example of a female brigade in an East Berlin

---

[8] Lothar Bisky, Irene Dölling, Michael Franz, Wolfgang Gersch, Irene Knoll, Rolf Richter, Waltraud Warnecke, "'Eine sonderbare Liebe' von Lothar Warneke," *Weimarer Beiträge*, 31, No. 2 (1985), 309-28.

[9] Stories on role reversals can also be found in the anthology by Edith Anderson, *Blitz aus heiterm Himmel* (Rostock: Hinstorff, 1975).

lightbulb factory — this is an exception in that most other women's films concentrate on private life. The frame for the plot is the attempt of a film student to make a film about the brigade. In this way, the problems the girls have with each other, with themselves, and with their supervisor surface. Like several of the Babelsberg productions of this time, the film *Alle meine Mädchen* wants to draw attention to the incongruencies in the social relations of people, to promote more mutual understanding and tolerance, self-confidence and self-realization, and individuality within the collective.[10]

Iris Gusner is also the director of one of two films dealing with a specific aspect of this topic: the relationship between partners of different nationality. Her film *Wäre die Erde nicht rund* (1981) is highly autobiographical. While studying geology in Moscow, a female student and a fellow-student from Syria become acquainted. They marry and have a daughter, but soon experience problems which derive from the different role expectations they have as a result of their socialization in different cultures. The marriage finally comes to an end when the woman realizes that as a woman she would not have a chance to work in her profession in Syria, while the man feels he must return to his home country because the condition placed on his being allowed to study was his later participation in the country's development.[11]

What has distinguished GDR "women's films" from most contemporary DEFA films is, not least, a deeper depiction of conflict which usually rejects happy-end solutions. The first film to demonstrate this very clearly — and in a stylistically new way as well — was one of the biggest DEFA domestic successes and became known beyond the borders of the GDR as well: *Die Legende von Paul und Paula* (1973). The director Heiner Carow made use of a story that, in spite of its almost fairy-tale typification, does not seem contrived. The heroine, with whom the audience can identify, lives life to the fullest;

---

[10] Another female group portrait was *Die Stunde der Töchter* (1981) by Erwin Stranka: the meeting of four sisters at their father's sickbed serves as the framework for the portrayal of four different women's life stories — a family panorama that also provides insight into problems specific to GDR society and the liberation or non-liberation of women.

[11] An earlier film had also dealt with the theme of love between partners of different national backgrounds: *Ein April hat 30 Tage* (1979) by Gunther Scholz. In this film the brief passionate relationship of a young single mother and an Argentinian living in exile in the GDR comes to an end when the Latin American is called back to his country to perform illegal party work.

and the story is told in a precise style of poetically exaggerated realism which is not afraid to use melodramatic elements. The screenplay is by Ulrich Plenzdorf, whose play *Die neuen Leiden des jungen W.* was at the same time becoming a similarly big box office success both in the GDR and the Federal Republic. The film centers around the young salesgirl Paula, who has two illegitimate children from two different men — in this respect she resembles Margit Fließer in *Der Dritte.* Paula falls in love with Paul, an established, married civil servant, who in the beginning hesitates to show his love for her because he thinks he cannot risk a divorce in his position. After he finally does leave his wife (who is characterized somewhat too one-sidedly as only pretty, superficial, and dumb), Paula dies during the birth of their child. Beyond the Moritat-like love story, the film reflects on conformity or the dialectics of the ideal and reality, and — marginally — on cinema itself. It supports a personality ideal that has much in common with the "total human being" portrayed by GDR poet and dramatist Volker Braun in *Kipper Paul Bauch,* which was produced for the stage at the same time; it argues for a socialist humanity which fills all human needs — emotional, sensual, and spiritual — equally.

The female image conveyed in the film was partially criticized by women, however. The East Berlin critic Regine Sylvester wrote:

> [Der Film] wirft aber Fragen auf, bedenkt man die Autorenwertung, die Paulas bedingungslose Unterwerfung, ihre Hingabe an den Mann, ihre Sprachlosigkeit dem Mann gegenüber (— sie bezieht zu ihrer Situation nur im Monolog Stellung —) kritiklos beläßt und durch Pauls endgültige Rückkehr in ihre Arme belohnt. Auch Paulas Tod bei der Geburt ihres dritten Kindes — die Gefahr war ihr und Paul bekannt, sie hat das Risiko auf sich genommen, um diese große Liebe ganz zu vollenden — hat mit Selbstaufgabe zu tun; oder auch mit Hilflosigkeit, anders als durch ein Kind die Dauerhaftigkeit einer Liebesbeziehung auszudrücken und zu erleben. [12]

---

[12] Regine Sylvester, "Film und Wirklichkeit," p. 100.

And the West Berlin feminist film magazine *Frauen und Film* published a multi-paged negative review which of course completely ignored the significance of the film in the context of previous GDR productions.[13]

New, too, was the depiction of a social milieu that had appeared on the screen in the so-called Berlin films of the mid-1950s and would reappear as a favorite site in several films in the early 1980s: the *Kiez* of Prenzlauer Berg. Included in this was the contrast between the unskilled, simple salesgirl Paula and the established civil servant Paul.

Problems in partner relationships caused by the couple's unequal social levels is the subject of Egon Günther's film *Die Schlüssel* (1972). The differences between Klaus, the somewhat coolly pedantic, ambitious mechanical-engineering student, and the amicably unspoiled worker Ric, whom he often criticizes, become evident on a vacation trip to Cracow in Poland. They are based not only on their different characters but on their differing social positions as well. Ric is proud of what she does, but she knows that she is "less changeable" and will always lag behind her friend. Her courage in making such a confession, which has a freeing effect on her, is of course followed by the sudden fear of losing her friend. Searching for him, she blindly runs in front of a tram: death brings all hopes and fears for the future irreversibly to a sudden end.

The polarity of different social positions in society is found once again in Evelyn Schmidt's film *Das Fahrrad* (1982). The heroine of this film, Susanne Becker, just under thirty years old, has left her husband and is earning a living for herself and her young daughter at a monotonous, unsatisfying job, finding diversion only in occasional meetings with friends in a disco. One evening she meets Thomas there, a young man from a good family, an engineer who has recently become head of the department for technical production. Susanne senses the social differences and reacts very hesitatingly to Tommy's apparent interest in her. Through this brief encounter she becomes even more aware of the tristesse of her existence. The next morning she stands crying at the hated stamping machine. Finally she risks breaking out of this daily monotony: she quits her job. But a new and better one cannot be found so

---

[13] Helke Sander and R. Schlesier, "'Die Legende von Paul und Paula' - eine frauenverachtende Schnulze aus der DDR," *Frauen und Film*, 1, No. 2 (1974), 8ff.

quickly, her money runs out, she borrows some, and when the child gets sick, she reports her bike as stolen to get the insurance money. The deception is discovered and she faces charges in court.

This casts a shadow on her happy relationship with Thomas, which has begun in the meantime; he has found a job for her in his firm and moved her into his well-cared for new apartment. Her confession provokes from him as first reaction: "What if someone in the firm finds out!" His concern over his clean company record is apparently more important to him than the new companionship. Susanne is disillusioned, and Thomas' later willingness to help her, which is shown when he succeeds in having the case transferred from court to a commission for conflicts within the firm, does not affect this disillusionment. The difference between two life standards becomes increasingly clear. After an ugly dispute Susanne moves out. The last sequence of the film shows her teaching her daughter to ride a bicycle: happily laughing, Susanne looks on as the little girl proudly rides by herself around the old fountain on the market square. The bicycle becomes a symbol of newly won self-assurance and independent activity.

Susanne resembles somewhat the main character in another film, which appeared in the movie theaters a little less than a year earlier: *Bürgschaft für ein Jahr* (1981), directed by Herrmann Zschoche. The script, written by Gabriele Kotte, is based on a novel by Tine Schulze-Gerlach, which in turn describes an actual happening. The novel however is set in Dresden, while the film takes place in Berlin. Nina Kern, twenty-eight years old and mother of three children, divorced from her frequently drunken husband, who had beaten her, is, in the opinion of the neighborhood, *asozial*. She hangs around with men and doesn't fulfil her motherly duties. All three children have been placed in a children's home. With her confused, sometimes touchingly naive spontaneity, the supposedly delinquent woman radiates a human warmth that immediately makes her likeable. What makes one shiver, on the other hand, is the behavior of all the "normal" people, who consider themselves so much better than the *Rabenmutter*, who in reality is so devoted to her children that she will do anything to get them back. Two *Bürgen*, citizens from the neighborhood, assigned officially by the court, are supposed to see to it that she improves beforehand.

With a new solid friend, Nina cleans up the apartment and cares for the youngest daughter, who has been given back to her for a probationary period. She pays for a short time of happiness with another man with renewed loneliness: the new man just spends a few enjoyable hours with her, and the far too *brav* but reliable other man has left in the meantime, too. What is left is the dull everyday work of cleaning the subway (a leitmotif to which the film repeatedly returns) and the children, with whom, after the release of the older two from the home, she will not be able to cope by herself — unsolved problems. At the end is a close-up of the resigned, sadly questioning face of Nina. Her adapting appears to be successful. Her claim to happiness is not yet resolved.

A film heroine who insists on her claim to happiness and who — along with Margit Fließer and Paula — became the most popular of all those mentioned here is Ingrid Sommer, better known as Sunny, the title heroine of Konrad Wolf and Wolfgang Kohlhaase's film *Solo Sunny*. Like Nina Kern, Sunny doesn't live in a chic new apartment but rather in a *Hinterhof* apartment in Prenzlauer Berg. The neighbors complain about her, too: her music is often too loud and she often has different men visiting her. Most of the time, however, the former factory worker travels around the countryside as a singer in a pop group playing *Kulturhäuser* in the provinces. Her insatiable drive to say what she thinks and her unwillingness to make concessions result in the loss of her job, and her love for a young philosopher who refuses to pursue a career fails as well due to her uncompromising expectations.

When, in addition to this private disappointment, she experiences a professional one — at her first big singing debut in a Berlin bar she comes up against the indifference of an audience which is only concerned with itself — she takes an overdose of sleeping pills, but is rescued. At the end she attempts a new beginning with a young band; whether or not she'll succeed remains open. "One must be able to be a personality without being famous," Sunny once says.

Along with Nina Kern (*Bürgschaft für ein Jahr*), Susanne Becker (*Das Fahrrad*), and Sabine Wulff, the heroine in a film of the same title by Erwin Stranka — these anti-heroines of DEFA films — Sunny belongs to the so-called "marginal figures" of society who moved into the center of DEFA productions at the beginning of the 1980s, and in so doing triggered a heated discussion. Advocates of the films countered the opponents of these atypical heroes saying that the very term "marginal figure" was alien to the socialist concept of humanity. Moreover, they could point to the success of most of the movies, the themes of which obviously hit a nerve of society. All these films address petit-bourgeois tendencies in GDR society — very frequently in connection with marriage themes in which women again play dominant and positive roles.

Heiner Carow's *Bis daß der Tod euch scheidet* (1979) was the most provocative of the films on this topic. The story of a young marriage, one of the too early and immature sort that frequently takes place in the GDR, is told in an unmistakably polemic fashion. The film is intended to show that neither an intact social environment — in this case, sympathetic colleagues at work — nor the heeding of well-intended advice are a guarantee of personal happiness. Sonja and Jens, barely twenty years old, pledge their eternal love for one another after their civil marriage ceremony; and at first things go well, or at least according to the book: *Our Family*, a wedding present from their colleagues at work. The problems begin with their first child; after spending the *Babyjahr* at home, Sonja wants to go back to her old job in the department store, but Jens is strictly against it. When Sonja goes back to school without his knowledge and earns her qualification as a skilled worker, he feels deceived. He beats her, gets drunk, runs away, and then is tearfully remorseful — a never-ending cycle. When Jens finds out that Sonja has aborted a child that had been conceived while he was drunk, the fighting breaks out once more, and in her desperation she watches emotionlessly as he picks up a beer bottle containing acid and drinks from it. A crass effect, but it is based on a true story; this first inspired Günther Rücker to write his screenplay.

The film ends the way it began: with a wedding celebration. This time Sonja's friend is getting married and she too receives the clever marriage book as a present, along with a *Gartenzwerg*. Sonja screams out her guilt, but after initial consternation no-one really wants to hear about it: the unpleasant truth could interfere with the harmony and joy of the celebration. How Sonja and the now mute Jens will cope with their guilt is left open.

It is not coincidental that the portrayal of interhuman relationships became a major topic in film as well as in all other areas of GDR art and literature in the late 1970s. Here there was the opportunity to discuss mistakes, something which had always been prevented where political questions were concerned. Here one could show and discuss — without prettifying — what was wrong and should be changed in regard to human relationships, especially those between men and women. Dealing with these questions is not an escape into the private realm; partnership and marriage can be viewed as a mirror of social problems.

In Frank Beyer's *Das Versteck* (1978), which is based on a script by Jurek Becker, a divorced husband seeks shelter with his ex-wife after a year of separation; pretending to be (wrongly) pursued by the police, he in reality wants to explore the chances for a new beginning. Despite a reconciliation, the woman in the end is frightened away from beginning her marriage all over again. Before this point is reached, however, they relive in flashbacks the main stages of their relationship, from the first rush of emotions to the typical signs of erosion, his egotistical indifference, her rebellion against conformity, convenience, boredom, and their mutual aversion to arguing. When the woman speaks of the necessity of discussing problems, because otherwise the unnatural peace and quiet of a cemetery prevails, one senses that not only the marriage is meant — especially since such pleas for more openness and honesty in both private and public life have recurred as a leitmotiv in several GDR films and books.

In Evelyn Schmidt's debut film *Seitensprung* (1980) a couple with a five-year-old son is presented as an average family: it is enclosed in an oppressive "home-sweet-home" idyll with firm rules and the fatal tendency to sweep problems under the carpet. One day a problem turns up — literally — at the front door in the form of the husband's twelve-year-old illegitimate daughter. It comes to light that the husband has been having an affair all along with the girl's mother, who has suddenly died. The brunt of the ensuing conjugal conflict is borne — as so often happens — by the child.

Herrmann Zschoche's film *Glück im Hinterhaus* (1980), a movie adaption of Günter de Bruyn's novel *Buridans Esel* (1968), was released at nearly the same time. De Bruyn's book had been one of the first literary discussions of the new *Spießer* mentality and consumer ideology in the GDR. The realization of Ulrich Plenzdorf's screenplay for the film was delayed for nearly a decade. It focuses on the mid-life crisis of a forty-year-old director of a local library in East Berlin who falls in love with a young female apprentice not only because of her outer charm but also because he sees in her a reincarnation of the ideals of his own youth. But the brief attempt to escape from his dull marriage, his career ambitions, and his high standard of living fails.

Roland Oehme, as he has said,[14] also proceeded from the assumption that there are innumerable extramarital affairs in the GDR when he made the film *Meine Frau Inge und meine Frau Schmidt* (1985). He wanted to experiment with the question of what would happen if such an affair took place openly instead of being kept secret. The subject had already been treated in a radio play of the same title by Joachim Brehmer in 1976, but there it was framed in the relatively harmless form of a dream. Oehme's film comedy presents the story as a modern fairy tale, whereby the realistic background of a fictitious GDR town prevents the mind game of "What would happen if . . ." from being viewed as simply a dalliance in a fool's paradise. Karl Lehmann is surprised when, at a company party, Brigitte Schmidt, the plant's nurse, asks him to father her child. The divorced Frau Schmidt assures the happily married Lehmann that there would be no other obligations, and thus he sees nothing standing in the way of accepting the offer, which he enjoys so much that he presses for repetition. After a brief irritation Lehmann's wife Inge agrees with Frau Schmidt to share Karl like sisters. In shifts he now spends one week at home with his legally married wife and daughter, and the next week with his other "wife." The compromise proves to be extremely fruitful. It not only revives the old love and makes him the happy father of Frau Schmidt's twins but also of Frau Inge's new offspring. It is society around them that can't refrain from malicious comments, although some people do show understanding for the happy threesome.

Up to this point one could dismiss the film as a typical male fantasy, but here the women seize the initiative once again and this time to Karl's initial discomfort. (As so often happens in GDR literature and films, in this case, too, the women are more active, more open to new ideas than the man.) What is fair for him seems only fair for Brigitte and Inge, too: each now takes a second lover, without planning to give up the first one. Karl leaves anyway, manifesting the old jealous Adam, until he realizes that this new, more humane

<hr>

[14] "Gespräch mit dem Regisseur Roland Oehme," *Progress-Pressebulletin Kino DDR*, No. 2, 1985.

way of living together can only work out if all have the same rights. For the sake of equality he divorces his wife Inge, and the whole extended family — augmented by the two additional men — celebrates the divorce with a feast on a tower overlooking the town. The director of the film, as he has stated, wanted to provide a catalyst — especially for young people — to bring about a discussion of how love, marriage, and living together might function in the future; Oehme views the film as an appeal for more humane relations between the sexes.[15]

Public response to Oehme's film was minimal; discussions took place only at film forums, and the critics' reviews were unanimously negative, although I suspect — as often happens in the West, too, in the case of radical films — aesthetic reservations were placed in the forefront in order to avoid discussing the provocative theme. In recent years, however, other DEFA films as well have failed to achieve the public response aroused by productions at the beginning of the 1980s.

Nor was Heiner Carow successful, as he had hoped, in repeating the success of *Paul und Paula* and *Bis daß der Tod euch scheidet* with his most recent film, *So viele Träume* (1986), although he wanted a connection to be made between the new film and the other two — *So viele Träume* as the concluding film of a trilogy of "women's films," as it were. The 33-year-old scriptwriter Wolfgang Witt based his screenplay on a factual report: *Die Hebamme* by Imma Lüning. Some aspects of the film are reminiscent of motifs from Carow's earlier films; one is reminded too of Egon Günther's heroine in *Der Dritte*. Drunken assaults had already been the problem of the couple in *Bis daß der Tod euch scheidet*. The heroine of *So viele Träume* was also once in love with a man who, with increasing frequency, beat her when drunk. A reason for his aggression was that he, a *Grenzgänger* between East and West Berlin, working in the East and living in the West, had for her sake stayed in the East when the Wall was built in 1961. When she couldn't take it any longer, she left him; pregnant, she settles in a town on the Baltic. The son that is born of this failed relationship is deaf and dumb. Carow does not hesitate to speak of disappointed hopes, unfulfilled desires, and the unredeemed claim to private happiness.

---

[15] Ibid.

As in his earlier films, Carow is *unbequem*, and, with his contrived story and the complicated narrative structure which uses flashbacks, dreams, and monologues, he expects more than a simple consuming of the film by the audience. At the beginning of the twenty-four-hour time span of the film, the heroine, a woman in her mid-forties, head midwife at a university clinic, returns home from the capital where she received a high official honor. At home, she is awaited by her half-grown son and her lover, who is twenty years younger. She is accompanied by a younger woman whom she has met on the train and invited to stay with her. To their surprise they soon discover that the younger woman is the midwife's daughter, whom she had left behind as a two-year-old child when she ran away from her husband. Breaking into the banquet room where the midwife is being honored, the daughter screams this at her mother. After this scandal the young woman tells her mother's lover about her own difficult childhood with a bad stepmother, her years in a home for juvenile delinquents, and two unhappy love affairs. Returning home after an upsetting night at the hospital, the midwife discovers that she has probably lost her lover to her daughter. At the end we see the woman riding on a train, just as she was in the beginning, but this time toward the unknown, again reflecting on memories and dreams.

Among the important aspects of Carow's film is that he, in the figure of his protagonist, mirrors a section of GDR history: the beginnings of women's emancipation and the optimism of the *Aufbau* years. When the family of the simple fisher boy, who has made her pregnant, automatically expects them to get married, she replies: "Ich kann doch nicht jeden heiraten, bloß weil er mich mal umgelegt hat. Jetzt haben wir eine neue Zeit. . . ."

Siegfried Kühn's film *Der Traum vom Elch* (1986), which came out soon after *So viele Träume*, stays more in the private sphere. The title is that of the novel by Herbert Otto, but the fact that both of these films about women deal with unfulfilled dreams seems to me to indicate a new trend toward resignation, a trend which can also be seen in the most recent example of the genre — *Die Alleinseglerin* (1987). Anna, the protagonist of *Der Traum vom Elch*, an anaesthesia nurse, about 30, divorced and childless, is in love with a man who loves his freedom and whom she sees only twice a year. After a crisis brought about by the suicide of her friend, who felt rejected by the man she loved, and by the hopelessness of her own new relationship with a married man who has little time for her, Anna parts with her dream, deciding not to wait any more for the rare meetings with her lover. What remains, so we can assume at the end of the film, is the compensative satisfaction she finds in her work.

Neither is personal happiness attained by the heroine of the most recent DEFA *Frauenfilm*: *Die Alleinseglerin* by Herrmann Zschoche, based on motifs from the autobiographical narrative by Christine Wolter. The film character Christine, divorced mother of a boy, inherits a sailboat from her father. The boat becomes a symbol of the testing of her strength, of her ability as a woman to persevere in a male-dominated society. In her determination to get the boat afloat again she risks her career as a literary scholar as well as her relationship with a new friend, and the chance for a new start with her ex-husband. When she finally sets out with the boat for the first time it runs aground on a sandbank. The final frame of the film shows her face, laughing defiantly. This is illustrative of the new tones of female self-irony which, along with the satirical portrayal of academe, give the film something of a humorous sovereignty, without diminishing the skepticism vis-à-vis change in male consciousness and the sober regard of the losses deriving from emancipation.

The development of emancipation in GDR films from the early 1970s to the mid-1980s can perhaps be summarized as the development from the propagation of a new female self-understanding and self-confidence to computing the price paid for it, as was shown in the last three films discussed. At the same time, these films manifest the particular quality of DEFA films: even when they deal with dreams, they never become dream factories. Far more than West German or American films, GDR films are a mirror of their society.

Filmography

Listed in chronological order according to the premiere date: title, year, author of script (S), director (D), leading actors (A).

Der Dritte, 1971, S: Günther Rücker based on Eberhard Panitz' story *Unter den Bäumen regnet es zweimal*; D: Egon Günther; A: Jutta Hoffmann, Barbara Dittus, Rolf Ludwig

Die Schlüssel, 1972, S: Helga Schütz, Egon Günther; D: Egon Günther; A: Jutta Hoffmann, Jaecki Schwarz

Leben mit Uwe, 1973, S: Siegfried Pitschmann, Lothar Warneke; D: Lothar Warneke; A: Cox Habbema, Eberhard Esche

Die Legende von Paul und Paula, 1973, S: Ulrich Plenzdorf, Heiner Carow; D: Heiner Carow; A: Angelica Domröse, Wilfried Glatzeder

Die unverbesserliche Barbara, 1977, S: Lothar Warneke; D: Lothar Warneke; A: Cox Habbema, Peter Aust

Das Versteck, 1978, S: Jurek Becker; D: Frank Beyer; A: Jutta Hoffmann, Manfred Krug

Sabine Wulff, 1978, S: Erwin Stranka, based on Heinz Kruschel's novel *Gesucht wird die freundliche Welt*; D: Erwin Stranka; A: Karin Düwel

Ein April hat 30 Tage, 1979, S: Carlos Cerda, Gunther Scholz; D: Gunther Scholz; A: Angelika Waller, Jurie Darie

Bis daß der Tod euch scheidet, 1979, S: Günther Rücker; D: Heiner Carow; A: Katrin Saß, Martin Seifert

Solo Sunny, 1980, S: Wolfgang Kohlhaase; D: Konrad Wolf, Wolfgang Kohlhaase; A: Renate Krößner, Alexander Lang, Heide Kipp, Dieter Montag

Seitensprung, 1980, S: Regina Weickert; D: Evelyn Schmidt; A: Renate Geißler, Uwe Zerbe

Glück im Hinterhaus, 1980, S: Ulrich Plenzdorf, based on the novel *Buridans Esel* by Günter de Bruyn; D: Herrmann Zschoche; A: Dieter Mann, Ute Lubosch, Jutta Wachowiak

Alle meine Mädchen, 1980, S: Gabriele Kotte; D: Iris Gusner; A: Lissy Tempelhof, Madeleine Lierck, Barbara Schnitzler, Monica Bielenstein, Viola Schweizer, Evelin Splitt, Andrzej Pieczynski

Dach überm Kopf, 1980, S: Ulrich Thein; D: Ulrich Thein; A: Renate Geißler, Dieter Franke

Unser kurzes Leben, 1981, S: Regine Kühn, based on the novel *Franziska Linkerhand* by Brigitte Reimann; D: Lothar Warneke; A: Simone Frost, Hermann Beyer, Christine Schorn

Die Stunde der Töchter, 1981, S: Erwin Stranka, Walter Stranka; D: Erwin Stranka; A: Ursula Karusseit, Dorit Gäbler, Karin Düwel, Petra Blossey, Dietrich Mechow

Bürgschaft für ein Jahr, 1981, S: Gabriele Kotte, based on Tine Schulze-Gerlach's novel of the same title; D: Herrmann Zschoche; A: Katrin Saß, Monika Lennartz, Jan Spitzer, Jaecki Schwarz, Christian Steyer

Wäre die Erde nicht rund, 1981, S: Iris Gusner, Günter Haubold; D: Iris Gusner; A: Bozena Stryjek, Rasim Balajew

Die Beunruhigung, 1982, S: Helga Schubert; D: Lothar Warneke; A: Christine Schorn, Hermann Beyer, Cox Habbema

Das Fahrrad, 1982, S: Ernst Wenig; D: Evelyn Schmidt; A: Heidemarie Schneider, Roman Kaminski

Kaskade rückwärts, 1984, S: Iris Gusner, Roland Kästner; D: Iris Gusner; A: Marion Wiegmann, Johanna Schall, Siegfried Höchst, Jaecki Schwarz

Eine sonderbare Liebe, 1984, S: Wolfram Witt; D: Lothar Warneke; A: Christine Schorn, Jörg Gudzuhn

Meine Frau Inge und meine Frau Schmidt, 1985, S: Joachim Brehmer, based on his radio play of the same title; D: Roland Oehme; A: Katrin Saß, Viola Schweizer, Walter Plathe

So viele Träume, 1986, S: Wolfram Witt, based on the documentary *Die Hebamme* by Imma Lüning; D: Heiner Carow; A: Jutta Wachowiak, Dagmar Manzel, Peter René Lüdicke

Der Traum vom Elch, 1986, S: Christa Müller, based on Herbert Otto's novel of the same title; D: Siegfried Kühn; A: Katrin Saß, Marie Gruber, Christian Steyer, Detlef Heintze

Die Alleinseglerin, 1987, S: Regine Sylvester, based on Christine Wolter's novel of the same title; D: Herrmann Zschoche; A: Christina Powileit, Johanna Schall, Manfred Gorr, Götz Schubert

Gender and the Work Ethic
in the Environmental Novels of
Monika Maron and Lia Pirskawetz

Nancy Lukens

In a recent essay on ecological criticism in GDR prose Hubertus Knabe speaks of what he calls a new "Endzeit-Literatur," a recent tendency in GDR literature to focus on fundamental issues of human existence in modern industrial society.[1] Knabe makes two points about the ecological discussion as reflected in GDR literature of the 1980s which I would like to pursue in this study. First, he asserts that, despite its radical critique of the scientific-technological revolution, this literature nevertheless implies the possibility of change within socialist society through a "sanfte Revolution des Bewußtseins" (p. 221). Secondly, Knabe notes that it is most often female authors and female protagonists who suggest new attitudes which may point the way to the survival of the planet: "Die Destruktion der Materie durch Umweltzerstörung oder Aufrüstung erscheint vorrangig als maskulin verursacht, so daß ein anderer Umgang mit der Natur auch eine Stärkung femininer

---

[1] Hubertus Knabe, "Zweifel an der Industriegesellschaft - Ökologische Kritik in der erzählenden DDR-Literatur," *Umweltprobleme und Umweltbewußtsein in der DDR*, ed. Deutschland Archiv (Cologne: Wissenschaft und Politik, 1985), pp. 201-50. Other studies of ecological criticism in GDR literature include Wolfgang Ertl, "Zivilisationskritik in der Literatur der DDR: Überlegungen zu Hanns Cibulkas *Swantow*," in *Studies in GDR Culture and Society* 7, ed. Margy Gerber et al. (Lanham/New York/London: University Press of America, 1987), pp. 81-94; Wolfgang Ertl, "Ökolyrik in der DDR: Eine Beispielreihe," in *Studies in GDR Culture and Society* 5, ed. Margy Gerber et al. (Lanham/New York/London: University Press of America, 1985), pp. 221-35; Horst Dieter Schlosser, "'Wenn sich im Kraftwerk die Turbine dreht. . .' - Literarische Auskünfte über die Arbeitswelt," in *Die DDR-Gesellschaft im Spiegel ihrer Literatur*, ed. Gisela Helwig (Cologne: Wissenschaft und Politik, 1986), pp. 51-84; and Eckart Förtsch, "Fragen 'menschheitsgeschichtlichen Ausmaßes' - Wissenschaft, Technik, Umwelt," in *Die DDR-Gesellschaft im Spiegel ihrer Literatur*, pp. 85-105.

65

Verhaltensweisen erfordert, wie Christa Wolf oder Irmtraud Morgner meinen" (p. 220).

In this regard, Knabe cites a significant programmatic passage from Morgner's *Amanda* in which she analyzes the relationship between the work ethic and the threat of the destruction of humankind:

> Alleinherrschendes Eroberungsdenken in Gesellschaft, Wissenschaft und Technik hat die Erde an Abgründe geworfen. Eroberungsdenken von Männern — eine Kulturzüchtung, nicht Männernatur. Diese Züchtung wurde bis zur Perversion, die Selbstvernichtung einschließt, hochgetrieben. Nur wenn die andere Hälfte der Menschheit, die Frauen, bestimmte, bisher nur für private Zwecke entwickelte Fähigkeiten und Tugenden in die große Politik einbringt, können atomare und ökologische Katastrophen abgewendet werden. Nur wenn die Männer und die von Männern geführten progressiven Regierungen erkennen, daß sie die Probleme der Weltpolitik und Ökologie und ihre eigenen ohne gewisse Fähigkeiten und Tugenden der Frauen nicht bewältigen und entsprechend handeln, kann der Planet gerettet werden.[2]

The appearance of Christa Wolf's Chernobyl narrative *Störfall* (1987) certainly adds force to Knabe's observation about the "Endzeit-Literatur" of the early 1980s.[3] Wolf's *Frankfurter Poetik-Vorlesungen* and the accompanying novel *Kassandra*, which both appeared in the West the same year as Morgner's *Amanda* (1983),[4] had already offered lucid analyses of the relationship between our culture's loss of the traditionally feminine virtues and its self-destruction.

[2] Irmtraud Morgner, *Amanda. Ein Hexenroman* (Berlin/Weimar: Aufbau, 1983; Darmstadt/Neuwied: Luchterhand, 1983), as quoted in Knabe, pp. 220-21.

[3] Christa Wolf, *Störfall. Nachrichten eines Tages* (Berlin/Weimar: Aufbau, 1987; Darmstadt/Neuwied: Luchterhand, 1987).

[4] Christa Wolf, *Voraussetzungen einer Erzählung: Kassandra. Frankfurter Poetik-Vorlesungen* (Darmstadt/Neuwied: Luchterhand, 1983); and *Kassandra. Erzählung* (Darmstadt/Neuwied: Luchterhand, 1983). The GDR edition: *Kassandra. Vier Vorlesungen. Eine Erzählung* (Berlin/Weimar: Aufbau, 1983).

Knabe's observation that such non-quantifiable, social aspects of the environmental crisis[5] are coming into focus in GDR literature, and the suggestion that women's contribution to a transformation of ecological consciousness may be essential to human survival seem worthy of further consideration. If one accepts the widespread notion that GDR literature functions as a seismograph of changing social consciousness,[6] it makes sense to consider to what extent specific works which thematize ecological issues reflect such social considerations. In particular, I am interested in the question of how gender relates to the criticism of the prevailing ethos of productivity found in recent prose dealing with environmental themes. My thesis is that works by women authors and/or featuring female protagonists who deal with environmental issues bring what Morgner calls "bestimmte, bisher nur für private Zwecke entwickelte Fähigkeiten und Tugenden" into the public sphere of ecological policy. A major question to ask of these works, to follow the logic of the *Amanda* passage, is whether those in decision-making positions — Morgner assumes they are men or dominated by men — recognize the urgency of learning traditionally female skills, virtues, and perspectives, and act accordingly.

In this article, I consider two novels of the 1980s that complement the arguments of Wolf and Morgner about gender, rationality, and the self-destructive cycle in which in-

---

[5] There is little published material available reflecting official GDR environmental policy discussion. As far as unofficial discussion and activities are concerned, one valuable West German source of information and documentation on church, regional, and local initiatives is Peter Wensierski and Wolfgang Büscher, *Beton ist Beton. Zivilisationskritik aus der DDR* (Hattingen: Scandica Verlag, 1981). One Western observer of evolving GDR ecological policy notes that ecological factors have increasingly been included in the criteria of effective economic planning, and asserts the importance of including "die gesellschaftliche Dimension des Umweltproblems" in this planning (Gerhard Timm, "Die offizielle Ökologiedebatte in der DDR," in *Umweltprobleme und Umweltbewußtsein in der DDR*, p. 132). Timm quotes a GDR economist writing over a decade ago who had already emphasized the need to include social factors in ecological planning, though he claimed these factors to be largely non-quantifiable and hence not reflected in planning statistics. Timm's reference is to Günter Streibel, "Umweltschutz und Umweltgestaltung als volkswirtschaftliche Aufgabe," *Wirtschaftswissenschaft*, 23, No. 8 (1975), 1147 (not p. 1148 as Timm cites).

[6] This thesis is at the core of Anita M. Mallinckrodt's recent study of the environmental discussion in the GDR, *The Environmental Dialogue in the GDR. Literature, Church, Party and Interest Groups in their Socio-Political Context* (Lanham/New York/London: University Press of America, 1987), p. 19. See also Knabe, p. 202.

dustrial society finds itself: Monika Maron's *Flugasche*[7] and Lia Pirskawetz' *Der stille Grund*.[8] Both novels have female protagonists whose professional work confronts them directly with the ecological dilemma: the trade-off between economical growth and the destruction of nature, between instrumental and more holistic views of how the environment should affect quality of life. In both novels, a community's economic welfare seems to depend on an industrial plant which at the same time poses a threat to the quality of life. In each, the author focuses on the female protagonist's approach to the problem and her way of relating to the authority structures at the workplace. Hence I will look at the interaction of prevalent notions of gender role and the work ethic in the actions of each protagonist. I will also briefly consider differences in the narrative strategies used by Maron and Pirskawetz and the possible relevance of these differences for their representations of gender and the work ethic.

Maron's protagonist Josefa Nadler is a journalist with the Berlin paper *Illustrierte Woche* who is sent to talk to workers and management at an outdated, soot-belching power plant in the city of B. (presumably Bitterfeld). Her assignment is to get a story on the problems facing "the dirtiest city in Europe" (p. 32). The old plant is being kept running, perpetuating the documented health problems of its workers and the local populace, even though a new plant has been built and is due to begin operation. Details of Josefa's visit to the plant and her reflections on the significance of what she saw and heard there are interwoven into the fabric of Maron's narrative. Her novel centers on the conflicts of values experienced by Josefa both at work and in her personal life as a result of her uncompromising approach to both. The often mentioned 180 tons of "Flugasche" (fly ash), which alert her to the urgency of the problem during her visit to B., symbolize both the ecological problem that is the subject of Josefa's assignment and the personal conflict she experiences between truth and compromise in journalism, between her confrontational style and the "realism" of her superiors and friends.

[7] Monika Maron, *Flugasche* (Frankfurt/M.: Fischer, 1981). An English version has appeared under the title *Flight of Ashes* (London/New York: Readers International, 1986), translated by David Newton Marinelli. Subsequent references to *Flugasche* will appear parenthetically in the text. Translations of passages are my own.

[8] Lia Pirskawetz, *Der stille Grund* (Berlin: Neues Leben, 1985). All subsequent references to this novel appear parenthetically in the text.

The object of Josefa's outrage is the "they" of the system in which she works. She rejects the "realism" of the prevailing work ethic which allows natural and human resources to be exploited for the sake of a kind of progress that can only serve a common good at the prize of human life. Josefa sees her co-workers as hypocritical and fearful of the truth: her immediate superior Luise, who is sensitive to the conflict and yet unwilling to accept a version of the story of B. that will not be approved by the editorial board; editorial director Rudi Goldammer, who goes home to listen to Mozart and write children's books in order to escape the thought of the 180 tons of ash (p. 126); and the men at the top of the Party hierarchy who threaten her with exclusion from the Party. Josefa wonders aloud to Luise why she sent her to cover such a story when, as an editor, Luise knows that if Josefa writes what she must write, it will not be printed and nothing will have been accomplished (p. 17). But Josefa quickly discovers that her editor has learned to fit into the subject-object instrumentality of the hard world of the media. She equates Luise's ability to function with "them," i.e., to placate her male superiors, with a refusal to see the fine layers of ash that fall "sachte wie Schnee" (p. 16). Luise chooses to believe that the residents of B. are smiling, when in reality they are squinting to keep the ash out of their eyes (p. 16). At this level, Josefa's isolation and rage are not gender-specific, but defined by power relationships:

> Gegen mein klägliches "Ich habe gesehen"
> stellen sie ihr unerschütterliches "Wir", und
> schon bin ich der Querulant, der Einzelgän-
> ger, der gegen den Strom schwimmt, unbe-
> lehrbar, arrogant, selbstherrlich. (p. 33)

Monika Maron, herself a freelance journalist with the Berlin *Wochenpost* since 1976, draws attention to the social implications of the ecology issue through an interior monologue of Josefa, who asks herself: Who has the right to decide that a coal-burning plant built in 1890 should keep its employees working under nineteenth century conditions, and to call it progress that most of the stokers are now women and in a socialist collective? Why have I never known about these conditions? — Because what the media elect to report are the products and the rate of production, not their connectedness to the economy of the environment and to human relationships:

Nichts über das Kraftwerk, kein Wort von den Aschekammern, die das Schlimmste sind. Warum sollen die waschwütigen Hausfrauen, die ihre Waschmaschinen schon für zwei Hemden in Gang setzen, nicht wissen, wer ihren löblichen Sauberkeitssinn bezahlt? Warum sollen die strebsamen Kleingärtner nicht daran denken, wessen Gesundheit ihre gut gedüngte Rosenzucht kostet? Vielleicht wollen sie es sogar wissen, vielleicht gingen sie vorsichtiger um mit ihresgleichen. (p. 21)

It is clear that Josefa's, and in all likelihood Maron's, hope for change in ecological policy is intricately bound up with an awareness of the need for more widespread consciousness of the connection between exploitation of the environment and exploitation of human beings. While numerous fantasy sequences show that Josefa associates exploitation with a male mode of thinking and relating, it is also evident that she attributes the pervasiveness of instrumental, subject-object patterns of relationship in both work and personal spheres to the willingness of women to accommodate themselves to this modality and conform to the image of muteness and powerlessness to effect change that has been prescribed for them. This requirement of muteness, an integral part of the male-defined work ethic prescribed for females, is also valid in regard to social change and revolutionary tradition. Josefa asserts in an outburst to her friend:

Das Schlimmste ist, . . . sie haben uns so viel über Revolutionen erzählt, daß ein Leben ohne Revolution ganz sinnlos erscheint. Und dann tun sie so, als sei für uns keine übriggeblieben. . . . Wir dürfen noch den Staub beiseite kehren, der dabei aufgewirbelt wurde . . . ich soll die Revolution von hundertachtzig Tonnen Flugasche reinwaschen, soll sie putzen und polieren mit Glanzmitteln aus der Sprühdose und soll sie als PS-gewaltiges Gefährt in die Zukunft auf Zeitungspapier anpreisen. Hinterher gehe ich zum Friseur und lasse mir die Haare blond färben, weil ich süchtig bin nach Veränderung. (pp. 101-02)

There is a significant stylistic equivalent in Maron's narrative to this image of the woman's scripted passivity. Maron's narrator alternates frequently between the first and the third person to convey her overall picture of the effect on female self-awareness of such subject-object thinking by people in authority at the workplace and in the socialization process. Speaking in the first person to her superior Luise, Josefa asserts her authority as a thinking, feeling, and initiating "I." By contrast, when narrating her own socialization or the admonitions and remonstrances she experiences at work for being frank — or in social settings where her identity and mode of behavior or her state of ill health are being evaluated by male colleagues, friends, or her son — the narrator refers to herself in the third person, a form of narration more suitable for a report card or an obituary.

On the other hand, there are jumps from the third person back to the first, from passivity to omnipotence. Josefa must endure the well-meaning advice of her two friends Christian and Brommel not to keep banging her head against the wall; in one such instance, the reader notes only a third-person reference to her muteness: "Ehe Josefa antworten konnte, sprach er weiter über ein Buch, das er gerade las . . . " (p. 112). It is only through narrative fantasy that the protagonist emerges a page later as an active subject with the capacity to say "I." She imagines herself as an octopus being held, growing wings, flying: "Ich habe viele Arme. Ich bin ein Tintenfisch" (p. 114). In a similar sequence, she imagines herself flying over the rooftops and being greeted, and, moreover, recognized and esteemed, by a young child: "Du bist Josefa, ich erkenne dich" (p. 71). By contrast, Josefa's creativity is not accepted in her professional world. In a confused, fragmented sequence toward the end of the narrative, Josefa, again in a third-person account, recalls the editorial session which marked her professional demise. Here, the author assumes the voice Josefa has been denied by ironically dramatizing the sexual politics of the situation. The Party boss Strutzer — "In der Haltung des Siegers . . . König Siegfried in der Herrscherpose" — announces: "Die Genossin Nadler hat eben selbst den besten Beweis für ihre krankhafte Selbstüberschätzung geliefert'" (p. 206).

Physical illness and delirium predictably follow, but only then does Josefa recognize the source of her dis-ease and, Maron implies, the source of our diseased environment and "Leistungsethik" as well:

Damals hatte Josefa zum ersten Mal be-
griffen, was die Leute meinten, wenn sie
von ihrem Privatleben sprachen. Sie hatte
bislang nie verstanden, wo die geheimnis-
volle Grenze zwischen einem privaten und
einem anderen Leben verlaufen sollte, wo
das anfing oder endete, das niemanden an-
ging und über das man nicht sprach. Mein
Mann, deine Frau, meine Sache, deine
Angelegenheit, eine besondere Art von
Leben, nur mittels besitzanzeigender Für-
wörter beschreibbar, Privateigentum, Be-
treten verboten, Vorsicht, bissiger Hund.
Josefa hatte weder ihre Ehe noch ihr Kind
als etwas ansehen können, das zu trennen
gewesen wäre von ihrem Leben mit Luise
oder Hodriwitzka oder Strutzer.

(pp. 207-08)

While Josefa learns the essential lesson of separating her
identity from the achievement others expect of her, the novel
closes with the laconic observation by the third-person
narrator that the "Höchster Rat" has learned nothing. Taking
two apparently unrelated actions, the male hierarchy wields
its two-edged sword over Josefa Nadler. First they resolve to
reconsider whether Comrade Nadler is worthy of membership
in the Party. They then proceed to claim her "Angelegenheit"
(p. 207) as their own as they do precisely what had been her
goal in the first place, but was unacceptable to them when it
came from her: they order the decommissioning of the ecologically irresponsible power plant in B. The price for Josefa's
"success," if it may be called that, is high indeed, Maron
implies, and no change has occurred in the prevailing ethos of
the expedient. The condescension of the all-male "Höchster
Rat" toward the "Cassandra" in their midst remains unbroken,
and the figures to whom she had looked for signs of a willingness to question and resist, Luise and the stoker
Hodriwitzka in the factory of B., are absent in the eight-line
narrative that ends the novel, the pronouncement of the
"Höchster Rat." Hodriwitzka has been run over in a suspicious
accident, Luise is co-opted by her superiors, and her scornful
comment earlier that Josefa is looking more and more like
"die Heilige Johanna auf dem Scheiterhaufen" (p. 129) comes
closest to describing the state in which Maron leaves her
protagonist. Maron's latest novel, *Die Überläuferin*, is even
more bleak in its implications. It is a sequel to *Flugasche* and

features a young woman who, leaving her place of work, is never missed, becomes paralyzed, and commits suicide.[9]

West German reception of *Flugasche* — the book was rejected for publication in the GDR — has been unanimously positive. Reviewers have often noted the irony of GDR cultural functionary Klaus Höpcke's comment at the 1981 Leipzig Book Fair to the effect that Maron's novel could have been published there if only the author had been willing to make changes to emphasize the positive aspects of the working person's experience.[10] Most have lauded the credibility Maron's account gains by avoiding one-dimensionality.[11] Only Ria Endres of *Die Zeit* mentions the gender-specific, as opposed to GDR-specific, conflicts faced by Josefa Nadler as she struggles for her "Recht auf Differenz," noting that this struggle lays bare a "regressive Struktur."[12]

In her 1985 novel *Der stille Grund*, Lia Pirskawetz, like Maron, addresses the syndrome of a diseased work ethic and distorted gender-role perceptions functioning to prevent responsible and collective decision-making on burning ecological issues. In contrast to Josefa Nadler, Pirskawetz' protagonist Carola Witt, a city government official in the Upper Elbe town of Lachsbach, undergoes a markedly positive development from a self-effacing, unhappy, and angry adolescent suffering from lack of parental affection to an assertive and powerful woman who is the moving force behind creative change in the ecological crisis facing the municipality. Like

---

[9] Monika Maron, *Die Überläuferin* (Frankfurt/M.: Fischer, 1986).

[10] Franz Josef Görtz, "Das Bißchen Sozialismus," *FAZ*, 25 November 1980; Uwe Wittstock, "Verordnetes Schweigen," *FAZ*, 4 April 1981; Siggi Liersch, "Ungewohnter Sozialistischer Realismus," *Diskus* (Frankfurt/M.), No. 3, 1981.

[11] Cf. Karl Corino, broadcast review of *Flugasche* on 16 July 1981, Norddeutscher Rundfunk 3, transcript on file at S. Fischer Verlag, Frankfurt/M. Corino disputes Klaus Höpcke's charge of "Schwarz-Malerei" in Maron's novel by pointing to its "happy end," i.e., the closing of the plant in "B." (he fails to note the irony of that ending in terms of the subjective experience of the disappearing narrator). Another critic refers to Maron's style of confronting conflict arising from the efforts to effect change as "behutsam," "unaufdringlich" (F. J. Görtz, broadcast review, Westdeutscher Rundfunk, 7 April 1981, on file at Fischer). Ria Endres ("Schwierig: Umgang mit Wirklichkeit," *Die Zeit*, 10 April 1981, Literaturbeilage, p. 6) credits Maron with breaking out of the "Starrheit einer sozialistischen Literaturtheorie" and locating her work "im Spannungsverhältnis zwischen Subjektivität und gesellschaftlicher Determiniertheit."

[12] Ria Endres, p. 6.

Maron, Pirskawetz focuses on the conflict between economic interests and the environment. Here the dilemma arises from the demands of economic development — greater productivity, more jobs and consumer goods could be obtained by allowing an economically more efficient factory to be built in an area under state environmental protection — and the need to preserve the natural resources of the region.

There are significant differences in the two female protagonists' approaches to their situation, however. Carola Witt is not an outsider to power, but only to male perceptions of it. As "Sekretär des Rates der Stadt," with a male "Sekretärin," she sets the tone from the beginning for a humorous but definite revision, from within the power structure, of conceptions of the workplace and assumptions about gender roles and criteria of achievement.

The narrative persona and the devices Pirskawetz employs in describing Carola Witt's working world suggest not victimization, as in Maron's novel, but potency in a world of patriarchal weakness. The use of the first person throughout the 430-page novel serves to reinforce a sense of the protagonist's strength to confront the contradictions and conflicts facing her. Carola moves from preoccupation with herself to a greater inner clarity and control of both the environmental situation of the city and her own personal and career situation. Using consciously ironic metaphors, the narrator plays on traditional attitudes about gender roles in the workplace. For example, as Carola reflects on the process by which a *Stadtratssekretär* must make decisions, she realizes how important the "Backfischideal" of her youth still is to her: "Wer nicht anständig entscheiden kann, soll lieber gar nicht entscheiden" (p. 7). Pirskawetz connects Carola's thinking as a professional with the eventual outcome of her love affair with the ruthlessly rational and productivist Albert, whose child she expects to be raising alone: "Könnte ich . . . mein Backfischideal nicht einfach sitzen lassen, wie eine Ungeliebte mit Kind?" (p. 7). By using the damsel-in-distress metaphor in reference to an ethos that she would find more convenient to ignore, the narrator ironically assumes the traditionally male position of control and exploitation, at the same time suggesting that it is unacceptable to abandon her sense of responsibility.

In another instance, Carola observes her own response to a temper tantrum by her male boss, the cantankerous mayor. Here again she ironically plays a traditionally male role, this time by distancing herself from his childish weakness: "Die Erregung des Bürgermeisters rührte mich damals nicht mehr als einen Wochenendvater die Tränen seiner Frau übers mißratene Kind. Und ich reagierte wie ein Familienpatriarch" (p. 18). In another setting, a City Council meeting at which the Mayor has abdicated and turned matters over to Carola as Secretary of the Council, the consistent use of feminine pronouns to refer to the male office secretary adds to the caricature of this figure, whom Carola calls "die Ikone" because of his pious inactivity and exaggerated deference toward the boss:

> Sie [die Ikone] hielt die schmalen Fingerspitzen wie zum Gebet aneinandergelegt und protokollierte nichts. Eine Diskussion ohne Reglementierung durch den Alten war für sie nichtexistent. . . . Und es war an mir, als erstes meine Sekretärin fruchtbar zu machen, auf daß sie ein brauchbarer Assistent würde. (p. 104)

If these rhetorical details serve to assure us of the narrator's confidence about having a voice in a man's job, we are also given ample evidence that the difficulty is less her perception of herself in her decision-making capacity, than others' problem with her as a woman in that role. The day after Carola makes an appearance at the village carnival festivities, she is reprimanded by the mayor, who calls her "Mädl, Mädl," vacillating between his dependence on her competence and his need to patronize her:

> du bist nicht irgendeine Sekretärin. . . . Wenn du irgendeine Tippmieze wärst, tätsch kee Wort verlieren. Aber so. Du bist Sekretär des Rates der Stadt. Du wirst amende mein Nachfolger im Amte. So eener geht nicht unter die Maulaffen und stellt die Waden zur Schau. (p. 92)

There are also numerous instances in which Pirskawetz' use of metaphor reinforces the message she is conveying about the traditional silencing of women's voices. It is implied that the absence of these voices and the uneven distribution of labor between men and women in the workplace and in public process contribute to an imbalance in the ecology of human relationships which in turn is reflected in imbalanced relationships between humanity and nature. In the turn-of-the-century interior narrative which makes up the core of the novel, Carola Witt is clearly the only person present addressing the founder of the *Naturschutz* movement, Professor Conwentz, with a substantive agenda related to ecological planning for twentieth century Lachsbach. Conwentz explains his plan to oppose the building of quarries on the Elbe, since, with current technology and small financial sacrifice, they can be located farther inland, thus preserving one of Germany's finest natural habitats from destruction (p. 266). Carola agrees. Suddenly the conversation is interrupted by Sander, the hotel owner who sells out to industry in order to avoid bankruptcy: Sander bends over Carola, brushes a strand of hair from her forehead and asks the professor, "Ist sie nicht eine reizende Person? . . . Halb Blaustrumpf, halb Märchenfee; halb Range, halb Gendarm" (p. 266). Carola's comment on this scene presumably reflects Pirskawetz' awareness of patterns that can be observed in her contemporary frame narrative as well:

> Damit war unsere Ideenkonferenz tot, hingeschlachtet mit dem immer gleichen Messer meiner männlichen Vormünder. Komischerweise war es egal, ob ich als weiblich oder unweiblich diffamiert wurde, der Effekt war immer derselbe: er schloß mich aus Männerangelegenheiten aus und damit aus allen Angelegenheiten von gesellschaftlichem Rang. (p. 266)

I cannot do justice in this short study to the epic breadth and multiple time frames of *Der stille Grund* or the wealth of literary and historical allusions Pirskawetz weaves into her narrative. Nor can I trace in detail the stages of Carola Witt's approach to the ecological debate or the positions and perspectives of all the other characters in both present-day and turn-of-the-century Lachsbach. In brief, Carola is fighting for a "third way" that acknowledges both the need for growth and the need to preserve the ecological balance of the area for future generations. Her eventual fiancé, Albert, argues that the present trend of exploitation of the environment goes back to the early capitalists and that if he had lived then he would have been on the other side, i.e., against the new factory (p. 132). Albert accuses Carola of trying to escape present reality: "Sie drücken sich noch vor der harten Realität. Machen auf Blumenkind und grüne Rebellion. . . " (p. 126). Present reality for Albert is the need for a new factory and his desire to become its *Betriebsleiter*.

Carola's analysis, on the other hand, combines the public and personal dimensions of the "verdrängte Seele" syndrome she sees everywhere, from Wilhelminian architecture and the productivist work ethic to the inability of Albert to acknowledge pain. She concedes that the roots of the syndrome are traceable to the turn of the century;[13] as she learns from her research in the city archives, there never had been a regional plan that would have allowed for a balance between growth and protection of resources. But it is not so much Carola's study of economics, her archival research or her previous experience as a textile worker which provide her with the bigger picture she misses in the instrumental mentality of her peers. What explains Carola's approach is her expanded "Seh-Raster," to borrow Christa Wolf's term from her *Frankfurter Poetik-Vorlesungen*.[14]

The holistic view of Wolf's seer Kassandra and of many of her female and male counterparts allows one to see connections where they might be conveniently suppressed or statistically ignored as a result of perverted priorities. Carola Witt's advantage in the ecological debate set up by Pirskawetz in *Der stille Grund* is attributable to the "bestimmte Fähigkeiten und Tugenden der Frauen" of which Morgner speaks in the *Amanda* passage cited above.[15] Both Wolf and Morgner suggest — and I am arguing that Pirskawetz is simply playing out this programmatic idea to its narrative hilt — that these "Fähigkeiten und Tugenden der Frauen" or, to put it in less gender-exclusive terms, the "erweiterter Blickwinkel,"[16] let light into the darker or less conscious areas of our being. In

---

[13] One GDR review of *Der stille Grund* justifies Pirskawetz' "phantastisch-utopischen Trick" (the carnival jaunt to historical Lachsbach) by asserting that the author is correct in locating the roots of today's environmental problems in the "Gründerjahre" (Marianne Krumrey, "Was wird aus dem Stillen Grund?" *Berliner Zeitung*, 2-3 November 1985). I am grateful to Dorothy Rosenberg for making her collection of GDR press reviews of Pirskawetz available to me.

[14] Christa Wolf, *Voraussetzungen einer Erzählung*, pp. 130-31. Cf. Christiane Zehl Romero, "'Weibliches Schreiben' - Christa Wolf's *Kassandra*," in *Studies in GDR Culture and Society 4*, ed. Margy Gerber et al. (Lanham/New York/London: University Press of America, 1984), pp. 15-29.

[15] Pirskawetz alludes to just this problem of certain traditionally female abilities which men have generally not been socialized to develop. Albert at one point describes his parents' sacrifices "um meine technischen Fähigkeiten zu fördern," whereupon Carola inquires irritably: "Haben Sie auch andere Fähigkeiten?" (*Der stille Grund*, p. 127).

[16] Wolf, *Voraussetzungen einer Erzählung*, pp. 130-31.

her narrative, Pirskawetz is doing just that, specifically with regard to the threatened relationship of humankind to its natural origins.

Whereas in Maron's *Flugasche* the protagonist bears the brunt of the conflict between her own need publicly to confront ecologically irresponsible conditions and the need of those with power to suppress that discussion, in Pirskawetz' novel the narrative itself is constructed to contain, absorb, and creatively exploit the conflict between the instrumental or productivist mentality and the urge to preserve life "im Stillen Grunde." A key to Pirskawetz' feminine dialectic in the ecological debate, as well as to her narrative strategy, is her unabashed rehabilitation of the subconscious, of dream and fantasy, of the carnival tradition, and grandmothers' and gypsies' wisdom. Not unlike Morgner in her *Trobadora Beatriz* and *Amanda*, Pirskawetz takes her characters and thus also the reader from present to past and back again in order to establish a historical continuity that includes both the personal and the public issues at hand. In this case, Carola Witt experiences the social status of women in the 1890s. At the same time, with the mind and expertise of a 1980s woman, she recognizes how the soul of the community is repressed as the financially beleaguered *Kurhotel* Sander sells out to industrial development at the expense of the environment. As a result of this sojourn into history, the *Stadtratssekretär* realizes that exploiting the area as a natural paradise for tourists will also destroy it. Thus the fantasy venture into the past is neither escapist nor nostalgic in its narrative function; it is a feat of carnival magic, which suggests reversibility. Not only temporal boundaries are crossed as the characters are whisked away by a gnome at the present-day *Fastnacht* and transported to the Lachsbach of the 1890s; in turn, the carnival atmosphere allows power relationships and values to be turned on their head by the fool figure Ekkehard, who features prominently as foil and rival to Albert in both the frame narrative and turn-of-the-century Lachsbach.

Pirskawetz' use of *Fastnacht*, carnival, fairy tale, and gypsy motifs, as well as romantic elements such as quotations of Novalis and nineteenth-century nature poetry, while perhaps somewhat excessive and stylistically uneven, certainly cannot be seen as frivolous avoidance of the conflict introduced with the ecological debate. Nor does the recurrence of the notion of *Heimat* signal a regressive tendency. On the contrary, Pirskawetz seems to be suggesting a radical re-thinking of the meaning of these traditional values.[17] When she uses the "Dornröschen" story, for example, it is with ironic gender role reversal. Carola fears that even she, who loves Albert, will not be able to wake him with kisses out of his century-long sleep, because only when he begins to feel his own pain will he wake up (p. 121). Elements such as the "Dornröschen" motif, which suggests the sleeping technological society dominated by instrumental thinking and repressing thoughts of deeper or ominous connections, do not provide escape routes to the past or to magic, but rather expand the "Seh-Raster" of the debate to include more than economics. The omnipresent fool Ekkehard serves Carola — both in the frame story of the mayor's office and in turn-of-the-century Lachsbach, where he is a quarry worker — as a reminder of the lost archaic power of connectedness to nature. In the end she takes up with the loyal and sensitive fool, who seems to be her source of energy and larger perspective as they return on Shrove Tuesday to modern-day Lachsbach to face the consequences of choices they had witnessed being made nearly a hundred years earlier.

And what is the outcome of the debate? Carola's "third way" prevails: the factory will be expanded, but relocated an hour away from Lachsbach, thus assuring jobs and consumer goods, but also preserving the *Naturschutzgebiet*. The frame story closes with an image of the carnival procession. Albert and Carola are looking out on the crowd from two very different perspectives: Albert waves "sieghaft lächelnd in sein privates Volk" (p. 428), content that he has contributed measurably to the welfare of the working people of Lachsbach, as production statistics will show. Carola, on the other hand, knows that her former co-workers in the factory will not like commuting, and notes that the encounters of hikers with the natural beauty of Lachsbach will never be found in a budget plan or in annual reports, nor will their satisfaction or dissatisfaction, or the presence of certain species of birds or breathable air, be converted to percentages.

The assumption made by the GDR economist Streibel that the social factors essential to ecological planning must be quantifiable to be included still seems operative,[18] at least as a

---

[17] Cf. Irma Hanke's study of the changing concept of *Heimat* in the GDR as reflected in recent GDR literature, "Heimat und Geschichte als Thema der DDR-Literatur," in this volume.

[18] Günter Streibel, "Umweltschutz und Umweltgestaltung als volkswirtschaftliche Aufgabe," p. 1147.

male mode of thinking to be criticized by a female public official in a 1985 novel. But Pirskawetz, unlike Maron, seems to suggest that the archaic power of fools and women to bring lost connections back into focus is stronger than the destructive power of one-dimensional thinking. In the final sequence of the frame narrative of *Der stille Grund* — and a final ironic gender-role reversal — Carola takes the "Rute der Fruchtbarkeit" from the "Flecklmann" who hops past their coach and orders the "Ikone," her male secretary, to call a special meeting of the *Stadtrat*.

> "Morgen ist Aschermittwoch."
> "Drum," sagte ich. "Wir werden uns Asche aufs Haupt streuen."
> "Ratssitzungen hat einzig und allein der Bürgermeister einzuberufen," erwiderte die Ikone. . . .
> "Es hilft nichts. Irgendwann muß ich Sie mit der Rute der Fruchtbarkeit schlagen."
> (p. 429)

And the future mayor thinks to herself, as she orders the secretary around with a mock authoritarian tone and barely camouflaged affection, that the man has potential if given a little room to learn to be creative.

Carola's non-confrontational but decisive approach from within the system and her irony which transforms rage can perhaps be seen as approximating Pirskawetz' perspective on the possibility of change in environmental policy in the GDR. One critic begins her review of *Der stille Grund* by quoting a Carola Witt maxim: "Wahrscheinlich fügt sich der Mensch in Dinge, sobald man sie ihm als unabänderlich darstellt" — and concludes emphatically: "Carola läßt nichts als unabänderlich gelten."[19] While most GDR reviewers of Pirskawetz' novel agreed that it tends to overwork metaphors and that it shows the stylistic unevenness of a first novel, they also welcomed Pirskawetz' use of a female protagonist as a model figure dealing constructively with a controversial public policy issue, and her skill at presenting a wide variety of perspectives on

---

19 Ingrid Kirschey-Feix, "Lia Pirskawetz. Der stille Grund," *Junge Welt*, 3 September 1986.

the problem.[20] One critic goes so far as to say that *Der stille Grund* "leistet einen Beitrag zur materialistisch-dialektischen Sicht unseres Umweltverhältnisses."[21] The positive reception of the novel and its popular style suggest that Pirskawetz may have captured one direction that GDR public consciousness of ecological issues is taking. Whether or not Maron's *Flugasche* — as is rumored — will soon be published in the GDR remains to be seen. In any case, the significance of both to the environmental discussion in the GDR should not be underestimated.

[20] Irmtraud Gutschke, "Zeitsprung auf den Boden der Tatsachen," *Neues Deutschland*, 4 December 1985, p. 4; "Traum und Wirklichkeit," *National-zeitung*, 17 November 1986; Krumrey, "Was wird aus dem Stillen Grund?"
[21] Krumrey, "Was wird aus dem Stillen Grund?"

Politics and Computers in the German Democratic Republic: The Robotron Combine

Gary Geipel

Americans and West Europeans have studied the processes of Soviet scientific inquiry and technological development for quite some time.[1] These researchers generally ask, "Does the political system of the Soviet Union influence that country's scientific and technological output?" Invariably, the answer is "Yes." Explaining just *how* Soviet communism has affected the USSR's scientific and technological output then becomes their more difficult and more important research task. The purpose of this paper is twofold: 1) to extend the question of how communism influences technological performance to the case of the German Democratic Republic; and 2) to focus on a single industrial firm, rather than the overall technological output of the country, in assessing links between politics and technological performance in the GDR. That firm is the computer manufacturer VEB Kombinat Robotron, with headquarters in Dresden.

That a relationship even exists between "politics" and "computers" is not self-evident. A person studying the success or failure of technological undertakings in the United States, for example, would not look first to federal policy for explanation. The firms involved in producing a certain technology would probably be studied as autonomous units, influenced by the general state of the economy and by the performance of

---

[1] See for example the study by Bruce Parrott, *Politics and Technology in the Soviet Union* (Cambridge: MIT Press, 1983); as well as *The Social Context of Soviet Science*, ed. Linda Lubrano and Susan Gross Solomon (Boulder: Westview, 1980); *Technology and Communist Culture*, ed. Frederic J. Fleron, Jr. (New York: Praeger, 1977); and *Industrial Innovation in the Soviet Union*, ed. Ronald Amann and Julian Cooper (New Haven: Yale University Press, 1982).

competing enterprises, but not by anything the government could call a technology policy. Quite the opposite is true in the case of the GDR. To a greater extent than in any Western state, the quality and quantity of available computer technology in the GDR can be traced to the success or failure of the country's political efforts to foster scientific and technological advance.

The GDR's Technological "Lag" and the Reform Imperative

In recent years, the popular media and many academic journals have carried accounts of the technological "lag" of the centrally planned economies behind the market economies. This lag is particularly wide in the field of information technology. It is no secret that the socialist countries have failed to produce computers or peripheral devices of a quality or quantity approaching Western norms. This situation is both embarrassing and costly to the leaders of the Soviet Union and the East-bloc countries. It raises doubts about the effectiveness of their political and economic orders, while jeopardizing their ability to remain militarily and industrially competitive with the capitalist West. In attempts to remedy their relative technological backwardness, the leaders of the Soviet bloc have studied and sometimes implemented changes in the structure of key socialist economic units and the relationships between them. This interest in *reform* usually focuses not on grand restructurings that would place the viability of one-party rule in question, but on smaller-scale moves toward greater efficiency within the context of central planning. Market elements and limited decentralization are often introduced, insofar as they promote this efficiency.

A particularly notable reform program was implemented in the GDR in the late 1970s. It has met with considerable success in some areas of the GDR economy and has apparently caught the attention of reform-minded planners in Moscow.[2] In essence, the top leaders of the Socialist Unity Party retain control over the broad strokes of economic planning while allowing enterprise managers to assume greater responsibility for the actual implementation of central plans. Enterprises in similar product areas are grouped together in giant *Kombinate* (combines), which typically include between ten and twenty factories and employ thousands of people. These combines are

---

[2] Cf. "East Germany: It's a Long Way from Prussia to Russia," *Economist*, 22 February 1986, pp. 47-50.

subordinate only to the appropriate industrial ministry, and their managers influence the entire production process — from research and development through manufacturing to the ultimate sale and use of the combine's products at home or abroad. The SED may still intervene, but its direct control is reduced.

In this scheme, responsibility for the production of computers in the GDR falls almost exclusively to the VEB Kombinat Robotron. Robotron is a combine of nineteen firms producing everything from typewriters and adding machines to mainframe computers. It is said to employ 70,000 people[3] and is one of seventeen combines subordinated to the GDR's Ministry for Electronics Technology.[4]

Robotron has gained attention in the West chiefly for its contributions to the Soviet bloc's unified system of computers. Robotron specializes in mid-range computers, a reference to their operating speed. Its machines are believed to equal and in most cases surpass in quality any comparably sized computers in Eastern Europe or the Soviet Union.[5] S. E. Goodman, a leading American specialist on Soviet-bloc computing, calls Robotron "the most cohesive and best-managed computer company" in any bloc country. He attributes this at least in part to "the relative freedom [Robotron] has to organizationally resemble and behave like a Western corporation."[6] This organizational resemblance does not mean that Robotron's products stack up even reasonably well against state-of-the-art Western computers. They do not. In an East European context, however, Robotron's success in producing viable computers and peripheral devices is indeed remarkable.

---

[3] Cf. Friedrich Wokurka, "GDR-USSR Computer Trade, Cooperation Outlined: Robotron Director Reports Achievements," *GDR Export*, No. 4, 1984, pp. 2-3.

[4] Cf. "Ministerium für Elektrotechnik und Elektronik," *DDR Handbuch*, 3rd ed., ed. Hartmut Zimmermann (Cologne: Wissenschaft und Politik, 1985), p. 901.

[5] This paper will not assess the technical performance of GDR computers in any detail. Such "technology assessments" of the GDR computer industry are conducted on a regular basis by researchers at the University of Arizona's Department of Management Information Systems under Seymour E. Goodman, and at the Forschungsstelle für gesamtdeutsche wirtschaftliche und soziale Fragen in West Berlin under Klaus Krakat.

[6] S. E. Goodman, "Socialist Technological Integration: The Case of the East European Computer Industries," *The Information Society*, 3, No. 1 (1984), 57.

The political influences on Robotron's performance will be studied here with reference to the three-stage process by which most computer firms apparently bring their products from conception to use: 1) setting product goals; 2) setting product specifications; and 3) marketing the finished product. These stages do not represent an iron law of how data-processing firms behave. Instead, they provide a manageable framework for studying the various types of decisions and structures that come into play during the development, manufacture, and sale of a computer.

Setting Product Goals

In a market-based economy, such as operates in the United States, a firm must produce what it can reasonably expect to sell. The American firm's task of deciding what to produce, therefore, requires an assessment of what the society needs (or can be made to believe it needs), as well as an assessment of the firm's ability to overcome its competition. In a centrally planned economy, such as the GDR's, a firm's production choices are determined in a far more complex manner. Robotron builds computers and enjoys high resource allocation priority in the overall GDR economy because of conscious political decisions — not as the result of unseen and inevitable market forces.

Robotron's production was politically legitimized in a process that may have delayed the timing and weakened the force of its entry into the computer field. The rise of a computer industry in the GDR depended in part on the SED leadership's acceptance that the use of machines and mathematical formulations in decision-making and industry (the science of "cybernetics") was compatible with Marxism-Leninism. Achieving this cohabitation of cybernetics and communist ideology was difficult everywhere in the Soviet bloc. Speculating on the roots of the so-called "anti-cybernetics movement" in the Soviet Union, Albert Parry surmised "a hidden, sickly fear in Stalin and his henchmen that the newfangled science of cybernetics, of programming, of servo-mechanisms, was just too deadly precise; that, if given leeway, it might somehow prove their vaunted 'science' of Communism, its alleged historical inevitability, all wrong."[7] Getting over this fear proved especially difficult in the GDR, where the legitimacy of communist rule — subject as it was to constant comparison with the situation

---

[7] Albert Parry, *The New Class Divided* (New York: Macmillan, 1966), p. 58.

"over there" in the Federal Republic — was even more in question than in the Soviet Union. The GDR was in fact the last East European country to reach an official peace with cybernetics; not until a 1962 SED conference on cybernetics was the open application of the discipline by GDR researchers tolerated.[8]

This outcome appears to have been the result of two factors. The first was the work of a scientist by the name of Georg Klaus, who took it upon himself to show that cybernetics and Marxism need not be enemies, that they can indeed be highly complementary. For Klaus, Marx was the first practitioner of cybernetics, and in a 1961 book entitled *Kybernetik in philosophischer Sicht* he managed to reinterpret key tenets of Marxism to demonstrate as much.[9] The second factor explaining the ultimate acceptance of cybernetics in the GDR was, ironically, a variation on the fears of illegitimacy that had kept the SED from embracing electronics-based decision tools in the first place. Favorable comparison with the Federal Republic, the SED leaders realized, could only be obtained if the GDR adopted the technologies that were already making West German industry an international force.[10] The adoption of automation and data-processing techniques was then explicitly linked to the GDR's "Scientific-Technical Revolution."

The relationship between Marxist ideology and computer science has never ceased to be on the minds of GDR leaders. It boiled over into open dissent, for example, in 1971, when a Politburo faction began a thinly veiled criticism of General Secretary Walter Ulbricht's enthusiasm about the application of technology to solving economic problems. Politburo member Kurt Hager warned of the danger that "the language of a particular scientific speciality [i.e., cybernetics] might become the political language of the Party" and that the Party would then cease to be a Marxist-Leninist party.[11] In his study of authority-building in the GDR after 1961, A. James McAdams argues that this debate on the nature of the Scientific-Technical Revolution was a key element in the opposition that

[8] Cf. "Kybernetik," *DDR Handbuch*, p. 780.

[9] Georg Klaus, *Kybernetik in philosophischer Sicht* (Berlin: Dietz, 1961).

[10] Cf. Steffen Werner, *Kybernetik statt Marx?* (Stuttgart: Bonn Aktuell, 1977), p. 215.

[11] Kurt Hager, *Einheit*, 26, No. 11 (1971), 1215, cited in "Kybernetik," *DDR Handbuch*, p. 780; my translation here and throughout.

forced Ulbricht's resignation in 1971.[12] To this day, it seems, the perceived contradiction between an all-out drive towards the computerization of GDR society and an adherence to traditional Marxist-Leninist tenets creates a significant drag on efforts to modernize.

Within the appropriate ideological bounds, however, the manufacture and use of computers in the GDR has been accepted by the political leadership since 1962 as absolutely necessary for the country's economic growth. The need for the GDR's economic reforms of the 1970s was clear: the country's industry was slipping further and further behind its Western counterparts; labor was being poorly utilized; and the proper technology for modernization efforts was simply not being produced. A vocabulary of reform evolved around these problems, including the notion of *Intensivierung* ("intensive" reform). As early as the Eighth Party Congress of 1971, *Intensivierung* was put forth as a central goal of GDR industry. The SED's own definition is as follows: "The frugal use of the means of production, resources, and labor so as to achieve the maximum necessary structural growth in national income with the minimum expenditure of human and material inputs."[13] This concept goes hand in hand with *Rationalisierung*, the "rationalization" or simplification of industrial processes.

The development of a strong microelectronics and data-processing industry was seen by the SED as an ideal means of attaining both *Intensivierung* and *Rationalisierung*. At a SED Central Committee meeting in 1976, for example, the Minister for Electronics Technology, Otfried Steeger, proclaimed that "the mastery of microelectronics is the central question of our continued development; its implications far exceed the field of electronics, because the application of this new technology will lead to *a new quality of Intensivierung*."[14] Steeger went on to describe an eight-point scheme by which the GDR could attain *Intensivierung* effects through microelectronics, including the development of a microchip research center, greater attention to training "qualified cadres" in information technology, and the Party's adoption of a "uniform strategy" in

---

[12] A. James McAdams, *East Germany and Detente* (Cambridge: Cambridge University Press, 1985), pp. 79-82.

[13] As quoted in Klaus Krakat, "Computerproduktion und Computereinsatz in der DDR," *FS Analysen*, No. 3, 1977, p. 27.

[14] *Neues Deutschland*, 11/12 December 1976, p. 7, as cited in Krakat, p. 55. My emphasis.

electronics governing the path from research through production.[15] Such a strategy was indeed adopted, and by the Tenth Party Congress in 1981, microelectronics was being singled out as the "main factor" in the general *Intensivierung* process.[16] Similarly, microelectronics was seen as a key to *Rationalisierung* in that it allowed for the automation of certain industrial processes, thus freeing up labor for other purposes.[17] Microelectronics has become Number One among the "key technologies" the SED is attempting to encourage in the 1980s; it has been a centerpiece of the Party's last two Five-Year Plans.[18]

In recent years, the SED has peppered the official GDR media with articles on computer-aided design and manufacturing (CAD/CAM) techniques, "flexible manufacturing systems," computer production figures, and the like. Klaus Krakat described how "CAD/CAM euphoria" swept the 1986 Party Congress: "Observers could have gotten the impression that the future of the GDR will only be mastered with the help of CAD/CAM."[19] At the same time, the SED has begun a serious effort to make significant numbers of GDR citizens computer-literate. In 1984, for example, the GDR's Ministry of Education — working with Robotron — announced plans to put 20,000 personal computers into the GDR's secondary schools by the end of 1986.[20] Robotron pledged itself to train the necessary computer instructors as well. (It is not believed that these goals were reached.) A basic course in data processing was offered for the first time in September 1986 at the country's 150 vocational/technical schools.[21] Again, Robotron machines made these courses possible.

In sum, Robotron's participation in the data-processing industry requires a backdrop of political and economic

---

[15] Krakat, pp. 55-57.

[16] Cf. Ronald D. Asmus, "Microelectronics, Robots, and Socialism in the GDR," *RAD Background Report/340 GDR*, 9 December 1981, p. 2.

[17] Asmus, p. 5.

[18] B.V. Flow, "5 More Years of 'Comprehensive Intensification' for the GDR's Economy," *RAD Background Report/6 GDR*, 17 January 1986, p. 3.

[19] Klaus Krakat, "Schlüsseltechnologien in der DDR," *FS Analysen*, No. 5, 1986, p. 123.

[20] John Kavanagh, "20,000 East German Schools to Get Micros," *Computer Weekly*, 22 March 1984, p. 7.

[21] Klaus Morgenstern, "Lehrlinge lernen am Computer," *Neues Deutschland*, 20 August 1986, p. 2.

legitimation in which the firm's technology is made to fit Marxist ideology; the firm's production goals are made to appear as essential national goals. The need to create this backdrop adds a feeling of tentativeness and an extra bureaucratic component to the process of computerization in the GDR.

Setting Product Specifications

With the general outline of its mission in place, Robotron is confronted on a recurring basis with deciding what standards its computers should embody, and how best to attain them. At the very outset of their computerization efforts, Robotron's planners had two key decisions to make. The first was whether to follow Western standards and the second was whether to seek compatibility with the rest of the Soviet bloc.

Robotron's decision to use Western computer architecture based on IBM standards is difficult to explain with complete certainty. No documents exist in the West on precisely when and how the choice was made. Nevertheless, educated guesses can be made as to the chief motivations behind this decision. The GDR's data-processing industry consisted of little more than adding-machine and typewriter production throughout most of the 1960s,[22] a time when the computer had not yet been totally legitimized within the SED hierarchy. When the Party finally fleshed out its views on cybernetics and realized that the GDR was lagging behind not only the West but other socialist countries as well in data-processing technology, it apparently concluded that a quick and proven fix was necessary. Copying seemed the best short-run means of catching up. The resulting "R-300" computer, based on IBM designs and unveiled in 1969, was of relatively good quality and was produced in respectable numbers.[23]

At about this same time, the Soviet Union began to push for genuine integration of CMEA's computer industry, an initiative that had lain dormant for almost a decade. According to Goodman, the Soviets had several important objectives: "to draw on the expertise of the East Europeans, to turn the East Europeans away from looking westward for this technology, to tighten economic ties, and to provide technical standardiza-

---

[22] Cf. Goodman, p. 44.

[23] Cf. Goodman, p. 44.

tion."[24] By the late 1960s, the Soviets had enlisted the participation of the GDR and four other East European countries in their plan to produce a family of compatible computers. Robotron's involvement made political and economic sense. First of all, its participation symbolized the GDR's willingness to assume important responsibilities within the bloc and demonstrate solidarity with Moscow. And, secondly, given that the SED had decided to build a respectable computer industry and automate other sectors of its economy, it was a sound choice to seek a CMEA arrangement that could supply the range of systems and technical cooperation that hard-currency limits and trade restrictions would prevent the GDR from obtaining in the West.

Having agreed in principle to build a unified line of computers, CMEA still had to settle on a basic design for this line. As Davis and Goodman write, this decision "was made only after some argument both within the USSR and among the CMEA partners. Nationalistic pride was an important factor in the argument favoring the use of a design of CMEA origin."[25] Ultimately, however, IBM architecture was selected as the CMEA standard. This was due in no small part to the efforts of Robotron representatives.[26] Far from implying a lack of "nationalism" on Robotron's part, the firm's efforts in the standardization debate seem to have been designed precisely to enhance its position in the CMEA computer program. Robotron was the only CMEA firm to have had broad experience in applying IBM architecture; this guaranteed it a leading role in the subsequent development of the bloc's unified systems. To push the IBM standard was thus the nationalistic thing for Robotron to do.

Once a general standard is set, a computer firm must ensure that the appropriate arrangements for design and manufacture are in place. It is generally in the firm's interest to minimize the time spent in getting a product from the drawing boards to the delivery trucks. The length of this process depends on three things: 1) the resources devoted to research and development within the firm itself; 2) arrangements for development partnerships with other firms or with research institutes; and 3) access to the components needed to manu-

[24] Goodman, p. 49.

[25] N.C. Davis and S. E. Goodman, "The Soviet Bloc's Unified System of Computers," *Computing Surveys*, 10, No. 2 (1978), 101.

[26] Cf. Davis and Goodman, p. 101.

facture a complete computer system. Politics is relevant to this process to the degree in which it encourages or impedes these conditions.

Robotron adopted a slogan in 1985 that goes something like: "The entire production of the combine must be revamped every three years."[27] This implies that the average age of Robotron's product line should be little more than three years. In its computers at least, Robotron has not lived up to this slogan; several of its machines have been in production for considerably longer than three years. Product lines at computer firms in the West are an average of little more than a year old.

Explaining such differences is not easy. Robotron seems to enjoy an abundance of in-house scientific manpower, claiming that it employs 9,000 scientists, designers, and engineers.[28] That figure implies that some 13% of Robotron's workforce is employed in research and development (R&D), which is comparable to the percentage of personnel devoted to R&D in most Western computer firms. Based on such numbers alone — even accounting for the fact that Robotron builds many other things besides computers — the GDR firm should be faring much better than it does. One can find a reason for the lack of success in the conditions under which R&D takes place in the Robotron combine. Continued bureaucratic control of investment decisions and research strategies is a drag on development, as are the minimal rewards available to productive scientists and engineers.[29] In addition, Robotron's shortcomings may have a great deal to do with its traditional lack of valuable R&D partnerships and its many problems in securing reliable supplies of components. Robotron's joint development projects have been limited to linkages with Soviet and other East European firms through CMEA's computer program. The CMEA partnerships have been rather one-sided for Robotron, which usually possesses the cutting-edge CMEA computer technology and helps firms from other countries more than vice versa. Until recently, domestic partnerships

[27] A. Polekhin, "Ritmy Robotrona," *Sotsialisticheskaya Industriya*, 28 June 1985, p. 3.

[28] Polekhin, p. 3.

[29] Cf. Fred Klinger, "Fortschritt im real existierenden Sozialismus - aktuelle Probleme und sozialkulturelle Hintergründe wissenschaftlich-technischer Innovation," in *Studies in GDR Culture and Society 7*, ed. Margy Gerber et al. (Lanham/New York/London: University Press of America, 1987), 95-113.

with GDR universities were also poorly utilized by Robotron. Now, according to a Western analysis published in 1985, "scientific cooperation" has become a new "key slogan" for the SED.[30]

Political initiatives of this type may enhance Robotron's R&D effort. Still, the firms will continue to face serious problems in translating its designs and models into significant production runs because of component supply problems. The largest GDR chip-manufacturing combine produces chips for all of CMEA, and Robotron's "share" is usually inadequate. It has almost nowhere else to turn.

Robotron's manufacturing problems are clearly of major political concern in the GDR. In 1982, the general manager of Robotron was quietly removed from his post, reportedly because of the firm's failure to meet production targets.[31] Such personnel changes, however, are probably not the kind of measures Robotron needs to redress problems caused by supply bottlenecks and lack of access to state-of-the-art research.

Marketing the Finished Product

Most Western computer firms are constrained in generating revenues only by the reach of their sales forces and by the demand for their products. If orders can be obtained, they will deliver on them. The same cannot be said of Robotron. As already described, Robotron is not producing computers in nearly the numbers it would like to produce them. Thus, it is constrained in its reach not by poor sales efforts or low demand but by low production capabilities. Beyond this, the computers and peripherals that Robotron *does* manage to produce are not simply sold to the first taker. Though Goodman finds that "by socialist standards, it appears to be inordinately motivated by export and profit,"[32] Robotron is not a profit — or revenue — maximizer in any traditional sense of those terms. Three factors, related to the GDR's political environment, regulate what Robotron can and can't do with its computers.

---

[30] Ross Alan Stapleton and Seymour Goodman, "Microcomputing in the Soviet Union and Eastern Europe," *Abacus*, 3, No. 1 (1985), 21.

[31] "Tempo zulegen," *Der Spiegel*, 12 May 1986, p. 79.

[32] Goodman, "Socialist Technological Integration," p. 57.

First, the GDR must commit a substantial portion of its industrial product to trade with the Soviet Union. An average of 39% of the GDR's total foreign trade is conducted with the USSR each year, making it East Berlin's largest trading partner by a wide margin.[33] The GDR relies on the USSR for virtually all of its oil, and for most of the other raw materials it needs to fuel its industry. In exchange for these commodities, the GDR is expected to supply the Soviet Union with finished goods — including textiles, machine tools, optical equipment, and, not surprisingly, computers. In 1984, 60% of Robotron's computer production was delivered to the USSR.[34] Given Soviet leader Gorbachev's campaign to extract more and better-quality goods from Eastern Europe in exchange for his country's energy supplies and patronage, Robotron's commitments to the Soviets may increase. In late 1985, the GDR and Soviet Union signed an agreement covering the 1986-1990 Five-Year Plan period that will raise the volume of their overall trade by six percent. A large percentage of the GDR's exports to the Soviet Union in that period will consist of electronics and microelectronics products — much of which can be expected to originate with Robotron. As Krakat writes, this huge obligation to supply the Soviet Union with computers will be carried out "despite domestic shortfalls in computer capacity."[35]

Secondly, the GDR's leaders must take steps to modernize the country's aged industrial base, while making at least some attempt to improve their people's living standards by increasing the availability of consumer goods. Recently, the GDR's planners have eased their restrictive investment policies, allowing a 25% rise in investments between 1984 and 1985, and a sustained high level in 1986. According to a report prepared by Radio Free Europe, this new investment policy "can only then achieve the much-needed modernization of East German industry if it is targeted on key technological areas"[36] — which the GDR seems to be doing. Robotron is a beneficiary of this investment policy since its computers are given priority application in other areas of the GDR economy and its own production capabilities are upgraded.

---

[33] Cf. Flow, p. 4, who relies on economic figures compiled by the GDR government.

[34] Cf. Wokurka, pp. 2-3.

[35] Klaus Krakat, "Ost-Technologie will eigene Wege gehen," *Computerwoche*, 21 March 1986, p. 49.

[36] Flow, p. 4.

Finally, the GDR needs significant, long-term sources of hard currency to service an estimated $6.6 billion total debt to Western banks and to boost living standards at home. The GDR is highly export dependent, deriving some 40% of its national income from trade with other countries. As already indicated, much of that trade is conducted with the Soviet Union. Another 28% of it, however, is conducted with the capitalist West, which serves as a source of hard currency.[37] The GDR's economic planners have no intention of giving this trade up; most indications are that they would like to expand it.

Robotron planners undoubtedly hope to play a part in the GDR's trade with the West, even though they are constrained by allocation problems (domestic needs and Soviet trade take priority) and by the technological shortcoming of their products in Western markets. For the most part, Robotron has limited itself to exporting peripheral devices to Western Europe. For example, some 10,000 Robotron printers were exported to the West in 1985; according to one account, they were particularly well received in a West Berlin department store.[38] One-third of the GDR's Western trade is focused on neighboring West Germany. Under a rider to the Treaty of Rome, the GDR can export goods to the Federal Republic tariff-free. This provision — which makes the GDR a de facto Common Market member — has been a tremendous boon to the GDR economy. Goods which might otherwise be non-competitive in the West manage to sell in West German stores by virtue of their low, tariff-free prices. At a press conference during the Leipzig Fair in the spring of 1986, Robotron spokesmen described plans to widen their distribution capabilities in France as well as increasing exports to the FRG.[39]

Conclusions

The framework used here shows that the Robotron Combine is structured, makes decisions, and relates with the outside world in ways that are very different from those that apply at Western computer firms. Although the argument can be made that American computer manufacturers are influenced by such political factors as American tax laws, federal

---

[37] Cf. Robert England, "Looking to New Technology to Revitalize Aging Industries," *Insight*, 16 February 1987, p. 34, who relies on economic figures compiled by the GDR government.

[38] Cf. "Tempo zulegen," p. 81.

[39] As reported by Krakat, "Schlüsseltechnologien in der DDR," p. 122.

oversight in their financial dealings, and trade disputes, the firms' basic existence — and the fundamental decisions they make on development strategy, production, and marketing — are not politically motivated in any meaningful sense. Virtually the opposite is true in the case of Robotron.

The political influences on Robotron can be grouped into three categories:

1) Social and ideological factors

The entire legitimation process surrounding cybernetics in the GDR can be seen as an attempt by the SED to evaluate how computing and industrial automation can be made to serve the needs of the country without affecting the leading role of the Party. While debates on the effects of technology also occur in non-communist societies, such debates tend to take place away from the locus of technological planning and implementation. In the West, the legitimation of new technologies — to the extent that it occurs at all — proceeds in tandem with the appearance of those technologies in the society. In the GDR, such legitimation is an *a priori* phenomenon. Even though Robotron's management, under the combine reform, has considerable leeway to set its own course, that management is a part of the ruling hierarchy that is still trying to come to grips with the computer.

The automation of industry is now a chosen goal, but debates over the role of the personal computer are still far from over. For now, GDR leaders appear to have adopted the position that making computers widely available to the average consumer is not "economical," given the lack of widespread computer literacy in the GDR and the existing emphasis on industrial applications of computing.[40] Unspoken, though just as important, of course, is the SED's desire to put off for as long as possible the growth of a politically threatening "hacker" subculture — which the widespread private use of computers would surely bring. Nevertheless, the GDR's leaders must be given high marks, in comparison with their socialist brothers, for recognizing a need not only for computer literacy but also for computer user groups that can communicate complaints and desires to Robotron. The resulting increase in the

---

[40] Cf. Klaus Krakat, "Auch Comecon-Länder haben CIM im Visier," *Computerwoche*, 22 May 1987, p. 40.

society's technological sophistication is an absolute prerequisite for Robotron's future success.

Of interest in the coming years will be the degree to which the SED encourages the expansion of data networks within the GDR, popularly accessible data bases, and data communications with the Western world. All of these developments, while desirable from an economic standpoint, are as yet hindered in the GDR by technological backwardness and continuing restrictions on the flow of information in general. Those of us studying the eventual impact of *glasnost* in the GDR should pay particular attention to its effects on the country's computer sector.

2) Politico-economic factors

Economic concerns alone seem able to gain primacy over ideological concerns in the GDR. The perception that the GDR's vital export sector would be seriously eroded without a commitment to the microelectronics industry is what placed Robotron on the pedestal it now shares with only a handful of combines in the GDR. Further, Robotron is able to do comparatively well as a Soviet-bloc computer manufacturer because of its organizational structure, which gives Robotron's managers decision-making authority on most issues, and has apparently done what the GDR's planners hoped it would do: shorten information flows, enhance coordination between branches of the firm, and provide greater flexibility in planning and administration.

3) International considerations

The position of the Soviet Union as the GDR's most important trading partner and political ally necessitates that the bulk of Robotron's computer production be shipped East — in exchange for the raw materials and foodstuffs that the GDR needs to survive. Robotron's production strategy is further influenced by its exclusive research and development ties to the Soviet Union and the rest of Eastern Europe. It remains to be seen if a growing trend in the West to ease export restrictions, combined with the apparent flowering of intra-German relations, will lead to meaningful joint ventures and the like between Robotron and Western computer firms as well.

The German-German relationship, regardless of its level of hostility or accommodation at a given point, has long been a force in the GDR's, and, by obvious extension, Robotron's drive to excel. Enhancing the economic and technological performance of the country vis-à-vis the Federal Republic is absolutely essential to the SED's quest for public legitimacy in the GDR. Whereas computing technology was once held back because of its perceived threat to the socialist underpinnings of the GDR, it is now touted as a "key technology" in the *strengthening* of the country's economy and society. Books and articles are published today in the GDR with the sole purpose of demonstrating to the country's citizens that computers were meant for socialism, and that they will bring the country closer to the communist ideal.[41] Pegged as bad or good, therefore, computers in the GDR have been defined in terms of their influence on the country's socialist orientation and economic performance. The Federal Republic, in all of this, is the inescapable point of comparison.

These three categories of political influence on Robotron are not mutually exclusive. Instead, they represent a fluctuating hierarchy of concerns that the SED and Robotron's planners must constantly confront. The planning, manufacturing, and marketing strategies employed by Robotron in the coming years will be key indicators of how far the SED is willing to go in realizing its goals of continued central control, increased domestic legitimacy, and international economic competitiveness.

---

[41] See, for example, Joachim Dubrau and Werner Netzschwitz, *Mikroelektronik: Wie verändert sie unser Leben?* (Berlin: Dietz, 1983).

Social Structure and the
Scientific-Technical Revolution:
Some New Sociological Questions in the GDR

Manfred Lötsch

Old and New Questions of Research on Social Structures

Interest in the empirical analysis of social structures began in the GDR toward the end of the 1960s. The evolution of this research can be traced above all in the publications generated by the Sociology Congresses of the GDR. The first conference, held in Berlin in 1969, was dominated by the search for relevant theses: definitions of the working class, of the class of collective farmers, of the working population; and the quantitative/statistical description of classes and social strata, i.e., the development and refinement of statistical instruments.[1] This first phase, which can be thought of as a period of basic self-definition, was, on the one hand, unavoidable — all new research begins with the quest for the right questions; but it also manifested a good many scholastic aspects, such as endless discussions about who really "belongs" to the working class.[2]

In the second phase, which began already in 1970, things became more concrete. On the basis of an initial study on the structure of the working class an attempt was made to combine empirical results with broader conceptual questions. The central issue of the study was the relationship between

---

[1] *Soziologie im Sozialismus. Die marxistisch-leninistische Soziologie im entwickelten gesellschaftlichen System des Sozialismus. Materialien der "Tage der marxistisch-leninistischen Soziologie in der DDR"*, ed. Wissenschaftlicher Rat für Soziologische Forschung in der DDR, Schriftenreihe Soziologie (Berlin: Dietz, 1970), pp. 402-35.

[2] See, for example, *Zur Sozialstruktur der sozialistischen Gesellschaft*, ed. Wissenschaftlicher Rat für Soziologische Forschung in der DDR, Schriftenreihe Soziologie (Berlin: Dietz, 1974).

"equality" and "social differences"; the study inquired about the objective bases of social differences in socialist society and how they were to be evaluated.[3] At the time the study was carried out, it was not at all a common assumption that essential social differences within and between classes are a stable phenomenon; on the contrary, the idea prevailed (not least in political thinking) that, once the old class differences were overcome, all other social differences would disappear within a relatively short period of time. The first studies showed that, in addition to "ownership relations," a second determinant of social differences had to be taken into consideration: the division of labor. Put briefly, the studies demonstrated that socialist society would have to cope with elements of social inequality for a long time to come.[4]

At the end of the 1970s sociological theory in the GDR underwent a development which brought about a profound change in conceptual thinking. Until then social differences had always been conceived of as ultimately negative; debate centered around how and in which time frame they could be overcome. Gradually it was realized that the issue is much more complicated than that. The third Sociology Congress, which took place in 1980, thus attempted to grasp the dialectics of social equality and social differences as a part of life in socialist society. After considerable discussion[5] widespread consensus was reached on the following points:

---

[3] Manfred Lötsch, "Über die soziale Struktur der Arbeiterklasse," in *Soziologische Probleme der Klassenentwicklung in der DDR. Materialien vom II. Kongreß der marxistisch-leninistischen Soziologie in der DDR, 15.-17. Mai 1974*, ed. Wissenschaftlicher Rat für Soziologische Forschung in der DDR, Schriftenreihe Soziologie (Berlin: Dietz, 1975), pp. 89ff.

[4] *Lebensweise und Sozialstruktur. Materialien des 3. Kongresses der marxistisch-leninistischen Soziologie in der DDR, 25. bis 27. März 1980*, ed. Wissenschaftlicher Rat für Soziologische Forschung in der DDR, Schriftenreihe Soziologie (Berlin: Dietz, 1981).

[5] See Manfred Lötsch, "Sozialstruktur und Wirtschaftswachstum," in *Wirtschaftswissenschaft*, 28, No. 1 (1980), 56-69; Joachim Freitag and Manfred Lötsch, "Sozialstruktur und soziale Mobilität," *Jahrbuch für Soziologie und Sozialpolitik 1981* (Berlin: Akademie, 1981), pp. 84ff.; Artur Meier, "Bildung im Prozeß der sozialen Annäherung und Reproduktion der Klassen und Schichten," *Jahrbuch für Soziologie und Sozialpolitik 1981*, pp. 116ff.; Manfred Lötsch and Gerhard Wörner, "Materielle Lebensbedingungen und Annäherungsprozesse," *Jahrbuch für Soziologie und Sozialpolitik 1983* (Berlin: Athenäum, 1983), pp. 161ff.; Ingrid Lötsch and Manfred Lötsch, "Soziale Strukturen und Triebkräfte: Versuch einer Zwischenbilanz und Weiterführung der Diskussion," *Jahrbuch für Soziologie und Sozialpolitik 1985* (Berlin: Athenäum, 1985), pp. 159ff.

1) Social equality remains a broad goal of social development in socialism. This goal must, however, be clearly distinguished from uniformity (*Gleichförmigkeit, Nivellierung*). One should not strive for a society in which position and life style are leveled to a common condition, but rather for a society in which all social groups and, finally, all individuals have equal possibilities and chances.[6]

2) This goal entails a long period of time; its essential precondition is a completely new dimension of the productive forces of society. This point will be elaborated upon below. At the same time, the overcoming of certain forms of social inequality are a present requirement of socialist society. This is especially true for status consistency on the lower level of society: for example, for the coincidence of heavy physical labor and physically harmful labor, of low levels of education and vocational training, unfavorable general living conditions, and lower social mobility.[7]

3) Certain social differences exist in socialist society not only because they have "not yet" been overcome, but because they result from the objective social conditions and in this sense are systemically necessary. This is true for differences that: a) are connected with the principle of distribution based on achievement, i.e., for differences deriving from the system of distribution; and b) for differences along the axis of work level, education, and training. At the fourth Sociology Congress (1985) new thought was given to the necessary and productive function of these social differences.[8]

Goals of Equality and Demands of Efficacy

This change in conceptual thinking in the late 1970s and early 1980s came about for reasons having little to do with the

---

[6] This is in keeping with the well-known formulation of Karl Marx and Friedrich Engels that it is a question of a society "worin die freie Entwicklung eines jeden die Bedingung für die freie Entwicklung aller ist" ("Manifest der kommunistischen Partei").

[7] See Artur Meier, *Soziologie des Bildungswesens* (Berlin: Volk und Wissen, 1974), esp. pp. 156ff. and 291ff.; Manfred Lötsch and Artur Meier, "Entwicklung des Verhältnisses von körperlicher und geistiger Arbeit und von Qualifikation und Bildung," in *Sozialstruktur der DDR*, ed. Rudi Weidig et al. (Berlin: Dietz, 1988).

[8] See *Soziale Triebkräfte ökonomischen Wachstums. Materialien des 4. Kongresses der marxistisch-leninistischen Soziologie in der DDR, 26. bis 28. März 1985*, Schriftenreihe Soziologie (Berlin: Dietz, 1986).

inner development of sociology in the GDR. Two factors are particularly important. In the 1970s the GDR, like other industrialized countries, changed over to an economic model which we define as "intensiv-erweiterte Reproduktion." This means that economic growth is to be realized not by the increased, or extensive, use of resources, but rather by heightened "rationalization." This change in the strategy of economic growth went hand-in-hand with new trends in the social structure. The quantitative labor force is no longer increasing, since the one source of new labor that existed — given the constant regression in the size of the population[9] — is now exhausted, i.e., women. Between the 1950s and 1970s the level of training of the work force grew extensively: at the end of the 1940s the ratio of unskilled and semi-skilled (*ungelernte, angelernte Arbeiter*), skilled workers (*Facharbeiter*), and those with degrees from technical colleges and universities was 75 - 23 - 2; at present it is 15 - 64 - 21. Today the structure changes only to the extent that older people leave and young people join the labor force. Since the mid-1970s the skills level of each new training year has been stable at 10 - 65 - 25.[10] The assumption is that this will remain the case in the foreseeable future. This is of considerable significance. As long as resources can be increased, holes in productivity can be compensated for extensively. With the end of extensive growth, the question of using resources effectively takes on new meaning.

Secondly, in the 1970s, at the latest, the challenge presented by the scientific-technical revolution became clear. Technological gaps could no longer be overlooked. Internationally the scientific-technical revolution entered a new stage which was mainly characterized by the broader and faster expansion of high technology. An important means which contributes to the acceleration of the process in the Western world — the international transfer of technology — is not available to the GDR (and other socialist countries) because of the Cocom barrier. It thus became necessary to develop a strategy which for the most part would rely on available potential in

---

[9] The population of the GDR decreased from 18,730,000 in 1949 to 16,640,000 in 1986. During the same time period the number of people working increased from 7,310,000 to 8,550,000. The number of working women rose from 2,890,000 to 4,200,000. *Statistisches Jahrbuch 1987 der Deutschen Demokratischen Republik* (Berlin: Staatsverlag, 1987), pp. 1, 17.

[10] Ingrid Lötsch, "Zur Entwicklung des Bildungs- und Qualifikationsniveaus in der DDR," *Jahrbuch für Soziologie und Sozialpolitik 1985*, pp. 511ff.

the GDR itself.[11] One can sum this strategy up by saying that the natural sciences and technical fields have become a first-rate growth factor in the GDR; economic growth and social progress are dependent on their development to a completely different extent than was the case under the conditions of the primarily extensive economic model.

This changed social context led to new emphases in sociological research. In the previous phases sociologists had addressed the development of the working class and the class of farmers — one could say that this was only natural since at this time (from the 1950s to the 1970s) the most interesting changes were taking place in these large social groups.[12] Special attention was given to those processes which we call "social approximation" ("soziale Annäherung"), with which is meant that class differences gradually lose their significance within the social structure. These developments supported the concept of a direct and short-term reduction of social differences in general.

One consequence of this idea was the belief that the development of the intelligentsia was also primarily a matter of overcoming social differences between this class and that of the workers and farmers. And this was certainly not entirely wrong. With regard to the intelligentsia as it developed from the old society, there really was profound change — for instance, the guarantee of equal opportunity and mobility with respect to higher education. As far as education and professional training were concerned, attention was first focused on the working class; the same was true for the mechanisms of distribution and thus for the development of income structures, etc.

In face of the question how the GDR's ability to meet the challenge of the scientific-technical revolution might be increased, a conclusion was reached which resulted in a fundamental conceptual change: structural developments which are aimed at overcoming social differences and which thus reflect

---

[11] See *Direktive des XI. Parteitages der SED zum Fünfjahrplan für die Entwicklung der Volkswirtschaft der DDR in den Jahren 1986 bis 1990* (Berlin: Dietz, 1986).

[12] See Siegfried Grundmann, Manfred Lötsch, and Rudi Weidig, *Zur Entwicklung der Arbeiterklasse und ihrer Struktur,* Schriftenreihe Soziologie (Berlin: Dietz, 1976); Kurt Krambach et al., *Genossenschaftsbauern - gestern, heute, morgen* (Berlin: Dietz, 1977).

the goals of equality, and structural developments which lead to efficient structures do not coincide. Concentrating on equality can result in an intelligentsia which, although similar to the working class, is not sufficiently productive. That is not to say, however, that the solution is to be found simply in the development of social differences; the problem is more complicated.

On the one hand, there are dysfunctional social differences, for example those which, aided by the relative weakness of certain aspects of the service sector, lead to the monopolizing of scarce goods and services and thus to differences in income and the material standard of living which contradict the principle of distribution based on achievement. On the other hand, there is dysfunctional equalization (*Nivellierung*) which does not achieve the goal criterion of "efficacy." Thus a dual social problem must be solved: the overcoming of dysfunctional social differences, on the one hand, and the development of progressive social particularity, on the other.

Contours of the Intelligentsia Issue in the GDR

The GDR has about 1% of the world's scientifically trained people, which may seem small but is considerably greater than its share of the world's population. For every 1,000 employees engaged in material production, the GDR has more than twice as many engineers and *Diplom* engineers as the Federal Republic.[13] "For every 10,000 inhabitants in the European COMECON countries in the mid-seventies there were 128 employees in the sciences, among them 42 scientists and *Kader* with doctorates. In the FRG, by comparison, there were 67, among them 17 scientists and engineers."[14] For every 10,000 people in the GDR there are 54 university and college-trained people working in research and development, in comparison with the United States, which has 25; Japan, 29; the Federal Republic, 17; England, 14; France, 12; Canada, 11; Sweden, 20; and Italy, 5.[15] All told, about 30% of all the scientists in the world work in COMECON countries.

---

[13] Harry Nick et al., *Ökonomie und soziale Wirksamkeit des wissenschaftlich-technischen Fortschritts* (Berlin: Dietz, 1986), p. 52.

[14] *Das Kaderpotential der Wissenschaft im Sozialismus*, ed. Lothar Kannengießer and Werner Meske (Berlin: Akademie, 1982), p. 168. My translation here and throughout.

[15] Ibid., p. 170.

These few data describe the problem quite precisely: productivity does not correspond with the potential. As a result of this, a study was undertaken under my direction at the Institut für Soziologie of the Akademie für Gesellschaftswissenschaften in 1986 to establish the causes of this discrepancy.[16] It is not possible to discuss the study in its entirety here, and I will focus therefore on one central aspect.

Values and Achievement Goals of Scientific Researchers

We started from the premise that subjective value orientations and achievement goals play a decisive role in scientific work; that actual performance correlates with these to a high degree and in an important way. Our assessment instrument, a standardized questionnaire, contained a rather large battery of indicators from which the content and level of such value orientations could be extrapolated. Our sample was divided into two groups: Performance Group 1 — 10% of the total sample, to which, on the basis of objective criteria, the most productive scientists and researchers were assigned; and Performance Group 2, which included the remaining 90% of those canvassed. We also distinguished between scientific work done in academia (university research) and in research facilities of plants and combines (industrial research).

The variables, in which value orientations are expressed, were studied on the basis of a complete correlation matrix using the methodology of factor analysis. The object was to determine whether, within the multiplicity of applied variables, complexes of connections could be ascertained from which the presence of specific behavioral strategies could be extrapolated. Three factors were extracted with the following shares of the explicative strength of the factor model: Factor 1, 52.8%; Factor 2, 39.3%; Factor 3, 7.8%. After the variables had been established, the factor loadings of which lie above the range of -0.4 and +0.4 and for which therefore a close relationship with the factors can be assumed, the content of the extracted factors could be easily identified. The variables constituting Factor 1 indicate high achievement goals and refined scientific ethics; we defined it therefore as the "Factor

---

[16] The sample comprised 2,950 people and was made up of complete canvassings of the entire scientific staff of two technical universities and the research facilities of an industrial combine (*Industriekombinat*) and subsamples in an additional technical university and in research facilities of two additional industrial combines.

of High Achievement Goals." Factor 2 is composed of orientations directed toward average performance goals; it thus received the designation "Factor of Job Orientation." Factor 3 expressed a high degree of commitment in regard to regular working time and was therefore called the "Factor of Extensive Work Readiness."

After this, the mean values of the factors were listed in increasing or decreasing order, which produced an initial overview. Illustration 1 shows the general level of the factors by groups: according to the direction of the arrow, the values included in the factors are either strongly or weakly characteristic. In order to heighten the clarity, the factor values were then calibrated to a mean of zero and a scatter of one, and the mean values and the standard deviation were calculated. The mean values of the groups plus/minus the standard deviation were then plotted into a system of coordinates. The graphic representation of the results shows the relative positioning of the groups in regard to the attitudes contained in the factors; the use of a system of coordinates (instead of a one-dimensional axis) makes it possible to compare two factors. The field thus created indicates the relative degree to which the attitudes contained in the factors are present in the groups. (See Illustrations 2-4.)

The first result consists of the fact that in both groups the direction of Factors 1 and 3 is the same, while the direction of Factor 2 is exactly the opposite. High achievement goals and the willingness to invest an above-average amount of time in attaining them coincide as tendencies. The next result, which can be seen in the graphs, seems more important: in general (Illustration 2), and even more in the case of Performance Group 1 for industrial research (Illustration 3), the groups overlap considerably, whereby the actual overlap is even larger than presented here, since the calculation and graphing procedure ($\bar{x} \pm 1$) includes only two-thirds of the sample.

Conclusions

The results presented here are characteristic of a larger problem in the GDR. While the GDR has a considerable pool of trained scientists and a system of higher education with an internationally comparable level of training, the social particularity of the top creative level of the intelligentsia is insufficiently developed. This is far less the case for academia than for industry, where the overlappings are so extensive that one can almost speak of a non-existent top level. There are several reasons for this:

1) The already mentioned overemphasis of "equalization," i.e., the reduction of social differences per se, has resulted in a loss of social particularity and, in many cases, a loss of status for the entire intelligentsia. This does not apply equally to all groups. It is far more true for engineers, for example, than for doctors or scientists in academia.

2) The extreme quantitative expansion of this stratum from the 1950s to the 1970s (it has increased approximately tenfold since 1949) has had an effect here. Here, too, the engineers are more affected than other groups.

3) All in all, there has been a leveling of income structures, once again especially for the technical intelligentsia. There is, to be sure, no direct connection between this and the under-developed value orientation of the intelligentsia; there is an indirect connection, however: the fact that scientific work is remunerated to more or less the same degree as work in material production strengthens the view that scientific work does not require an unusual commitment (Factor 3).

4) Industrial research, as opposed to academic research, does not have a long tradition. It began to be significant in the 1950s, and its real development took place in the 1960s and 1970s. While academic research could look back on a centuries-old tradition, industrial research has faced a conflict: its specific tasks make it impossible to assume the principles of academic research; and its own history is too brief for it to have fully established its own mechanisms for scientific work.

5) Connected with this is the fact that the functional principles of material production were largely carried over to this area of scientific research — partly out of necessity, but partly also in an exaggerated and nonsensical fashion. On the one hand, industrial research is subject to the rules and con-straints of the production process: it is part of a planned whole; research and development have set deadlines to meet (not only in socialist society, of course). On the other hand, the greater functional, physical, and social proximity to the working class results in researchers and workers being treated "equally": they are bound by the same strict working-time regulations; the pay level of the workers serves as the measure for the salaries of the members of the intelligentsia

employed there; and engineers and technical staff are often mobilized when workers are needed in material production.

6) Here, too, especially in the case of industrial research, the insight that top researchers flourish best around other outstanding scientists has not been fully appreciated. Most of the GDR's outstanding people in scientific and technical research are employed in academia. Industrial researchers tend to be younger; they encounter fewer emulatable models personally. This, too, is a consequence of the quantitative expansion mentioned above.

The conceptual conclusions to be drawn from the analysis I have sketched here are both simple and difficult. The basic conclusion is simple: socialist society needs an intelligentsia which, on the one hand, is not separated in an elitist way from the working class, but which, on the other hand, does not sacrifice, as a result of leveling, all of its social particularity (education, way of life, interests, values). It particularly needs a creative elite with well-defined social characteristics; it is a mistake to believe that outstanding scientific achievements can be reached by average people working under average conditions. The practical solution is difficult. There's a proverb that says that the opposite of a mistake is also a mistake. Solutions can be sought and found only within the framework of the basic values of socialist society; the alternative to harmful leveling cannot be greater social inequality. In essence it is an optimization problem with unknown criteria for the optimal. What we know for sure is that social leveling and social inequality are equally unacceptable. The optimal point between these two extremes depends on two decisive factors: the obtainable degree of effectiveness; and social acceptance. This second factor is also determined by two different things: the value concepts of the working class which do not allow for a special social status for the intelligentsia, and the value concepts of the intelligentsia which press for a special status. In a society that views itself as unified and cooperative, as socialist society does, disparate interests can be balanced only with consensus. In closing, let me say that this particular issue will require a good many more debates.

Transl. Margy Gerber

108

Illustration 1: Simplified Synopsis of the Mean Values of the Factors

	Factor 1	Factor 2	Factor 3
Sex:			
Male Female	↑	↓	↑
Educational Status:			
Promotion B *Promotion A* Diploma No diploma	↑	↓	↑
Institutional Sector:			
Academic research Industrial research		↓	↑
Performance Rating:			
Group 1 Group 2	↑	↓	↑

Management Function:

Factor 1	Factor 2	Factor 3
Senior manager Middle manager Project leader Junior manager Asst./sr. asst. Staff member ↑	Senior manager Middle manager Asst./sr. asst. Junior manager Project leader Staff member ↓	Senior manager Middle manager Asst./sr. asst. Junior manager Project leader Staff member ↑

Function Groupings:

Factor 1	Factor 2	Factor 3
Manager Appl. research Basic research Development Inform. process. Other Aux. functions ↑	Basic research Manager Applied research Inform. process. Aux. functions Development ↓	Manager Basic research Applied research Inform. process. Aux. functions Development ↑

Illustration 2

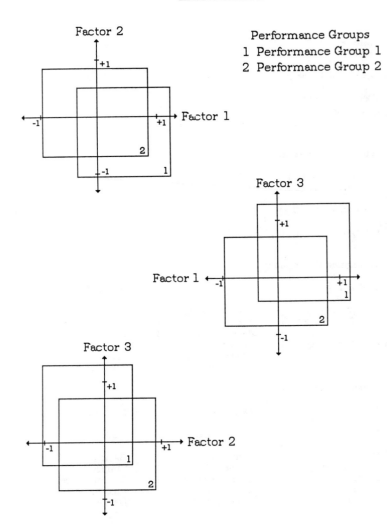

Illustration 3

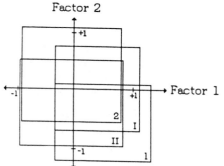

Performance Groups

1 Performance Group 1
2 Performance Group 2
   in Indust. Research

I   Performance Group 1
II Performance Group 2
    in Acad. Research

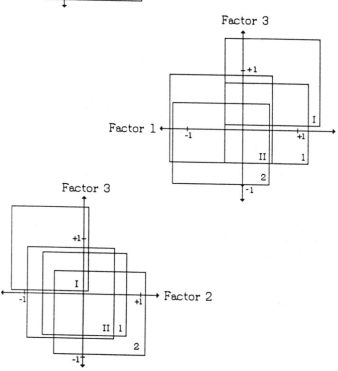

111

Illustration 4

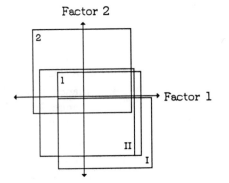

Performance Groups

1 Performance Group 1
2 Performance Group 2
  in Development,
  Construction,
  Production Prep.

I Performance Group 1
II Performance Group 2
  in Basic Research

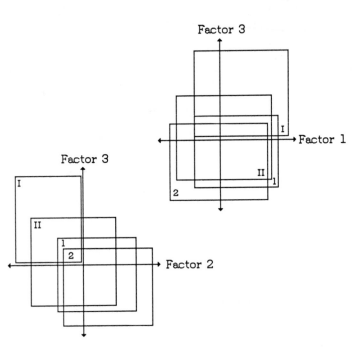

Heimat und Geschichte
als Thema der DDR-Literatur

Irma Hanke

In dem Bericht *Störfall*, in dem Christa Wolf aus Anlaß von Tschernobyl über die Folgen modernen Wissenschaftsverständnisses und seine Umsetzung in die Praxis nachdenkt, schildert sie eine Episode, die plötzlich die Situation von 1945 wieder ins Gedächtnis bringt. Am Abend dieses "bis zu seiner letzten Minute makellos gebliebenen Tages,"[1] den die Erzählerin in ihrem Wohnort in Mecklenburg verbringt, begegnet sie, aus dem Dorf heimkehrend, auf dem eigenen Grundstück einer Familie. Diese betrachtet das Haus, in dem der Vater nach dem Krieg aufwuchs — seine eigene Schwester, als Kind an Typhus gestorben, müsse auf dem Grundstück begraben sein, berichtet er. Die Eindringlinge werden von der Erzählerin eher unwirsch abgefertigt — auch sie und ihr Bruder haben zu dieser Zeit Typhus gehabt, da kommen Erinnerungen auf — und sie fährt fort:

> Ich habe mich umgedreht und im Gegenlicht, weil die Sonne schon hinter das Dach gerutscht war, das Haus liegen sehen, und sein Gesicht, das mir bis dahin fast immer freundlich erschienen war, hatte sich zur Fratze verzerrt. Da ich es mir abgewöhnt hatte, Augenblicksstimmungen nachzugeben, habe ich mir dieses in Wahrheit gräßliche Gefühl mit einer Überanspannung, mit einer seelischen Erschöpfung erklärt und bin ohne zu zögern ins Haus gegangen. Aber vergessen habe ich diesen Augenblick nicht mehr können, auch wenn ich es schon lange gewußt habe, daß jede Haut reißen und

---

[1] Christa Wolf, *Störfall* (Darmstadt/Neuwied: Luchterhand, 1987), S. 82.

aus den Rissen die Ungeheuer quellen können. Daß das Stützwerk hinter den Fassa-
den von Zeit zu Zeit zusammenzubrechen
pflegt; daß ganze Wegstücke unmittelbar
vor uns in Bodenlose zu versinken lieben.

(S. 85)

Was ist da geschehen? Das scheinbar private Refugium, das
Haus als sicherer Ort — es hat eine Geschichte; eine Geschichte, die die Zufälligkeit der eigenen Existenz, die das
vorläufig Vordergründige der selbst geschaffenen Ordnung ins
rechte Licht rückt. Heimat wird un-heimlich; ist selbst
geprägt durch eine Vergangenheit, die in die Gegenwart
nachwirkt. In der Situation, die Christa Wolf schildert, ent-
steht daraus eine existentielle Schocksituation: ein für sie spe-
zifisches Erlebnis. Aber die besondere Verknüpfung von Heimat und Geschichte — und zwar als Sichtbarwerden der Vorgeschichte des heutigen Staates in den Strukturen der
Gegenwart — scheint mir ein Charakteristikum der DDR-
Literatur, dem nachzugehen sich lohnt.

Wer immer sich mit dem Begriff "Heimat" befaßt, stößt auf
Bündel unaufgedröselter Assoziationsketten. Gegen Heimat, so
Günter Kunert, "gab es kein Argument, gibt es noch immer
keines, denn es ist nicht nur ein beschmutztes, verbrauchtes,
weil mißbrauchtes Wort, es ist zugleich nach und trotz aller
Relativierung ein vom Tabu geschütztes Fantasma."[2] Kunert
vermutet, daß die deutsche Betonung des engen — und übrigens unpolitischen — Heimatbegriffs gegenüber dem National-
bewußtsein eine holzige Frucht vom Baum des deutschen
Partikularismus sei, und als solche eo ipso mit dem Ruch von
Idylle und Rückständigkeit behaftet.

Tatsächlich wurde der Begriff seit dem 19. Jahrhundert so
emotional überfrachtet und vor allem in den Zeiten des
Nationalsozialismus derart gegen Rationalität und eine Kultur
der Vernunft ausgespielt, daß er vernünftiger Diskussion nicht
mehr zugänglich schien. In der Bundesrepublik der Nach-
kriegszeit haben vor allem die Vertriebenenverbände die Vokabel politisch besetzt; in der Gesellschaft erhielt und verbreitete sich zudem jene lokale Trachtenvereinskultur mit der
Pflege volkstümlicher Tradition und des "Echten," die selbst
wieder auf Nostalgie beruht, also auf dem Bedürfnis nach

---

[2] Günter Kunert, "Heimat als Biotop," *Politik und Kultur*, 14, Nr. 1 (1987), S.
10.

Harmonisierung und bleibender Identität, das einen Reflex auf den raschen Wandel der Industriegesellschaft darstellt. Erst während der beiden vergangenen Jahrzehnte kam es zu einer Umorientierung. Regionale Vielfalt wurde als Widerstandspotential gegenüber der vereinheitlichenden Industriekultur entdeckt, dem Protestpotential unterdrückter Schichten wurde nachgespürt, gegenkulturelle Bewegungen entwickelten eigenes Selbstbewußtsein. Die lebensweltlichen Bezüge des Heimatbewußtseins wurden herausgestellt, die Notwendigkeit dessen, was Ralf Dahrendorf Ligaturen nennt.[3] Typisch sind in diesem Verständnis der lokale oder regionale Bezug und die sozialpsychologische Komponente; nationale Töne fehlen hier.

In der DDR sind die Begriffe "Heimat" wie auch "Geborgenheit" sogleich in einem eindeutigen Sinn besetzt worden: als "sozialistische Heimat." Heimatgefühle, gebunden an Territorium und Milieu der ersten kulturellen Prägung des Menschen, stehen nach offizieller Auslegung der Lexika[4] in harmonischer Verbindung mit sozialistischem Vaterlandsbewußtsein, das sich auf die Nation bezieht: diese erscheint — darin wird die Herkunft des Marxismus aus dem 19. Jahrhundert sehr deutlich — als die quasi erstrebenswerte Einheit, als notwendiges Zwischenglied auf dem Weg zum Inter-Nationalismus. Heimatgefühle dürfen sich keinesfalls in borniert-partikularistischer Beschränktheit von ihr absetzen. Betont wird schließlich ein wichtiger weiterer Aspekt von Heimat: der des "Heimischwerdens." Er gilt für ehemalige Emigranten wie für Vertriebene: wenn etwa Hermann Kant im *Impressum* von den Familien spricht, die aus Eydtkuhnen oder Liegnitz kamen und nun mit ihren Kindern ein Recht auf Heimat anmelden, "ein Recht auf die Heimat Weißleben an der Börde,"[5] dann enthält das sowohl eine Wendung gegen die Bundesrepublik wie eine positive Auslegung des sozialistischen Heimatverständnisses.

Faktisch gibt es auch in der DDR einen starken Trend zur Regionalisierung und zur Entwicklung von Heimatkultur. Gefördert wird die lokale und Heimat-Geschichtsschreibung, mit Akzent vor allem auf der Geschichte der Arbeiterbewegung. Neuerdings, nicht zuletzt im Zusammenhang der Debatten um

---

[3] Ralf Dahrendorf, *Lebenschancen* (Frankfurt a.M.: Suhrkamp, 1979), S. 51.

[4] Vgl. hierzu die fast identischen Formulierungen in *Kulturpolitisches Wörterbuch*, 2. Aufl. (Berlin: Dietz, 1978), sowie Roland Opitz, "Heimatfindung und Vertrauen," in *Literatur und Geschichtsbewußtsein*, hrsg. v. Manfred Diersch und Walfried Hartinger (Berlin/Weimar: Aufbau, 1976), insb. S. 188.

[5] Hermann Kant, *Das Impressum* (Frankfurt a.M.: Fischer, 1975), S. 120.

kulturelle Identität,[6] kam es zu einer verstärkten Aufwertung gerade der regionalen Besonderheiten, die sich im Verlauf der Geschichte der auf dem heutigen Territorium der DDR gelegenen Länder (so die offizielle Formulierung) herausgebildet haben.

Schwierigkeiten bereitet dabei in der Theorie weiterhin zweierlei: einmal das oben erwähnte "Widerstandspotential" der Heimatkultur, das den Vorstellungen einer demokratisch-zentralistisch durchorganisierten Gesellschaft widerspricht,[7] sodann das Verhältnis zur Geschichte. Als Vorgeschichte der DDR gilt die Geschichte der gesamten deutschen Nation. Dabei wird zwischen historischem Erbe (also der Gesamtheit des Überlieferten) und den Traditionen unterschieden. Erbe *muß* übernommen, aber nur Traditionen sollen bewußt herausgestellt werden; sie besitzen zugleich eine Leitbildfunktion im Sinne des historischen Fortschritts.[8] Da die Geschichte der deutschen Einigung im 19. Jahrhundert vorwiegend von Preußen getragen wurde, fiel in den letzten Jahren das Licht besonders auf die "zwei Gesichter Preußens."[9] Preußen wird insofern nicht nur als ein von reaktionären Junkern beherrschter Staat, sondern zugleich als ein Motor fortschrittlicher Entwicklung gesehen. Diese Aufwertung fand einen

---

[6] Zusammenfassend: Helmut Hanke und Thomas Koch, "Zum Problem der kulturellen Identität," *Weimarer Beiträge*, 31, Nr. 8 (1975), 1237-64; sowie Irma Hanke, "Sozialistischer Neohistorismus? Aspekte der Identitätsdebatte in der DDR," in *Die DDR in der Ära Honecker. Politik, Kultur, Gesellschaft*, hrsg. v. Gert-Joachim Glaeßner (Opladen: Westdeutscher Verlag, 1988), im Erscheinen.

[7] Vgl. H. Hanke und Th. Koch, "Zum Problem der kulturellen Identität," S. 1259.

[8] Siehe vor allem Horst Bartel, "Erbe und Tradition in Geschichtsbild und Geschichtsforschung der DDR," *Zeitschrift für Geschichtswissenschaft*, 29, Nr. 5 (1981), 385-94. Der Aufsatz leitete eine sich länger hinziehende Debatte zum gleichen Thema ein. Zur Bedeutung Preußens vgl. die Zusammenfassung bei Johannes Kuppe, "Kontinuität und Wandel in der Geschichtsschreibung der DDR. Das Beispiel Preußen," *Aus Politik und Zeitgeschichte, Beilage zur Wochenzeitung Das Parlament*, B 20/21, 17. Juni 1986. Vgl. auch Irma Hanke, "Sozialistischer Neohistorismus," a.a.O.

[9] Ingrid Mittenzwei, *Friedrich von Preußen. Eine Biographie* (Berlin: Deutscher Verlag der Wissenschaften, 1979; Köln: Pahl-Rugenstein, 1980) leitete mit ihrer Darstellung eine differenziertere Bewertung Preußens ein. Vgl. dazu auch die das Erscheinen des Buches begleitenden Thesen: Horst Bartel, Ingrid Mittenzwei und Walter Schmidt, "Preußen und die deutsche Geschichte," *Einheit*, 34, Nr. 6 (1979), 637-43, insbes. 643.

breiten Widerhall in der öffentlichen Diskussion.[10] Daß zur spezifischen Vergangenheit der DDR noch andere regionale Traditionen zählen, ist von Autoren aus der DDR häufiger vermerkt, von außen jedoch viel seltener registriert worden.[11]

Fragen wir nach dem Verhältnis von Heimat und Geschichte in Literatur und Literaturtheorie der DDR, so sehen wir, daß die Reflexion über Geschichtsbewußtsein in der Theorie stets einen wichtigen Platz eingenommen hat.[12] Die Auseinandersetzung mit dem Thema "Heimat" wurde bewußt erst sehr viel später aufgenommen. Als die Zeitschrift *Neue Deutsche Literatur* in Vorbereitung des 35. Jahrestages der DDR das Thema "Erfahrung Heimat" aufgriff, waren die theoretischen Beiträge eher dürftig und bezogen sich typischerweise auf das "Heimischwerden." "Wir schaufelten uns ein Vaterland her," sagt Hermann Kant einleitend zu dem Heft,[13] und gibt der Vokabel damit sogleich wieder einen politischen Akzent, der sich auf die *ganze* DDR bezieht, also auf den Prozeß der Ausbildung der sozialistischen Nation.

Jedoch läßt sich unschwer anhand der dort entstandenen Literatur eine literarische Topographie der DDR mit regionalen Bezügen entwickeln, angefangen bei der sorbischen Literatur. Wir können dabei einmal die Schilderung typischer Handlungsorte (wie Leipzig oder Berlin) unterscheiden, sodann die Bindung an Landschaften, oder den Verweis auf regionale Mentalitäten. Schließlich wird, sehr häufig, die Heimatbeziehung über Literatur vermittelt. Wenn etwa Fontane die Sicht auf märkische Verhältnisse bestimmt oder Erinnerungen an die phantastische Realität E.T.A. Hoffmanns in die Darstellung Berlins eingehen, dann ist auch dieser Blick auf Gegenwärtiges geschichtlich bestimmt; er erfaßt in die Gegenwart hineinreichende Lebensformen. Solch ein reflektiertes Verhältnis zur eigenen Umgebung läßt die vorgebliche

---

[10] Sie fand ihren Weg bis in die Theater. Vgl. Claus Hammels Drama *Die Preußen kommen*, das 1981 in Rostock uraufgeführt wurde (Stückabdruck in *Theater der Zeit*, 36, Nr. 9 [1981], 61-72).

[11] Vgl. die Betonung anderer regionaler Traditionen in den letzten Werken Strittmatters (Erwin Strittmatter, *Der Laden* [Berlin/Weimar: Aufbau, 1983]; auch bei Joachim Walther, *Bewerbung bei Hofe* (Berlin: Neues Leben, 1982).

[12] So z.B. auf dem VII. Schriftstellerkongreß von 1973. Vgl. hierzu Volker Brauns Referat "Literatur und Geschichtsbewußtsein," in ders., *Im Querschnitt. Gedichte, Prosa, Aufsätze* (Halle/Leipzig: Mitteldeutscher Verlag, 1978), S. 331-38.

[13] Hermann Kant, "Ein einfaches Wort," *Neue Deutsche Literatur*, 32, Nr. 10 (1984), 6.

Naivität von "Heimatdichtung" im gängigen Sprachgebrauch gar nicht erst aufkommen. Auf einige Façetten dieses Heimatbildes möchte ich im folgenden kurz verweisen, und zwar am Beispiel einiger Gedichte und zweier Prosatexte.

"[V]äterlicherseits, mütterlicherseits" heißt ein Gedicht von Wulf Kirsten, das die Geschichte bislang nicht geschichtsfähiger, d.h. wortloser Geschlechter nachzeichnet:

> am webstuhl saßen sie in stickiger,
> niedriger stube, bleichgesichtige
> hungerleider sie alle auf lebenszeit,
> denen der brotkorb immer eine etage
> zu hoch hing. . . .
>
> . . . ein geschlecht von handwerkern
> und kleinbauern, nie aus dem dunkel
> getreten seiner und meiner leibeigenen
> geschichte. . . .[14]

Die in der Familiengeschichte überlieferten "Auffälligen" dieses Geschlechts verbleiben im gleichen Bereich des Bodensatzes der Geschichte. Der Aufruhr, der Protest gegen das "ewig und drei tage im göpel gehn" (S. 109) führt zu Lebensläufen, die Soziologen wohl als Individualisierung von gesellschaftlichen Konfliktlagen beschreiben würden: Ausbrüche ins Abseits. Der Seemann, den es nach Ostindien verschlägt, der Vagabund, der Garnhändler — andere Rollen hält die Gesellschaft für ihre Unruhe, "als ob ein weberschiffchen tschickte / und tschackte in seiner Brust" (S. 109) — nicht bereit. In ihre "leibeigene Geschichte" bleibt noch der Sohn, der Versemacher, eingebunden: Vergangenheit ist in ihm "aufgehoben."

Einen anderen Zugang zur Geschichte finden wir bei Volker Braun. "Landwüst" heißt der Ort im Vogtland, auf den er sich bezieht.[15] Die Erinnerung an die Vorfahren bestimmt auch bei ihm den Blick auf die heimatliche Landschaft. Aber zugleich scheint die Öffnung zur Zukunft viel gewisser. Natur ist geprägt von Geschichte, und Geschichte, noch unbehauen, unfertig, wird neu bearbeitet: "Natürlich bleibt nichts. / Nichts

---

[14] Wulf Kirsten, "väterlicherseits, mütterlicherseits," *die erde bei Meißen* (Leipzig: Philipp Reclam jun., 1986), S. 109.

[15] Volker Braun, "Landwüst," in ders., *Gegen die symmetrische Welt* (Frankfurt a.M.: Suhrkamp, 1974), S. 64-65.

bleibt natürlich." Natur, die gestaltete Natur, die den Autor anzieht, die ihm vertraut ist:

> Noch unter dem Dorf
> Unter Brachdisteln und Fladern verschollen
> Spür ich ein Dorf
> Meiner Vorvoreltern Schlag
> Und aufgebrannt der Welt ein Fleck
> Zum Leben. (S. 64)

— diese Natur ist zugleich Material der Geschichte. Braun hat im Interview mit Silvia Schlenstedt davon gesprochen, daß er sich in "Landwüst" bewußt einer Landschaft stelle, in die er sich natürlicherweise mischen könne. "Es ist die Landschaft meiner Vorfahren, die dort vor 300 Jahren Zimmerleute und Müller waren. Ich kann da überhaupt nur reden, indem ich mich als mehr oder weniger vermischten Fortsatz dieser Geschichte sehe."[16] Solche Sichtweise führt sogleich in die tieferliegende Erinnerung des Bauernkriegs — eine Geschichte von Gewalt und Unterdrückung, aber eben auch von Aufstand und gegenwärtiger Revolution. Im Gedicht verweist er darauf: "Eisern noch / Strahlt der Morgenstern hier." Die Gewalt, damals gegen den Adel gekehrt, richtet sich in der neuen Welt auf die Bezwingung der Natur: "Traktoren / Traben unter den Peitschenlampen."

Die Prägungen der Vergangenheit werden bei Kirsten und bei Braun unter je anderer Perspektive wahrgenommen: ärmliches Volk bei Kirsten; bei Volker Braun hingegen gilt das Andenken nicht Duldern, sondern Rebellen. Die Größe der in der Gegenwart aufgenommenen geschichtlichen Bewegung wird von Braun unterstrichen durch die bis in Form und Wortwahl reichenden Hölderlin-Anklänge.

Eine eigene Bedeutung hat das Thema "Preußen" in der DDR-Literatur. Die Erinnerung an sein historisches Erbe ist zwiespältig. Darüber wird nicht nur in Drama und Roman reflektiert, sondern auch in der Lyrik. Preußen verkörpert eine Mentalität und eine Haltung, die auf die heutige Gesellschaft durchschlägt. Knapp hat das Kurt Bartsch in seinem Epigramm über den Wechselbalg DDR zusammengefaßt:

---

[16] Volker Braun, "Interview," in ders., *Es genügt nicht die einfache Wahrheit* (Frankfurt a.M.: Suhrkamp, 1976), S. 118.

Friedrich, im schönen Monat Mai, und Stalin
Begatten sich im Park von Sanssouci.
Das Kind, das sie gebären (Rabenväter!)
Wächst hinter preußisch dicken Mauern auf.[17]

Der gleiche Autor hat in dem Gedicht "Märkische Kleinstadt" das Verstaubte, scheinbar Zeitlose des alten Preußen
gezeichnet: "Kartoffeln wachsen hier und welke Jahre."[18] Die
Parolen des neuen Staates setzen sich nicht durch gegen die
zerfallende Vergangenheit: "laut ein Transparent / Verkündet
Zukunft, die im Sommer bleicht" — Poesie des Trostlosen.

In Peter Huchels Gedicht "Brandenburg" wird der Brand-
geruch der Kiefernheide wahrgenommen mit den Augen
Kleists: "*Ach, wie die Nachtviole lieblich duftet!*"[19] Bilder stei-
gen auf: der rote Ulan, der Tanz mit den Bauerntöchtern. Nur
der Schluß erinnert an das vergängliche Prinzip Preußens: "Im
Wasserschierling / versunken / die preußische Kalesche."

Der Aufweis bleibender Strukturen, vormärzlicher Lebensformen findet sich übrigens keineswegs nur in Rückblicken
auf Preußen. Wulf Kirsten etwa geht ihnen nach in einem
Kleinstadtporträt des Meißner Landes: "wege nach S."[20] Die
Straßen, an denen alle Bäume abgeholzt wurden, und die
"tugendfloskeln," mit denen sie gepflastert sind, scheinen das
einzig Heutige an der liebevoll entwickelten Idylle mit "strie-
zelbäckern" und Reseda. Aber diese Idylle täuscht — es ist
eine Idylle gegen die Zeit. Die Beharrlichkeit der Lebensformen ist eher ein Produkt der Ängstlichkeit der von der
Geschichte gebeutelten Stadt, die nie aus dem Ruch der ärm-
lichen Verhältnisse herausgekommen ist. Das hat auch das
Verhalten zur Politik geprägt: man hat nie große Sprünge
wagen können. Da lernt sich die Fügsamkeit:

stadtbrände, kontributionen, pestjahre.
der segen gottes versagte immer aufs neue.
selbst die kommunalgarde verspätete sich
zur revolution in der landeshauptstadt. (S. 54)

[17] Kurt Bartsch, "Liaison," in ders., *Kaderakte. Gedichte und Prosa* (Reinbek:
Rowohlt, 1979), S. 85.

[18] Kurt Bartsch, "Märkische Kleinstadt," in *Kaderakte*, S. 86.

[19] Peter Huchel, "Brandenburg," entnommen: *In diesem Lande leben wir.
Deutsche Gedichte der Gegenwart*, hrsg. v. Hans Bender (Frankfurt a.M.:
Fischer, 1980), S. 139.

[20] Wulf Kirsten, "wege nach S.," in *die erde bei Meißen*, S. 54-55.

Kirsten hat dieses Motiv in einem Prosatext, dem Klein-
stadtbild der imaginären Stadt Kleewunsch,[21] in der literarischen Landschaft irgendwo zwischen Seldwyla, Schilda und
Abdera angesiedelt, satirisch aufgenommen: seine Gegen-
wartsbezüge sind unübersehbar.

Auch Günter de Bruyn bezieht sich in zwei Erzählungen,
die das Thema Heimat und Geschichte aufgreifen, ausdrück-
lich auf den Vormärz. So in *Märkische Forschungen*.[22] Hier
geht es um das Wie der Auseinandersetzung mit der eigenen
Vergangenheit. Der Historiker Menzel hat eine Wissenschafts-
karriere aufgebaut, indem er den vergessenen fortschrittli-
chen Historiker und revolutionären Dichter Max Schwedenow
für die sozialistische Kulturtradition "erschloß." Als ein Ama-
teurhistoriker, der Lehrer Pötsch, entdeckt, daß Schwedenow
zum Schluß seines Lebens Reaktionär und Zensor Metternichs
wurde, wird er von Menzel aus der Wissenschaft heraus und in
die Rolle des Sonderlings gedrängt. Als liebenswürdig-skurrile
Existenz lebt er weiter in seinem Heimatort — auf der hoffnungslosen Suche nach dem vollkommenen Beweis. Das Phan-
tom der Wahrheit, dem der armselige Lehrer nachjagt, hat vor
den festen Karriereinteressen Menzels keinen Bestand. In die
neu sich bildenden Traditionen der jetzigen Gesellschaft haben sich schon längst wieder Interessen geschoben, die aus
dem Aufrechterhalten und Fördern bestimmter Mythen Ge-
winn ziehen. Dies eigentlich kritisiert de Bruyn. Aber für
unser Thema wichtiger scheint mir ein zweites: Dem, der
diesen Erfolg nicht teilen kann, bleibt der Part des Kauzes,
das heißt, er entwickelt Verhaltensweisen, wie sie im Jean
Paulschen Kuhschnappel oder in Kirstens *Kleewunsch* nahe-
liegen, die nur beschränkte Lebensmöglichkeiten bieten.
Denn auf die Gegenseite derer will er sich nicht schlagen, die,
wie ein Historiker im Westen, den Lebensweg Schwedenows
für die höhere Ehre Metternichs vereinnahmen wollen.

Dieser westliche Historiker übrigens spricht von den Fun-
damenten des Neuaufbaus in Europa — Sicherheit, Stabilität
und Frieden, die er nach dem Vorbild eines "gesunden Kon-
servatismus" (S. 148), wie er in der Restaurationszeit des vergangenen Jahrhunderts herrschte, propagieren will. Metter-
nich als Exponent dieser Gesinnung wird daher gegenüber
Pötsch gepriesen:

[21] Wulf Kirsten, *Die Schlacht bei Kesselsdorf. Kleewunsch* (Berlin/Weimar:
Aufbau, 1984).

[22] Günter de Bruyn, *Märkische Forschungen* (Frankfurt a.M.: Fischer, 1979).

> Das Biedermeier, Zeit nostalgischer Sehn-
> sucht heute, Zeit der Ruhe und Geborgen-
> heit, war sein Werk. Seine Größe wurde uns
> bisher verstellt durch preußisch-deutschen
> Nationalismus und durch Fortschrittsgläu-
> bigkeit. Da Hitlers Krieg das eine, Atomtod
> und Umweltvergiftung das andere für uns
> zerstört haben, können wir die Bedeutung
> dieses wahren Friedensfürsten erst jetzt
> wieder erkennen. (S. 148)

Der so Angesprochene allerdings hatte den damaligen inneren
Frieden Deutschlands als "Friedhofsruhe" bezeichnet — übrigens ist so auch das ganze Kapitel überschrieben.

De Bruyns Verweise auf den Vormärz sind unmißverständ-
lich, wenn das Zitat auch deutlich macht, daß er die jetzige
Zeit meint, und zwar durchaus nicht nur die engere Heimat
der DDR, wie westliche Kritiker annahmen. Deutlicher noch
scheinen biedermeierliche Verhaltensmuster im jüngsten
"Heimatporträt" de Bruyns durch, dem Roman *Neue Herrlichkeit*, der unweit von Schwedenow spielt.[23] Erzählt wird eine
Geschichte der Gegenwart, aber verwendet werden Topoi der
Vergangenheit. Sie werden angewandt auf das mit sanfter
Ironie gezeichnete Bild vom liebenswürdig-schwachen Sohn
des mächtigen Vaters mit seinen landesväterlichen Attitüden;
sie erscheinen im Porträt der jungen Unschuld vom Lande,
die verlassen wird, oder der seelenvollen Nachbarsfrau; auch
die Sicherheit, mit der die Mechanismen funktionieren, nach
der gehobene Kreise unter sich bleiben, spielt auf die
vergangene Welt an. Signalisiert wird somit, daß sich in der
neuen Gesellschaft die alten, die "heimatlichen" Strukturen
nur zu gut erhielten (wobei übrigens, und dieser Filter darf
nicht vergessen werden, der Gleichheitsanspruch der neuen
Gesellschaft stets gegenwärtig bleibt).

Einar Schleefs *Gertrud* (1980), nur im Westen veröffentlicht,[24] ist ein Werk völlig anderer Art. Hier herrscht ein
Geschichtsverständnis vor, bei dem Gegenwart und Vergangenheit wie selbstverständlich ineinander übergehen. Es gibt
keinen Glauben an einen irgendwo sich durchsetzenden Fortschritt mehr. Eine mit klarsichtigem Haß gezeichnete Verket-
tung von Gewalt, Verrat, ängstlicher Anpassung, Arbeit, Über-

---

[23] Günter de Bruyn, *Neue Herrlichkeit* (Frankfurt a.M.: Fischer, 1985).

[24] Einar Schleef, *Gertrud* (Frankfurt a.M.: Suhrkamp, 1980).

lebenskampf, Karrieresucht bestimmt das Geschehen. Die engen kleinstädtischen Verhältnisse, wie wir sie auch bei Bartsch und Kirsten finden, bewahren Geschichte und reproduzieren Geschichte in immer gleichen Formen:

> In der Stadt engem Gewerche hat ein
> Mensch da Platz. Hinter mir scheppert die
> Halde, hoch schleift das Förderband. Ab-
> raum. Von hier, entfernt, sieht die Stadt
> anders aus, inne verstrickt. Rauch der
> Bahnhofskessel, Qualm vom Taubenberg.
>
> (S. 85)

Schleef beschreibt, in einem mit Rückblenden durchsetz-ten inneren Monolog der Mutter und in Briefen, die sie an den Sohn richtet, den Lebenslauf dieser Frau und ihrer Fami-lie in einer Kleinstadt des Ostharz, in Sangerhausen. Erzählt wird verknappt, verkürzt, in einem völlig eigenen Sprach-duktus, der sich an die besondere Sprachentwicklung in die-ser Gegend anlehnt, "Geschichte von unten," die in die Ver-gangenheit hineinreicht; die zugleich immer auf das engste verknüpft ist mit der Vergangenheit der Stadt. Kindheits-erinnerungen werden durch historische Bezüge überlagert: Arminius und Flavus, der grinsende Totenkopf am Rathaus als Wahrzeichen von Sangerhausen, die Großmutter am Webstuhl kurz vor ihrem Tode, die, sektiererisch, nur noch "Kober-sprache" (S. 376) spricht, dies alles gekoppelt an Familien- und Ortsgeschichte. "Jede Ecke mir verbunden," heißt es an einer Stelle, "das Vergangene gegenwärtig weiß nicht warum . . . . Was macht die Gegend aus uns, daß wir eigenartige Leute sind" (S. 119).[25]

Der Autor sieht in den Bauernkriegen nicht das Signum des Neuen, wie Braun, sondern ihr Ersticken in blutigem Schrecken. Erinnerungen an diese Vergangenheiten überla-gern den Alltag: Zeitebenen und Wahrnehmungsebenen schie-ben sich ineinander. Insofern ist es der Erzählduktus, der die eigentliche Aussage enthält und das Wie der Erfahrung ver-deutlicht: die Geschichte der Gewalt, die Verstrickungen des Dürftig-Engen, die Zähigkeit des Überlebens von Familien un-ter allen politischen Ordnungen.

---

[25] Vgl. die aufschlußreiche Interpretation dieses Werks: Horst Domdey, "Abkehr von Fürstenaufklärung. Beobachtungen zu Einar Schleefs Buch 'Ger-trud'," in *Probleme deutscher Identität. Jahrbuch zur Literatur in der DDR*, Band 3, hrsg. v. Paul Gerhard Klussmann und Heinrich Mohr (Bonn: Herbert Grundmann, 1983), S. 35-65.

Fragen wir zum Schluß nach einigen Erklärungen für die historische Tiefendimension des Heimatverständnisses in der DDR. Da ist zunächst einmal die selbstverständliche Vertrautheit mit der Blickweise des Historischen Materialismus. Dies setzt Kenntnisse der Vergangenheit voraus, der geschichtlichen Entwicklung, die zum Heute führt. Wichtiger noch scheint mir, daß der Blick für die Geschichte der bislang im Nebel der Sprachlosigkeit versunkenen Geschlechter geschärft wird — Geschichte als Geschichte der bislang Unterdrückten — und daß die materialistische Betrachtungsweise dazu anhält, die Gegenwart als historisch geprägt — geworden und nachwirkend — anzusehen. Hinzu kommt das in der DDR übliche ständige Hervorheben der Bruchstelle zwischen alter Gesellschaft und neuer Gesellschaft; gerade die Betonung des Zukunftsaspekts läßt die Strukturen der Vergangenheit umso eindringlicher hervortreten.

Schließlich spielt hier auch die besonders intensive Beschäftigung mit der eigenen Literatur eine Rolle, die in der DDR zeitweilig an die Stelle der Auseinandersetzung mit gegenwärtigen weltliterarischen Strömungen treten mußte. Zudem hat die Tatsache, daß eine Flucht nach außen, ein Sich-Verlieren an fremde Welten kaum möglich war, vermutlich zu eingehender Introspektion geführt. Sie hat aber auch über die Beschädigungen der eigenen Geschichte nachdenken und die Übermacht der Vergangenheit in der eigenen Umgebung erkennen lassen. Der Blick in die Vergangenheit entspringt durchaus der Reflexion über die Bedingungen des eigenen Fortschritts; nur in Brauns "Landwüst" erscheint Geschichte als ein wirklich für Veränderung offener Prozeß.[26]

Andererseits war der Zugang zum Erfahrungsbereich Heimat weniger politisch verstellt als in der Bundesrepublik; und bestimmte äußere Bedingungen fördern diese Sichtweise. So hat Günter Kunert von der Illusion von Zeitstillstand gesprochen, die sich aus dem Eindruck geringen baulichen Wandels in der DDR ergebe. Das "anheimelnde" Bild der Vergangenheit korrespondiere mit der biologischen Verfaßtheit des Menschen: Heimat als Biotop.[27] Aber diese Welt ist auch in der DDR zunehmend der Zerstörung ausgesetzt. "Moderni-

---

[26] In den späteren Werken Brauns läßt sich allerdings auch eine Veränderung des Zeitbewußtseins konstatieren, vgl. z.B. Volker Braun, "Das innerste Afrika," in ders., *Langsamer knirschender Morgen* (Frankfurt a.M.: Suhrkamp, 1987), S. 61-63.

[27] Günter Kunert, "Heimat als Biotop," S. 13f.

sierung" heißt der Geist, der, einmal gerufen, die Gesellschaft auf spezifische Weise vorantreibt: besonders kraß wird das sichtbar am Vorgehen der sozialistischen Großproduktion in der Landwirtschaft. Hier — bei der Zusammenlegung und Begradigung einer geschichtlich gewordenen Landschaft — wird der Verlust einer menschlichen Dimension deutlich und führt zu Erbitterung und Protest. Wulf Kirsten spricht ihn aus, wieder unter Rückgriff auf ein Goethesches Bild, in "das haus im acker."[28] Zerstört ist die vertraute Umgebung, "die heimat verödet / zum allerweltsbezirk und niemandsland." Einzig und allein die beiden Alten harren noch aus, nach ihrem Tod wird auch ihr Haus wegplaniert werden, und es bleibt nur die Klage: "alles versunken! verschlungen / vom reißwolf des fortschritts was einst / mir gehört hat wie dem vogel die luft" (S. 108).

Die Gewalttätigkeit gegenüber der Natur — hier gilt sie nicht mehr als Ausdruck revolutionärer Kraft. Gewichen ist die Hoffnung auf Veränderung der Welt — zumindest scheint Veränderung in dieser Form nicht mehr der begrüßenswerte Weg. Und so bleibt auch hier das Bewußtsein von Verlorenheit — oder die Ahnung, wie in dem einleitenden Text bei Christa Wolf, daß Heimat nur noch das vorläufig, auf Abruf, uns Gegebene bleibt.

---

[28] Wulf Kirsten, "das haus im acker," in *die erde bei Meißen*, S. 106-08.

Alltagserfahrung? Bemerkungen zur Darstellung des Todes in der neueren DDR-Literatur

Magdalene Mueller

> "Wenn der Kommunismus gesiegt hat und die sozialen und ökonomischen Probleme gelöst sind, dann beginnt die Tragödie des Menschen."
>
> (Heiner Müller)[1]

Dialektischem Ermessen zufolge bezieht die Frage nach der Qualität des gesellschaftlichen Lebens auch die Frage nach der Qualität des individuellen Sterbens mit ein. Hier soll uns beschäftigen, wie diese existentielle Erfahrung in der sozialistischen Gesellschaft der DDR reflektiert wird. Der Marxismus-Leninismus der DDR integriert die Geschichte des einzelnen Menschen in den als gesetzmäßig verstandenen historischen Gesamtprozeß. Indem an Hegels Satz "Das Ganze ist das Wahre" angeknüpft wird, kommen "Brüche, Niederlagen, Zerstörungen, Katastrophen in der Geschichte nur als Verbindungsglieder zu dem ganz Anderen, Neuen"[2] zur Geltung.

Doch wurden extreme existentielle Grenzerfahrungen wie das Sterben und der Tod, die in der vormarxistischen Gesellschaft traditionshalber von den Institutionen der Religion verwaltet worden waren, im philosophischen Diskurs der DDR vernachläßigt. Das führte zu Versäumnissen in der theoretischen Aufarbeitung bestimmter Alltagserfahrungen. Erst in den letzten Jahren scheint diese Problematik immer mehr öf-

---

[1] "Der Dramatiker und die Geschichte seiner Zeit: Ein Gespräch zwischen Horst Laube und Heiner Müller," in *Theater 1975. Jahrbuch von 'Theater heute,'* S. 123; zu Heiner Müllers poetologischer Verarbeitung vom Tod vgl. Florian Vaßen, "Der Tod des Körpers in der Geschichte. Tod, Sexualität und Arbeit bei Heiner Müller," in *Heiner Müller. Text + Kritik*, Nr. 73 (1982), S. 45-57.

[2] Vaßen, "Der Tod des Körpers," S. 45.

fentlich diskutiert und kulturpolitisch verarbeitet zu werden.[3] Wenn der marxistische Philosoph Branko Bošnjak im Tod die "Urquelle jeder Religion" sieht,[4] so kann daraus keineswegs geschlossen werden, daß "die Darstellung des Todes in der sozialistischen Literatur Aufschluß über das Verhältnis zum Religiösen zu geben verspricht," wie es beispielsweise Michael Rohrwasser haben möchte.[5] Auch wenn die Kirchen vom Staat gewissermaßen toleriert werden, und sich die Oppositionsbewegungen zu diesen als "Kirche von unten" besonders im Friedenskampf artikuliert haben, bleibt in der marxistischen Gesellschaftstheorie der DDR die Religion weiterhin grundsätzlich als "Opium für das Volk"[6] bestimmt.

Daß der Tod in der Philosophie der DDR explosives Gedankengut in sich haben könnte, deutet die Vorsichtigkeit an, mit der Sterben und Tod thematisiert werden. Jürgen Hauschke verweist darauf, daß "Sterben und Tod nicht im Zentrum" der "marxistisch–leninistischen Weltanschauung" stehen, gibt aber zu, daß es sich dabei "um essentielle und existentielle, jeden Menschen tief bewegende Probleme" han-

---

[3] Zur Alltagsdiskussion vgl. Toni Hahn, "Umfassende Intensivierung – Inhalt sozialistischen Alltags und Alltagsbewußtseins?" *Deutsche Zeitschrift für Philosophie*, 34, Nr. 8 (1986), 728-33; Iring Fetscher, "Der Tod im Lichte des Marxismus," in *Grenzerfahrung und Tod*, hrsg. von Ansgar Paus (Frankfurt/M.: Suhrkamp, 1978), S. 290ff. Siehe auch die in den 80er Jahren gehäuft auftretenden Veröffentlichungen zur Sterbebetreuung: Susanne Hahn und Achim Thom, *Sinnvolle Lebensbewahrung – humanes Sterben. Positionen zur Auseinandersetzung um den ärztlichen Bewahrungsauftrag gegenüber menschlichem Leben*, Weltanschauung heute, Bd. 40 (Berlin: Deutscher Verlag der Wissenschaften, 1983); *Sterblichkeit und Lebenserwartung. Analyse des Gesundheitszustand der Bevölkerung im europäischen Vergleich der Deutschen Demokratischen Republik*, hrsg. von Günter Ewert und Hildegard Marcussen (Berlin: Volk und Gesundheit, 1981); Günter Baust und Uwe Körner, "Weltanschauliche Aspekte der modernen Medizin," *Einheit*, 40, Nr. 1 (1983), 94-100; *Betreuung Sterbender. Tendenzen – Fakten – Probleme*, hrsg. von Kay Blumenthal-Barby (Berlin: Volk und Gesundheit, 1982).

[4] Zitiert nach Ferdinand Reisinger, *Der Tod im marxistischen Denken heute. Schaff – Kolakowski – Machovec – Prucha* (München/Mainz: Kaiser und Grünewald, 1977), S. 45.

[5] Michael Rohrwasser, "Über den Umgang mit dem Tod in der sozialistischen Literatur," *Frankfurter Hefte*, 38, Nr. 3 (1983), 65.

[6] Vgl. *Philosophisches Wörterbuch*, hrsg. von Georg Klaus und Manfred Buhr (Leipzig: Bibliographisches Institut, 1972): "Glaube, religiöser," S. 224-25; "Kirche," S. 274-75; "Religion," S. 475-81; vgl. auch Ursula Wilke, "Diskussion über gegenwärtige Entwicklungstendenzen in der Ethik," *Deutsche Zeitschrift für Philosophie*, 34, Nr. 9 (1986), 839-42.

dele.[7] Indem er der Literatur therapeutische Funktion zu-
weist, da sie "ein Angebot möglicher Hilfe" (S. 940) geben
könne, scheint er keine grundsätzlichen, sondern nur funk-
tionelle Probleme zu vermuten.

Die Sensibilisierung für die Problematik des Todes hat in
der Gesellschaft der DDR mehrere Gründe. Der uneinge-
schränkte Fortschrittsglaube ist durch die weltweite ökologische und atomare Bedrohung gebrochen worden. Daran gekoppelt ist eine Vereinsamung des Individuums, das Lebens-
sinn in der Arbeit finden soll, ihn aber nicht nur daraus
schöpfen kann. Zusätzlich haben die sogenannten Zivilisa-
tionskrankheiten als ökologische Begleiterscheinungen der
modernen Industriegesellschaft die Auseinandersetzung mit
dem Tod intensiviert. Seit dem Aufkommen der neuen Frie-
densbewegung Anfang der 80er Jahre ist es besonders der
drohende Atomtod, dem immer mehr kritische Aufmerksamkeit gewidmet wird.

Im folgenden werde ich mich mit der literarischen Darstellung individueller Todeserfahrung beschäftigen. Vor allem
werden mich hier der Alters- und Unfalltod sowie der Krebs-
tod interessieren. Folgende Werke werden besprochen: Jurij
Brězan, *Bild des Vaters* (1983); Egon Richter, *Der Tod des
alten Mannes* (1983); Uwe Saeger, *Nöhr* (1980); Günter de
Bruyn, *Neue Herrlichkeit* (1984); Charlotte Worgitzky, *Heute
sterben immer nur die andern* (1986); und Christoph Hein,
Der fremde Freund (1982). Angestrebtes Ziel ist, die von den
Schriftstellern dargestellten Todeserfahrungen im gesellschaftlichen Kontext der DDR zu analysieren. Weiterhin in-
teressiert, wie die Autoren die durch Sterben und Tod aktuell
gewordenen existentiellen Fragen literarisch beantworten.
Methodisch sollen Blochs im 52. Kapitel von *Prinzip Hoffnung*
unterbreiteten marxistischen Überlegungen zum Tode als der
"stärksten Nicht–Utopie" Beachtung finden.[8]

---

[7] Jürgen Hauschke, "'Den Enkeln meines Vaters'. Vaterfiguren – ein Aspekt
der Poetologie Jurij Brězans," *Weimarer Beiträge*, 32, Nr. 6 (1986), 940.

[8] Ernst Bloch, *Das Prinzip Hoffnung* (Frankfurt/M.: Suhrkamp, 1977), S.
1297ff. Im 52. Kapitel hat Bloch eine bunte Phänomenologie möglicher Gedanken zum Tod aufgezeichnet. In seiner Philosophie des Noch-Nicht geht er
davon aus, daß die positiven Möglichkeiten der Welt noch nicht herausge-
bracht sind. S (Subjekt) ist noch nicht P (Prädikat). Das Dunkel des gelebten
Augenblicks ist Ausgangspunkt seiner Philosophie. Bloch vermutet, "daß der
Tod im Dunkel des gelebten Augenblicks eine philosophische Wurzel hat, ja
daß beide die *gleiche* Wurzel haben" (S. 1386-87).

Ausgangspunkt meiner Darstellung ist die von Irmtraud Morgner in *Amanda* aufgeworfene Frage, wie in der DDR–Gesellschaft mit dem Tod "eigenverantwortlich" umgegangen werden könnte, und welchen Stellenwert der Tod innerhalb der marxistisch–leninistischen Gesellschaftstheorie einnehmen sollte:

> Wir haben Gott abgeschafft, schön und gut.
> Aber die Gegenstände, mit denen sich Reli-
> gion beschäftigt, konnten wir nicht ab-
> schaffen. Tod, Krankheit, Zufall, Glück, Un-
> glück — wie lassen sich die unerbittlichen
> Wechselfälle des Lebens eigenverantwort-
> lich meistern? Wer ohne Gott lebt, kann
> Verantwortung nicht delegieren. Er muß
> diese Last immer allein tragen. Bei Ent-
> scheidungen kann er den Zweifel über de-
> ren Richtigkeit nicht loswerden, indem er
> sich mit der Vorsehung beruhigt. Schwer
> ist das, liebe Genossen, wenn man nicht
> vom Glück begünstigt bleibt.[9]

Morgner spricht in *Amanda* den gewaltigen Verlust an, den der Tod eines geliebten Menschen hinterläßt. Dieser Tod bleibt in seiner Privatheit stehen; sein Stachel trifft. Morgner geht die Todesproblematik radikal an. Im Unterschied zu anderen Schriftstellern stellt sie nicht den Sterbensprozeß eines Menschen dar, sondern läßt die betroffene Triebwagenfahrerin Laura Salman programmatisch einen kritischen Brief an die Zeitschrift *Neue philosophische Blätter* schreiben: "Freilich" verstehe sie, daß der Marxismus "eine junge Wissenschaft" sei und "vorerst noch alle Hände voll zu tun" habe "mit politischen und gesellschaftlichen Zuständen im engeren Sinne" (S. 153). Auch habe sie den Eindruck, daß die Philosophen der DDR "solche Gegenstände bevorzugen, die die Klassiker schon mal angefaßt oder doch wenigstens berührt haben, und daß Philosophie für Fachleute geschrieben wird von Fachleuten, von 'Berufsdenkern' grob gesagt" (S. 153). Da sie die Beantwortung der Frage nach dem Tod innerhalb des Marxismus mangelhaft findet, fordert Laura Salman eine "Philosophie oder etwas, wofür" sie "bisher keinen Namen" wisse, "für Nichtfachleute. Über täglich zu bewältigende, unabweisbare, elementare Lebensereignisse" (S. 153).

---

[9] Irmtraud Morgner, *Amanda. Ein Hexenroman* (Darmstadt/Neuwied: Luch-terhand, 1983), S. 152.

In der sozialistischen Literatur der 20er und 30er Jahre herrschte noch ein heroisches Todesbild vor, das "die Verheißung einer Unsterblichkeit im Kollektiv"[10] vermitteln wollte. Dieses Todesbild, das aus der propagandistischen Funktion der Literatur des kämpferischen Marxismus zu verstehen ist, wurde in den 40er und 50er Jahren in der DDR weitertradiert.

Unter dem Eindruck des antifaschistischen Kampfes und aus der Erfahrung des amerikanischen Exils hat Ernst Bloch im *Prinzip Hoffnung* den Tod des roten und kommunistischen Helden in klassischen marxistischen Kategorien bestimmt. Nach Blochs Auffassung kommt nur die

> eine Art Menschen . . . auf dem Weg zum Tod fast ohne überkommenen Trost aus: der rote Held. Indem er bis zu seiner Ermordung die Sache bekennt, für die er gelebt hat, geht er klar, kalt, bewußt in das Nichts, an das er als Freigeist zu glauben gelehrt worden ist. . . . Der Himmel . . . ist keinem roten Materialisten da; dennoch stirbt dieser, als Bekenner. . . . Das macht: er hatte vorher schon aufgehört, sein Ich so wichtig zu nehmen, er hatte Klassenbewußtsein. . . . Und diese Gewißheit des Klassenbewußtseins, individuelle Fortdauer in sich aufhebend, ist in der Tat ein Novum gegen den Tod. (S. 1378–80)

Bloch hatte aber bereits im *Prinzip Hoffnung* seine Zweifel an dieser künstlichen Erhöhung des marxistischen Todes laut werden lassen: "Daß der Name des Märtyrers im Herzen der Arbeiterklasse eingeschreint ist, gibt diesem Namen keine Augen, kein leibhaftig anwesendes Dasein zurück, auch er liegt als Leiche weitab vom intendierten Ziel" (S. 1300). Blochs Bestimmung der Nahziele verhindert für ihn eine Opferung der lebenden Menschen für das künftige Glück der Menschheit.

Auch wenn die "Todesverachtung aus der Zeit der heroischen Revolution" (S. 1382) abgeschlossen ist, wenn die "Hingabe des eigenen Lebens für die künftige Sache" (S. 1300) nicht mehr gesellschaftlich notwendig sein wird, ist damit der Tod noch keinesfalls aufgehoben: "der Tod, als Beil des

---

[10] Rohrwasser, S. 57.

Nichts gedacht, die härteste Nicht–Utopie" (S. 1289–90) bleibt bestehen. Vorhanden ist noch "der naturhafte Tod, als der durch keine gesellschaftliche Befreiung berührbare" (S. 1381).

Obwohl die DDR noch keine klassenlose Gesellschaft ist, signalisieren die Darstellungen des Todes in der Literatur, daß der "naturhafte Tod" ins Zentrum des Bewußtseins gerückt ist. Der rote Kämpfer, soweit er überlebt hat und nicht nur in der Erinnerung der Enkel lebt, ist selbst im Alltag der DDR untergetaucht, ist gealtert und führt das Leben eines Pensionärs. Die aktive Bewältigung des Alltags, die Bewährung im so sehr veränderten Kampf, ist von der zeitweise fast eintönigen Ruhe des Alltags abgelöst worden. Da die Lebenssorge noch nicht total überwunden ist, stehen soziale Probleme der Altersbewältigung im Vordergrund.

Die Forderung, "eigenverantwortlich" mit dem Tod umgehen zu lernen, die Laura Salman in Morgners *Amanda* stellt, ist eine praktische Umschreibung dessen, was Bloch in seinen philosophischen Überlegungen zur Problematik eines naturhaften Todes spekulativ angedeutet hat:

> Die Vermittlung mit dem *Naturhaften* daran ist nun gerade für die befreite, solidarisch gewordene Menschheit ein spezifisch welthaftes, weltanschauliches Problem. Desto mehr, als nach abgeschaffter Armut und Lebenssorge sich die Todessorge besonders hart erhebt, gleichsam ohne das Unterholz übriger, banaler Depressionen. Die Vermittlung mit dem Subjekt der Gesellschaft ist in der klassenlosen gelungen, jedoch das hypothetische Subjekt der Natur, woraus der Tod kommt, liegt auf einem anderen Feld, auf einem weiteren als dem des geglückten sozialen Einklangs. (S. 1381–82)

Die Sorge um diesen von Bloch bestimmten naturhaften Tod ist mehr oder weniger offenes und verstecktes Thema der literarischen Produktion der 80er Jahre in der DDR. In einigen literarischen Zeugnissen wird diese Sorge stärker mit Elementen des roten Kämpfers vermischt, in anderen weniger. In wieder anderen wird sie zur Anklage an eine nicht ausreichende Sterbehilfe benutzt. Alle diese Entwürfe artikulieren Bereiche der Entfremdung im menschlichen Erleben.

Obwohl Autorinnen wie Christa Wolf und Maxie Wander in vielbeachteten Werken das Problem behandelten,[11] wurde die eigentliche breitenwirksame Diskussion um den Tod in der DDR nicht durch diese Frauen, sondern durch den in Fortsetzungen erschienenen Vorabdruck von Jurij Brězans *Bild des Vaters*[12] in der populären Zeitschrift *Für Dich*[13] ausgelöst. In den publizierten Leserbriefen wurde Brězans "Gestaltung des würdevollen Sterbens"[14] ausnahmslos angesprochen und ließ daraus schließen, daß auch andere Bürger der DDR genauso wie Laura Salman auf den Tod mit Kopflosigkeit und tiefem Kummer reagieren.

Jurij Brězans *Bild des Vaters* sowie Egon Richters *Der Tod des alten Mannes*[15] behandeln den "'einfachen und normalen'" Alterstod.[16] Ihre literarischen Ansätze könnten als paradigmatisch für die Annahme gelten, daß im Kommunismus "der Tod als Abschluß eines erfüllten Lebens . . . zu einem 'natürlichen' Ende" wird und "seine Bedrohung für das Individuum" verliert.[17] Das Sterben selbst ist ein langsames, rationalisiertes Abschiednehmen vom bisherigen politischen und persönlichen Leben. Rückblickend geht die Analyse ins Individuelle und darüber hinaus gleichzeitig ins Gesellschaftlich–Historische. Das Gemeinsame der Sterbenden ist ihre positive Erinnerung an eine politische Vergangenheit in der Arbeiterbewegung und im Kampf gegen den Faschismus. Stationen der Kindheit, Jugend, des Erwachsenwerdens, kurz alle Lebensphasen werden als besonders erinnerte Erlebnisse mit ihren eigenen Höhen und Tiefen geschildert; Knotenpunkte des gelebten Lebens werden reflektiert, ehemalige Entscheidun-

[11] Christa Wolf, *Nachdenken über Christa T.* (Darmstadt/Neuwied: Luchterhand, 1969); Maxie Wander, *Leben wär' eine prima Alternative. Tagebuchaufzeichnungen und Briefe* (Darmstadt/Neuwied: Luchterhand, 1983).

[12] Jurij Brězan, *Bild des Vaters* (Berlin: Neues Leben, 1982).

13 Vgl. "Leserbriefe," *Für Dich*, Nr. 24, 1983 und Nr. 26, 1983 sowie Hannelore Hammer, "Gespräche mit Jurij Brězan," *Für Dich*, Nr. 17, 1983, S. 30-32, Charlotte Burkhardt, "Leserfragen beantwortet Jurij Brězan," *Tribüne*, 14.6. 1983, S. 5 und Uwe Körner, "Für und Wider: 'Bild des Vaters' von Jurij Brězan," *Weimarer Beiträge*, 30, Nr.1 (1984), 94-110.

[14] Hauschke, S. 958; Brězan hatte seinen Roman mit dem Motto beginnen lassen: "*Ein Leben vollendet sich in großer Würde, und wer Zeuge war, meinte nun zu wissen, daß keiner so aus dem Leben gehen könne, der nicht so durch das Leben gegangen sei. Was aber ist das: in Würde durch das Leben gehen?*" (S. 7).

[15] Egon Richter, *Der Tod des alten Mannes* (Rostock: Hinstorff, 1983).

[16] Uwe Körner, "Für und Wider: 'Bild des Vaters,'" S. 99.

[17] Vaßen, "Der Tod des Körpers," S. 48.

gen hinterfragt, schuldhaftes und schuldbesetztes Geschehen entwirrt. Die Protagonisten sind voller charakterlicher Schattierungen und haben ein erlebnisreiches Leben hinter sich. Sie werden auf quasi säkularisierte Weise als rote Helden gezeichnet, die nicht ohne Fehler und menschliche Schwäche sind.

Diese Entwürfe unterscheiden sich jedoch in dem, was in den Leserbriefen zu Brězans Roman als "würdevolles" Sterben bezeichnet worden ist. Während Brězans Protagonist Tobias Hawk noch alle kleinen Wichtigkeiten seines Lebens regeln kann und nach eigenem, ans Alte Testament gemahnenden Beschluß[18] bewußt im Kreise seiner Lieben stirbt, findet der Tod des alten Mannes in Richters Roman im sterilen Krankenhaus statt. Der Sterbende ist mit bewußtseinsvernebelnden Spritzen vollgepumpt und kann den Schleier nur manchmal zerreißen, um sich den geschichtsinteressierten Fragen seines jugendlichen Bettnachbarn, der Sohnesstatt vertritt, zu stellen. Darüber hinaus wird keine persönlich menschliche Sterbehilfe geleistet, allein die chemische steht aufgrund eines notorischen Personalmangels zur uneingeschränkten Verfügung und wird von den behandelnden Ärzten und pflegenden Schwestern ohne kritische Hinterfragung in Hülle und Fülle verabreicht.[19]

Brězans *Bild des Vaters* bringt eine Idealisierung des Sterbens. Der Sterbende kann aus Lebenssattheit seinen eigenen

---

[18] Bei Brězan heißt es wörtlich: "Der alte Mann sah noch einmal alles. Novemberland, dachte er und einigte sich mit sich selbst auf eine Lebensfrist von acht vollen Tagen. Er starb in der letzten Minute des zehnten Tages" (S. 9). In diesem Zusammenhang sei an einen Gedankengang Blochs erinnert. In einem Gespräch mit Siegfried Unseld sieht Bloch den Satz "Und Abraham starb alt und lebenssatt" als "falsch" und "gefährlich" an. Er erklärt: "Der Tod ist doch ein Beilhieb für die allermeisten, auch wenn sie alt sind. Also das scheint mir etwas Vergangenes und uns nicht mehr Nachlebbares aus Zeiten zu sein, in denen auch das Individuum noch nicht ausgebildet war, sondern nur der Stamm, das Stammesleben" ("Über Tod, Unsterblichkeit, Fortdauer. Ein Gespräch mit Siegfried Unseld, 6.8.1969, in Königstein/Taunus," in Bloch, *Ergänzungsband zur Gesamtausgabe. Tendenz – Latenz – Utopie* [Frankfurt/M.: Suhrkamp, 1978], S. 329).

[19] Zu diesem Fragenkomplex vgl. *Grenzsituationen ärztlichen Handelns*, von einem Autorenkollektiv unter Leitung von Uwe Körner, Karl Seidel und Achim Thom, Medizin und Gesellschaft, 13, 3. Auflage (Jena: Gustav Fischer, 1984); Heinz Arnold, *Medizinische und soziale Betreuung materiell sichern. Der sozialistische Staat. Theorie – Leitung – Planung* (Berlin: Staatsverlag, 1979); Joachim Glomb, Eike Glomb und Bernd Rößler, *Gestaltung des Betreuungsmilieus im Krankenhaus*, Medizin und Gesellschaft, 20, 2. Auflage (Jena: Gustav Fischer, 1984).

Tod bestimmen. Die Kategorie der Eigenverantwortlichkeit ist für den Protagonisten Tobias Hawk insofern kein Problem, als er im Kollektiv aufgeht. Bei Richter ist von einem so idealisierten Tod wie bei Brězan nichts zu merken. Das Sterben wird zu einer willentlichen Verlängerung des körperlichen Lebens seitens der Ärzte ohne ausdrückliches Einverständnis des Sterbenden. Eine Eigenverantwortlichkeit wird ihm nicht zugestanden.

Bei Charlotte Worgitzky sind in *Heute sterben immer nur die andern*[20] die Morphiumpräparate für die sterbende Krebskranke Maria notwendige und unentbehrliche Schmerzmittel, die ihr einen sanften Tod verschaffen. Diese Mittel akzeptiert sie allerdings erst zu allerletzter Stunde; im Verlauf ihrer Krankheit hat sie sich in hilflosem Widerspruch und sinnloser Revolte gegen den tödlichen Krebs geweigert, schmerzlindernde Mittel zu gebrauchen. Wie kann einer Krebskranken ihr bevorstehender Tod vermittelt werden, und wie können die Freunde und Verwandten verantwortungsbewußt mit ihr umgehen — diese Fragen stehen im Mittelpunkt der Erzählung. In diesem Punkt unterscheidet sich das Werk nicht von Entwürfen westlicher Länder. Nach Worgitzky hat ihre Gesellschaft keinerlei Freiräume für die langwierige, häusliche Betreuung Krebskranker eingerichtet; sie benennt diese sozialen Mißstände. Dem Sohn wird es unmöglich gemacht, in den letzten Wochen vor dem Tod stündlich um seine Mutter zu sein, denn er muß täglich zur Uni gehen. Nur in den letzten Tagen vor ihrem Tod kann er von seinem Universitätsstudium freigestellt werden. Die emotionale und physische Erschöpfung derer, die täglich um die Sterbende sind, deutet die Ich-Erzählerin an: "Wäre ich nicht zur Buchmesse gefahren, hätte das meiner Arbeit nicht geschadet; ich *wollte* fahren. Es war Flucht: Mal einen Tag entfernt sein vom Ort des Sterbens, nicht erreichbar, auch nicht am Telefon" (S. 97).

In de Bruyns *Neue Herrlichkeit*[21] handelt es sich um die demonstrierte Unfähigkeit, alte Menschen mit ihrer ausgelöschten Arbeitskraft noch sinnvoll in die Gesellschaft zu integrieren. Nachdem sie keine Arbeit mehr ausführen können, ist auch ihre Selbstverwirklichung zu einem Stillstand gekommen. Das Altersheim ist eine Barackensiedlung, die sich als Sterbefabrik entpuppt und deren Luft von einem scharfen

---

[20] Charlotte Worgitzky, *Heute sterben immer nur die andern* (Berlin: Der Morgen, 1986).

[21] Günter de Bruyn, *Neue Herrlichkeit* (Frankfurt/M.: Fischer, 1984).

Geruch nach Urin erfüllt ist. Ungleich schwerer als der Gestank sind die hoffnungslosen Gesichter der alten Menschen zu ertragen. Diese sind "stumpf und bewegungslos" und die Augen sind "vollkommen leer" (S. 182). Das Alters- und Pflegeheim ist ein Wartesaal des Todes, in dem einsames Sterben an der Tagesordnung und Menschlichkeit ausgespart ist. Die zerstreute alte Frau Tita ist medikamentös in einen Dämmer- und Dauerschlaf versetzt worden. Ihre altersbedingte Zerstreutheit ist medizinisch als nicht heilbarer "Altersschwachsinn" diagnostiziert worden. Durch Medikamente soll dieser "gedämpft" und der ihn begleitende Fluchttrieb gehemmt werden, so daß die "innere und äußere Ruhe chemisch hergestellt" (S. 197) werde. Die sie behandelnde Ärztin gibt zu, daß "Lethargie und Mangel an Bewegung" (S. 197) nicht gut für sie seien, verschanzt sich aber hinter dem offenkundigen Personalmangel, der es eben notwendig mache, die alten Menschen mit Hilfe chemischer Mittel passiv zu halten.

In dieser Romanrealität einer umfassend verwalteten Gesellschaft ist das natürliche Sterben aus der Familie ausgelagert und in die tödliche Einsamkeit des Altersheimdorfes verlegt worden, in dem der Mangel an emotionalen Bindungen das Sterben beschleunigt. Neben der Kritik an der Funktionärsgesellschaft verkörpert *Neue Herrlichkeit* auch eine Anklage an eine Leistungsgesellschaft, in der "alt sein" mit "arbeitspolitisch unnütz" gleichgesetzt wird. Auch Richters Kritik zentriert sich auf die mangelnde menschliche Sterbehilfe und die Medizin, die sich zu sehr auf die Chemie verläßt. Die Sterbenden bei Richter und die Bruyn werden im Namen der Medizin entmündigt; de Bruyn klagt an, daß Eigenverantwortung nicht integral ist.

Durch die Verurteilung zu Hilflosigkeit und Passivität würde die "Macht der stärksten Nicht-Utopie" als Hoffnungslosigkeit überhand gewinnen, wäre da nicht die jüngere Generation, die zumindest bei Richter aus dem Leben der alten lernen will. Somit scheint die Sehnsucht nach einer besseren Welt durch. Sie ist wesentlich, indem die Weitergabe der widersprüchlichen Lebens- und Kampferfahrungen des alten Mannes inspirierend auf den jungen Bettnachbarn wirkt. Damit wird angezeigt, daß es Zukunft in der Vergangenheit gibt. Das ist der entscheidende Unterschied zu Brězans Darstellung, der den Sterbenden im Kollektiv aufgehen läßt und keine Sehnsucht nach einer besseren Welt artikuliert. Bei Richter wird die Problematik des Sterbens und des Todes noch mit einer traditionellen Kämpfermentalität angegangen.

"Die Enkel fechtens besser aus," ist das Motto, bleibt aber insofern ambivalent, als die potentielle Selbstverwirklichung im Gespräch mit dem Jugendlichen durch betäubende chemische Mittel behindert wird. Wie de Bruyn und Worgitzky zeigen, ist die sozialistische Gesellschaft verbesserungswürdig und harrt des Engagements der Jüngeren. So ausgesprochen deutlich wie bei Richter wird bei ihnen aber dieses Mandat nicht weitergegeben.

In dem Roman *Nöhr* von Uwe Saeger wird der Tod in dreifacher Weise behandelt: der vorgetäuschte Tod des Protagonisten Nöhr, der Tod seiner Mutter (wird nur als Beerdigung erinnert) und der seines Stiefvaters.[22] Der vorgetäuschte Unfalltod erinnert zunächst an einen gehobenen Kriminalroman,[23] hat seine Wurzeln aber in der problemreichen Identitätssuche des Ingenieurs Nöhr. Es handelt sich bei Nöhr um Lebensangst, die sich im Leiden an der Entfremdung zu seiner Frau und zu seiner Arbeit äußert.[24] Sein Aufenthalt in der psychiatrischen Anstalt hat ihm nur zeitweise Linderung verschaffen können.

Nöhrs Stiefvater, der sich zeitlebens über die Kirchgänger lustig gemacht hat, kehrt kurz vor seinem eigenen Tode vorsichtshalber noch in den Schoß der Kirche zurück, kann sie ihm doch etwas bieten, was die Gesellschaft der DDR nicht leisten kann: die Vergebung der Schuld und den Schutz, der von der kirchlichen Tradition auszugehen scheint. Er kann erst sterben, nachdem der Pfarrer ihm seine Sünden vergeben hat. Die Flucht in die Kirche wird zwar vom Stiefsohn als Marotte des Sterbenden betrachtet, ist aber als hilflose Angst vor dem Tod zu verstehen, die als mangelnde Eigenverantwortlichkeit interpretiert werden kann.

Neben Brězans Roman gehört Christoph Heins *Der fremde Freund* zu den meistdiskutierten Büchern der letzten Jah-

---

22 Uwe Saeger, *Nöhr* (Rostock: Hinstorff, 1980).

23 Der Tod im Kriminalroman ist ein ganzer Fragenkomplex für sich. In welchem Ausmaße die Kriminalliteratur ein Indiz für die Todesfaszination ist, kann hier nicht weiter diskutiert werden. Vgl. dazu Helmut Birkhan, "Kulturanthropologische Bemerkungen zu Tod und Sterben in Mittel- und Westeuropa," in *Gegenwart als kulturelles Erbe. Ein Beitrag der Germanistik zur Kulturwissenschaft deutschsprachiger Länder*, hrsg. von Bernd Thum (München: Iudicium Verlag, 1985), S. 196.

24 Saegers Behandlung der Entfremdungsproblematik ist der Fragestellung des Dramatikers Müller vergleichbar. Vgl. Anmerkung 1.

re.[25] Anläßlich der Beerdigung ihres unerwartet verstorbenen Freundes erinnert sich die Ich–Erzählerin scheinbar teilnahmslos an ihn und ihre distanzreiche Beziehung. Seine Ironie und selbstdestruktive Lust an lebensgefährlichen Autofahrten hatten sie zeitweise befremdet. Sie wußte, daß er sich nicht vor dem Tod fürchtete. Schlimmer sei es für ihn, so hatte er oft gesagt, nicht wirklich zu leben. Bei einer Streiterei vor einer Kneipe ist er von einem Jugendlichen tödlich verletzt worden. Offen bleibt, ob es sich nur um einen tragischen Unglücksfall handelt, oder ob Henry das tödliche Abenteuer suchte. Auf Henrys Freundin, die Ich-Erzählerin, wirkt sein plötzlicher Tod gerade deswegen so schockierend, da er so sinnlos ist; überrascht ist sie dagegen nicht (S. 148).

In seiner Novelle schneidet Hein eine verwandte Thematik an: die literarische Verarbeitung der Bestattung. Bei Hein wird die Form der Bestattung an sich bezweifelt. "Beerdigungen und Krankenhausbesuche bei Bekannten" waren für den verstorbenen Henry "so etwas wie fremde Ehestreitigkeiten, die man mit anhören mußte" (S. 12-13). Sie waren ihm "unangenehm" und machten ihn "passiv." "Vertane Zeit. Atavistische Totenkulte. Ein uneingestandenes Spiel mit einer noch immer nicht aufgehobenen Ewigkeit" (S. 13) nannte er sie und fragte:

> wer trägt wen zu Grabe. . . . es gibt Beerdigungsinstitute, die es professionell erledigen, optimal. Wozu die persönliche Anwesenheit. Zusammengehörigkeit mit einer Leiche? Woher rührt das Interesse, beim Verbuddeln, Verbrennen dabeisein zu wollen. Zu müssen. Der, den man liebt, ist es nicht. (S. 13)

Heins Roman zeigt, wie sehr die Bestattungsrituale in der DDR die gleichen sind, wie sie aus der abendländischen Kulturgeschichte bekannt sind. Sofern in den hier behandelten Werken über die Beerdigung berichtet wird, wird sie seitens der Kirche vorgenommen. Die Würdigung des Toten steht im Zentrum der Feier. Die Angehörigen und Freunde übernehmen die öffentliche Trauerarbeit in bekannter Form. Die Beerdigung hat auf jeden Fall den Anschein einer feierlichen Ge-

---

[25] Christoph Hein, *Der fremde Freund* (Berlin/Weimar: Aufbau, 1982). Die westdeutsche Ausgabe trägt den Titel *Drachenblut* (Darmstadt/Neuwied: Luchterhand, 1983). Im folgenden wird aus der westdeutschen Ausgabe zitiert.

staltung. Wenn der Plattenspieler rauscht (Hein, S. 15), die Grabträger angetrunken sind (Saeger, S. 124), die Beerdigung als Massengeschehen abläuft und die Trauergäste große Aufmerksamkeit darauf verwenden müssen, um auch zu der richtigen Trauerfeier zu gelangen (Hein, S. 13-14), so reflektiert das einen fehlerhaften Betrieb und vermittelt einen ironischen Einblick in die Alltagswirklichkeit der DDR.[26]

Zusammenfassend möchte ich folgendes festhalten: die hier besprochenen literarischen Verarbeitungen der Todesproblematik zeigen, daß das Sterben und der Tod grundsätzliche Probleme für die Bürger der DDR bleiben. Gleichzeitig machen sie deutlich, daß damit begonnen worden ist, den Tod als Alltagserfahrung im Sozialismus zu bedenken.

Blochs philosophische Überlegungen zum Tod scheinen mir im Diskurs eines sozialistischen Umgangs mit dem Tod deshalb wichtige Impulse geben zu können, da er erstens den roten Kämpfer als ein "Novum gegen den Tod" definiert und zweitens sich spekulativ über eine klassenlose Gesellschaft äußert, die nach der "heroischen Revolution" weiterhin mit dem Tod als natürlichem konfrontiert bleibt. In dieser Bestandsaufnahme hat er wesentliche Probleme entfaltet, die Gegenstand der philosophischen Diskussion der DDR werden müßten. In der noch nicht klassenlosen Gesellschaft der DDR bestimmen zwei wesentliche Voraussetzungen die literarische Diskussion um den Tod: erstens ist — wie Morgner ausführte — durch die Abschaffung der Religion nicht auch deren Thematik aufgehoben worden; und zweitens sind die Tode der roten Helden obsolet geworden. Dadurch ist ein ideologisches Vakuum entstanden, das theoretisch aufgearbeitet und besetzt werden sollte. Ein emanzipierter materialistischer Umgang mit dem Tod sollte den einzelnen befähigen, die Angst vor dem Sterben und vor dem Tod in eine Neugierde darüber, was da denn nun ist, umzuwandeln.[27] In dieser Hinsicht könnte

---

[26] Ein sozialistischer Umgang mit der Leiche ist meines Erachtens durchaus ein diskussionswürdiges Thema. Mir leuchtet es keinesfalls ein, daß die Kirchen – wie in der hier untersuchten Literatur dargestellt – geradezu ein Monopol als Verwalterinnen von Tod und Sterben in diesem Dienstleistungsbetrieb haben. Selbstverständlich gibt es auch sozialistische Begräbnisse, nur werden diese eigentümlicherweise hier nicht dargestellt. Meines Erachtens stehen noch Diskussionen aus, die sich auf ein "kulturelles Erbe" im Fragenzusammenhang Sterben und Tod beziehen. Zum kulturgeschichtlichen Umgang mit Tod und Sterben und der Tradition der Rituale vgl. Birkhan, S. 184ff.

[27] Bloch, *Das Prinzip Hoffnung*, S. 1384.

eine Diskussion über Blochs Überlegungen zum Tod durchaus befruchtend wirken.

"Gegenwärtige Zeit die auch in Zukunft / Vergangenheit heißt wie die meine": DDR-Reminiszenzen in Sarah Kirschs *Katzenleben* und *Irrstern*

Christine Cosentino

In dem 1984 von Sarah Kirsch veröffentlichten Lyrikband *Katzenleben* befindet sich ein Gedicht, "Blaue Kugel," in dem die Dichterin über die enge Welt von "meines Vaters Vater" nachdenkt.[1] Am Schluß des Gedichtes schaltet sie vom Sein des Großvaters auf die Eigenbefindlichkeit um und zieht ein aufschlußreiches Fazit:

> Es ist ein merkwürdiges Gefühl
> Ihn so aufrecht zu sehen in seiner
> Gegenwärtigen Zeit die auch in Zukunft
> Vergangenheit heißt wie die meine.

Diese poetische Aussage steht in auffälligem Gegensatz zu einem Statement, mit dem Kirsch sechs Jahre früher, im April 1978, in einem oft zitierten "Gespräch mit Schülern" aufgewartet hatte: "Man muß nach vorne leben und nicht nach rückwärts. Was nichts damit zu tun hat, daß wir uns nicht für alles, was in der DDR passiert, sehr interessieren. . . ."[2]

Kirsch machte sich damals in ihrem Bezug zu einem "Wir" zum Sprecher einer Gruppe ehemaliger DDR-Kollegen, lehnte jedoch das Etikett "Exilliteratur"[3] kategorisch ab. Die Frage

---

[1] Sarah Kirsch, "Blaue Kugel," in dies., *Katzenleben* (Stuttgart: Deutsche Verlags-Anstalt, 1984), S. 73. Der Band wird im folgenden mit dem Buchstaben *K* abgekürzt. Seitenzahlen befinden sich im Text der Arbeit.

[2] Sarah Kirsch, "Ein Gespräch mit Schülern," in dies., *Erklärung einiger Dinge (Dokumente & Bilder)* (Ebenhausen bei München: Langewiesche-Brandt, 1978), S. 45.

[3] Ebd.

einer sogenannten zweiten deutschen Exilliteratur à la Fritz J. Raddatz[4] möchte ich hier nicht noch einmal neu aufwerfen, da sie müßig ist. Die Uneinigkeit ehemaliger DDR-Schriftsteller bezüglich dieses Themas während der Westberliner Flücht-lingsgespräche (1980) hat dies wohl deutlich bewiesen.[5] Einer sinnvollen Untersuchung wert ist allein der Einzelfall. In diesem Konnex sei kurz an Peter Schneiders Erzählung *Der Mauerspringer* erinnert, dessen Psychogramme deutsch-deutscher Schizophrenie um die Frage kreisen: "Wo hört ein Staat auf und fängt ein Ich an?"[6]

Ich frage mich — und das als eine Art Up-date zu früheren Arbeiten über Kirschs im Westen entstandene Werke[7] — ob der DDR-Staat im Sinne Peter Schneiders in Sarah Kirschs letzten Werken zu wirken aufgehört hat bzw. ob die Künstlerin nach ihrer zum "Umzug" verharmlosten Einreise in den We-sten nun wirklich, wie angestrebt, ein "deutschsprachiger Schriftsteller, weiter nichts"[8] geworden ist.

Kirschs Dichtung in der DDR, wie auch immer skeptisch zweifelnd, war ein unterkühltes Loyalitätsbekenntnis zu ihrem Staat. Die Dichterin selbst wollte sie innerhalb des DDR-Kontexts als "politisch" verstanden wissen; allerdings nicht im Sinne der operativen Schlagkraft eines Volker Braun, sondern "politisch in einem sehr weiten Sinn, indem ich eigentlich nur will, daß das Lebensgefühl einer bestimmten Zeit sich in diesen Gedichten widerspiegelt."[9] Ist Kirsch in der BRD jetzt

---

[4] Fritz J. Raddatz, "Die zweite deutsche Exilliteratur," *Die Zeit*, 12. August 1977.

[5] Siehe hierzu Dennis R. McCormick, "Wolf Biermann and 'die zweite deut-sche Exilliteratur': An Appraisal after Nine Years," in *Studies in GDR Culture and Society 6*, ed. Margy Gerber et al. (Lanham/New York/London: University Press of America, 1986), 187-203.

[6] Peter Schneider, *Der Mauerspringer* (Darmstadt/Neuwied: Luchterhand, 1984), S. 107.

[7] Siehe hierzu u.a. meine Arbeiten "Von 'italienischen Amseln' und 'proven-zalischen Eulen': Sarah Kirschs westliche Dichtungen 'Drachensteigen' und 'La Pagerie,'" in *Studies in GDR Culture and Society 2*, ed. Margy Gerber et al. (Washington, DC: University Press of America, 1982), 87-98; "Sarah Kirschs Lyrikband 'Drachensteigen': Eine Neuorientierung?" *Michigan Germanic Studies*, 9, Nr. 1 (1983), 63-74; "'Ich gedenke nicht am Heimweh zu sterben': Überlegungen zu Sarah Kirschs Lyrikband 'Erdreich,'" *GDR Monitor. Special Series*, 4 (1984), 121-33.

[8] Hans Ester und Dick von Stekelenburg, "Gespräch mit Sarah Kirsch," *Deutsche Bücher*, 9, Nr. 2 (1979), 107.

[9] Kirsch, "Ein Gespräch mit Schülern," S. 11.

vorwiegend zur "unpolitischen" Dichterin geworden, oder kann man in den beiden Bänden *Katzenleben* (1984) und *Irrstern* (1986) hintergründig echohaft noch immer DDR-politische Resonanzen hören? Im offenen "Spielraum"[10] letzterer Werke glaubt der hellhörige Leser in der Tat Signale über das Unvermögen der Dichterin wahrzunehmen, widersprüchliche Emotionen zu relativieren. Die Konzentration auf DDR-spezifische Reminiszenzen, die ich zu erkennen glaube, ist *eine* Leseart unter vielen, aber, scheint mir, eine durchaus berechtigte.

An widersprüchlichen Äußerungen über die DDR, ähnlich den bereits erwähnten, mangelt es nicht in Sarah Kirschs Werken bzw. in Gesprächen, die sie geführt hat. "In der DDR könnte ich nicht mehr schreiben," teilt sie 1978 in einem Interview mit.[11] Zwei Jahre später überrascht sie ihre Leserschaft in einem ansonsten kritischen Interview dann plötzlich mit Worten, die nicht nur distanziert freundlich, sondern erstaunlich positiv sind:

> Ich bin nach wie vor außerordentlich froh, daß ich dort aufgewachsen bin. . . . Ich möchte wirklich nicht woanders aufgewachsen sein, weil ich einen Standpunkt bekommen habe, ich möchte sagen: einen Klassenstandpunkt, und ein ungeheures Gefühl für Gerechtigkeit und Ungerechtigkeit, was mir woanders vielleicht hätte abgehen können.[12]

Im poetischen Gewand, in Gedichtform, verkündet sie in ihrem ersten im Westen erschienenen Lyrikband *Drachensteigen* (1979) zunächst Begeisterung über ihre neugewonnene Bewegungs- und Reisefreiheit. In einem in Italien entstandenen Gedicht, "Dankbillett," heißt es entsprechend: "ach wie danke ich meinem vorletzten Staat, daß er mich hierher kata-

---

[10] Ebd., S. 13.

[11] Mathias Schreiber, "'In der DDR könnte ich nicht mehr schreiben.' Auskünfte über Schriftsteller-Alltag und Literatur. Gespräch mit Sarah Kirsch," *Kölner Stadt-Anzeiger*, 17. Januar 1978.

[12] Michael Rehsche, "Momente, die nicht wiederkommen . . . 'Weltwoche'-Interviews mit zwei ehemaligen DDR-Schriftstellern," *Die Weltwoche*, 22. Oktober 1980, S. 19.

pultierte."[13] Im Band *Erdreich* (1982) glaubt man dann bereits emotional und gesellschaftlich Unausgegorenes, Zwiespältiges aufzuspüren, in der Entdeckung von Affinitäten zu dem russischen Dekabristen Rylejew etwa, dem Dichterkollegen, dessen Kampfeshaltung gegenüber dem "verdunkelten Stern de[m] gehaßten geliebten"[14] ihm zum Verhängnis wurde.

Gesellschaftliche Verunsicherung registriert man aber auch im häufigen Anklingen von Themen des Unsteten, Wechselhaften, Temporären — eines Schwebezustandes der Unentschlossenheit, der sich vielleicht am augenfälligsten in dem Gedichttitel "Vorläufige Verwurzelung" (*K*, S. 12-13) aus dem Band *Katzenleben* niederschlägt. Der Titel überrascht etwas, denn in einem zwei Jahre früher veröffentlichten Gedichtzyklus, "Reisezehrung," in dem von einer fiktiven Transitfahrt durch die DDR die Rede ist, erschien der Gestus des Provisorischen noch von dem festen Vorsatz verdrängt: "Ich gedenke nicht am Heimweh zu sterben. / Unauslöschlich hab ich die Bilder im Kopf / Die hellen die dunklen."[15] Rundet man die Vielfalt widersprüchlicher Äußerungen mit einer frühen, Optimismus ausstrahlenden poetischen Aussage aus dem Jahre 1979 ab — "Die Zeit heilt Wunden."[16] — so fragt man sich, wie weit die Wunde nach rund zehn Jahren BRD-Aufenthalt nun wirklich vernarbt ist. Die Antwort auf diese Frage ist weitaus komplexer als die simplifizierenden, apodiktisch wirkenden Worte eines Interviewers aus dem Jahre 1982 es wahrhaben wollen:

> Sie hat sich mit aller Entschiedenheit auf ihre neue Situation eingelassen, auf die Erfahrungen des Abschieds, des Reisens ins vormals Unerreichbare und des Ankommens in einer zweiten Heimat, die sie auf dem Lande, in einem niedersächsischen Dorf gefunden hat.[17]

---

[13] Sarah Kirsch, "Dankbillett," in dies., *Drachensteigen* (Ebenhausen bei München: Langewiesche-Brandt, 1979), S. 26.

[14] Sarah Kirsch, "An Rylejew," in dies., *Erdreich* (Stuttgart: Deutsche Verlags-Anstalt, 1982) , S. 36.

[15] Sarah Kirsch, "Reisezehrung," in *Erdreich*, S. 44.

[16] Sarah Kirsch, "Italienische Amseln," in *Drachensteigen*, S. 27.

[17] Jörg-Dieter Kogel, "'Die Bilder bedeuten, was sie sind.' Gespräch mit der Lyrikerin Sarah Kirsch," *Süddeutsche Zeitung*, 15. April 1982, S. 16.

Ein abgeschlossener gesellschaftlicher Integrationsprozeß, ein "Angekommensein," bedarf kaum der kontinuierlichen Neubetrachtung und sollte Erinnertes neutralisiert haben. Aber ist dem im Falle Sarah Kirschs so?

An direkten Bezugnahmen zur DDR gibt es auf den ersten Blick in den beiden Bänden *Katzenleben* und *Irrstern*[18] relativ wenige. Im Gedicht "Katzenleben" (*K*, S. 74) klingt der Biermann-Eklat an. In "Querfeldein" (*K*, S. 83) wird von abgehörten Telefongesprächen mit "Elke," vermutlich Elke Erb, zwischen "Mecklenburg Brandenburg" und der BRD berichtet. In "Die Fähre" (*I*, S. 6) schweifen die Gedanken beim Anblick der für ortsfremde Chauffeure angebrachten roten Fahnen nach "Apolda und Moskau." Im Prosatext "Vergangenheit" (*I*, S. 23) wird mit Trauer eines "Franz" gedacht, wahrscheinlich Franz Fühmanns, der "in der Charité liegt aufn langwierigen Tod." Unter dem Titel "Nach Jahren im Winter" (*I*, S. 61) stellen sich plötzlich Gedanken an das Ostberliner Hochhaus ein, in dem Kirsch wohnte, und letztlich, in einer "Mondnacht" (*I*, S. 31), wird mit Unmut und Wehmut des "Ländchen[s]" gedacht.

Allgemein läßt sich feststellen, daß die meisten Texte in der Lyriksammlung *Katzenleben* und in dem Kurzprosaband *Irrstern* um das Thema "Natur" kreisen, um die Marschlandschaft Schleswig-Holsteins im Wechsel der Jahreszeiten, die begrenzte Welt des Gartens, die gefährdete Natur. Auffällig ist in diesem Kontext die vordergründige oder hintergründige Reflexion ökologischer oder nuklearer Bedrohung in der Form von Warngedichten. Strukturell steht karg Deskriptives neben komplexer bildlicher Subjekt-Objekt-Verschmelzung, und neben monotonerem, sachlicherem Sprechen glaubt man — seltener jetzt — die für Kirschs DDR-Werke so typische Vieltonigkeit des "Sarah-Sounds"[19] zu hören.

Die spezifische Art der Mischformen von Gedichten, mit denen sich die Künstlerin in der DDR einen Namen gemacht hatte, das Ineinanderblenden von resignativ-hoffnungsvoller Natur-, Liebes- und Politthematik, findet man in ihren westlichen Dichtungen selten, wahrscheinlich weil sich Kirschs

---

[18] Sarah Kirsch, *Irrstern* (Stuttgart: Deutsche Verlags-Anstalt, 1986). Der Band wird im folgenden mit dem Buchstaben *I* abgekürzt. Seitenzahlen befinden sich im Text der Arbeit.

[19] Peter Hacks, "Der Sarah-Sound," in ders., *Maßgaben der Kunst. Gesammelte Aufsätze* (Düsseldorf: Claassen, 1977), S. 268.

Erwartung vom Zustandekommen eines neuen kreativen gesellschaftlichen Spannungsverhältnisses in der BRD nun doch nicht so recht erfüllt hat.[20] Man gewinnt eher den Eindruck, daß die Künstlerin ihrer bereits in der DDR deutlich wahrnehmbaren Neigung zur Introversion jetzt in stärkerem Maße nachgibt — der "Kunst in sich selbst / Verloren zu gehen" ("Gasthaus," *K*, S. 35) — weil es, wie sie in dem Alptraumgedicht "Doppelter Boden" andeutet, in einer widersinnigen Welt ohnehin völlig gleichgültig ist, wo man lebt, ob in der BRD oder DDR. Im poetischen Gefüge eines fiktiven Verhörs in der westlichen Welt wird der lyrische Sprecher in ein "Wasserfaß mit dem doppelten Boden" gestoßen: "Ich kam in Karl-Marx-Stadt raus in einer ähnlichen Lage. O Deutschland hoch in Ehren sang der Kanari im Sicherheitstrakt" (*I*, S. 45).

Dem Leser fällt in diesem resignativen Sinne existentiellen Auf-sich-selbst-Gestellt-Seins Kirschs häufiges Aufnehmen des Bildes der Katze, oft der "roten Katze" auf, das Suggerieren — wie ein Rezensent es faßte — "ein[es] Zustand[es] *dazwischen* . . . ," also "seßhafte[r] Ambulanz."[21] Erwähnenswert sind ebenfalls die in diesem Bild sich brechenden Assoziationen von Unabhängigkeit, Eigenwilligkeit, Unkontrollierbarkeit, Freiheit und einem Vorsatz von Keinem-Gehören-Wollen ("Unausweichliche Kälte," *K*, S. 88). Das "vorige Leben" im "Ländchen" ("Mondnacht," *I*, S. 31) wirkt unterschwellig weiter fort. Wenn man nach rund zehn Jahren die Worte

> Erinnerung im Winter nach Jahren ich schlage
> einen Drudenfuß vor die Tür bin mir dankbar
> daß ich entkam
> ("Nach Jahren im Winter," *I*, S. 62)

liest, so wird unmißverständlich klar, daß die Trennung eine äußerst schmerzhafte und traumatische gewesen sein muß. In diesem Sinne kristallisieren sich zwei Hauptthemen in den Bänden *Katzenleben* und *Irrstern* heraus: Trennung und die Gestaltung einer neuen Lebensqualität in — wie die Dichterin ironisch kommentiert — "Vorläufige[r] Verwurzelung." Diese beiden Aspekte spiegeln die ambivalente Haltung der Künstlerin zur DDR, "die hellen, die dunklen" Seiten, wie sie es in

---

[20] Vgl. Ester und von Stekelenburg, "Gespräch mit Sarah Kirsch," S. 121.

[21] Peter Horst Neumann, "Sarah Kirschs grüne Entscheidung. Der neue Gedichtband 'Katzenleben,'" *Die Zeit*, 13. April 1984, Literaturteil, S. 1.

dem bereits erwähnten Gedichtzyklus "Reisezehrung" aus dem Band *Erdreich* angedeutet hatte.

Das Thema der "Trennung" durchdringt ein weitgefächertes Beziehungsgeflecht von Variationen wie u.a. Abschied, Zäsur, Auslöschen, Trauma. Für Günter Kunert, der ein Nachwort zu dem 1985 erschienenen Auswahlband *Landwege* geschrieben hat, manifestiert sich dieser Abschiedsgestus vorrangig als auf die Landschaft orientierte Bewußtseinshaltung des "Fremdgewordensein[s]."[22] Aber auch andere Sinngefüge lassen sich herstellen: Angst vor der Trennung von einem geliebten Menschen, Trennung als Ausdruck der vom Ich gefürchteten Gefahr des Selbstverlustes, als politischer Abschied vom vorigen Leben, d.h. Angst vor gesellschaftlichem Identitätsverlust, vor der Auflösung der Ich-Stabilität. Es fällt auf, daß das Thema der Trennung oft in Bildfelder eingebettet ist, die auf etwas Vergangenes ("Vergangenheit," *I*, S. 23-24) weisen, auf Versunkenes ("Wenn das Eis geht," *K*, S. 29), aus dem Unterbewußtsein Gehobenes, Traumverlorenes ("Beständig," *K*, S. 43), in der Stille Erinnertes ("Die Stille," *K*, S. 72). Auffällig ist ebenfalls das häufige Anklingen des Themas von Trauma und Mattigkeit (z.B. "Nördlicher Garten," *K*, S. 44) und — schlaglichtartig immer wieder neu hervorgehoben — von Verfolgungswahn und Beschattetwerden ("Katzenleben," *K*, S. 74; "Die Verdammung," *K*, S. 75), von Anschwärzen ("Sanfte Jagd," *K*, S. 89) oder Verpfiffenwerden ("Raben," *K*, S. 63).

Daß es sich hier u.a. um die versuchte Verarbeitung von Trennungstrauma aus dem vorigen Leben handelt, das dem Dichter-Ich durch die Kunst überwindbar scheint, läßt sich dem Assoziationsbereich des bereits erwähnten Bildes der Katze entnehmen, des spezifischen Katzenbildes etwa in dem Prosatext "Mondnacht," wo die Katze unter einem "Hirtenmantel aus dem vorigen Leben" schläft: "Die Kätzin träumt wohl verborgen sie solle ein Mensch sein verzieht ihren Mund. Erwacht schüttelt was ab . . . " (*I*, S. 31). Das Versatzstück "sich schütteln" bzw. "etwas abschütteln" taucht häufig in Kirschs in Ost und West veröffentlichten Lyrikbänden auf. Es weist generell auf Befreiungsversuche irgendwelcher Art, auf Selbstbehauptung und Triumph, auf das Verschmerzen eines zerbrochenen Liebesverhältnisses etwa, das

---

[22] Günter Kunert, "Nachwort. Ein Spiegel mit mir darin," in Sarah Kirsch, *Landwege. Eine Auswahl 1980-1985* (Stuttgart: Deutsche Verlags-Anstalt, 1985), S. 172.

— wie es z.B. in dem Gedicht "Elegie 2" der *Zaubersprüche* der Fall ist — durch gewaltsames Zusammenschweißen von Elegischem und Schnoddrigem ironisch reflektiert wird: "Ich bin der schöne Vogel Phönix / Schüttle mich am Morgen, sage / Pfeif drauf!"[23] Dieser Triumphgestus erscheint in den westlichen Dichtungen wesentlich abgeschwächt.

Im konkreten Sinne des Abschütteln-Wollens, des Bilanzierens, ist das Gedicht "Katzenleben" ein besonders beredtes Zeugnis von verarbeiteter oder nichtverarbeiteter DDR-Problematik. Nimmt man Sarah Kirsch beim Wort und sieht ihre Bilder als "das, was sie eigentlich sagen und sind. Keine Rätsel für irgendeine höhere Bedeutung,"[24] dann "lieben" die "Dichter" die von ihnen beobachteten Katzen, weil sie sich in deren Nicht-Kontrollierbarkeit und Freiheit wiedererkennen. Auf der Folie von Baudelaires "Les Chats" schwenkt Kirsch dann allerdings doch wieder vom empirisch-erfahrungsgemäßen auf den privat-psychologischen Bereich um und projiziert Subjektives ins Objektive. Die Katzen schütteln sich, können Erlebtes jedoch nicht völlig abschütteln. Eine Wahnvorstellung dauert fort:

> Aber die Dichter lieben die Katzen
> Die nicht kontrollierbaren sanften
> Freien die den Novemberregen
> Auf seidenen Sesseln oder in Lumpen
> Verschlafen verträumen stumm
> Antwort geben sich schütteln und
> Weiterleben hinter dem Jägerzaun
> Wenn die besessenen Nachbarn
> Immer noch Autonummern notieren
> Der Überwachte in seinen vier Wänden
> Längst die Grenzen hinter sich ließ.
> (*K*, S. 74)

Auch im Gedicht "Wenn das Eis geht" wird per Rückblende "Versunkenes" gehoben, treibt der Strom der Erinnerungen Erlebnissplitter ins Bewußtsein, die mosaikartig zusammengeblendet ein Bildgefüge von Schmerz, Dissonanz und Trauma evozieren:

---

[23] Sarah Kirsch, "Elegie 2," in dies., *Zaubersprüche* (Ebenhausen bei München: Langewiesche-Brandt, 1977), S. 19.

[24] Jörg-Dieter Kogel, "'Die Bilder bedeuten, was sie sind.' Gespräch mit der Lyrikerin Sarah Kirsch."

Abgeschnittene Locken Heiligenbilder
Treiben darin ersäufte Katzen und
Freundesleichen zuhauf viel Spreu wenig
Weizen gelangt auf den Mühlstein mitunter
Stöhnt das Getriebne bleibt stehn
Was sich verfangen hat bricht mir
Womöglich das Herz. . . . (*K*, S. 29)

Aus der spezifischen Verzahnung der Bilder "Abgeschnittene Locken," "Heiligenbilder," "Treiben," "ersäufte Katzen" und "Freundesleichen" läßt sich eine Brücke zu einem anderen Gedicht Sarah Kirschs, genannt "Unauslöschbares Bild" (*K*, S. 51) schlagen, das seinerseits wiederum in einer von der Dichterin zwar verneinten,[25] vom Leser jedoch assoziierbaren Beziehung zu einem Gedicht Volker Brauns, "Der Müggelsee," zu stehen scheint. Über die dichterische Intention und die Wirkung eines Gedichtes bzw. über die durchaus nicht immer konvergierenden Kräfte des Unbewußten und Bewußten im Prozeß einer Gedichtentstehung hatte die Dichterin sich einmal mit der lakonischen Festlegung geäußert: "Gedichte verwandeln sich manchmal."[26] Bei aller Vielschichtigkeit von Kirschs "Unauslöschbare[m] Bild" glaubt der Leser hier in der Tat eine solche "Verwandlung" bzw. ein Zusammenspiel mit Brauns "Müggelsee" aufzuspüren, in dem man Kirschs Gedicht als eine Art Gegenentwurf zu dem von Braun angeschlagenen Thema der Biermann-Ausbürgerung und des "Untergangs" der unter verschiedenen Bedingungen in den Westen abgetriebenen Dichterkollegen lesen kann. Auf dem Hintergrund von Klopstocks Ode "Der Zürchersee" reflektiert Braun in seinem 1979 in der BRD veröffentlichten Gedicht bitter über die "Freude" — ein Klopstocksches Schlüsselwort! — einer imaginierten Kahnfahrt mit Dichterfreunden der Lyrikbewegung der sechziger Jahre, von denen Bernd Jentzsch, Reiner Kunze, Wolf Biermann und Sarah Kirsch explizit bei Namen genannt werden: "Aber aus dem Kahn / Kippen sie, / . . . / Und sie gehen unter."[27] Kirschs Gedicht suggeriert Freude des Überlebens. Sie spricht von einem "gewaltige[n] Anblick, das bewirken die Dolomiten nicht nicht der Zürichsee in verschiedener schöner Beleuchtung. Ruckartige Freude, die Gewißheit auf der Erde zu stehen. /. . . / Nur die Erfahrung

[25] Aus meiner Korrespondenz mit der Autorin.

[26] Kirsch, "Ein Gespräch mit Schülern," S. 12.

[27] Volker Braun, "Der Müggelsee," in ders., *Gedichte* (Frankfurt a.M: Suhrkamp, 1979), S. 121.

steckt in den Knochen" (*K*, S. 51). Abgetrieben, aber nicht untergegangen; wieder Boden gewonnen und von vorn begonnen. Aber wie gestaltet sich die neue Lebensqualität der Künstlerin im Westen?

Klopft man Kirschs Gedichte nach DDR-Reminiszenzen ab, so scheinen die "dunklen" Seiten, die Schattenseiten, zunächst zu überwiegen. Aber lesen wir da richtig? Aus der vordergründigen Gestaltung der bundesdeutschen Welt, d.h. des begrenzten Privatbereiches in der Landschaft Schleswig-Holsteins, lassen sich hintergründig Schlüsse über erinnerte "helle" DDR-Realität ziehen. Man nimmt in Kirschs westlichen Dichtungen einen deutlich vorherrschenden Gestus des betont Privaten, oft Resignativen, Monotonen und Passiv-Apathischen wahr sowie ein Hervortreten von Bildmotiven, die Auflösung und verschwimmende Konturen suggerieren. Aus dem Nicht-Existieren irritierender Reibungsflächen in der BRD und aus dem von der Künstlerin bevorzugten gesellschaftlichen Nicht-Involviertsein läßt sich paradoxerweise deduzieren, daß Kirsch bei aller Skepsis der DDR gegenüber ihre besten, aktivsten und illusionsreichsten Jahre in eben diesem Erlebnisbereich verbracht hat. Kirsch selbst faßt es überzeugend in dem Interview von 1980, in dem sie von ihrem enttäuschten Glauben an große historische Augenblicke in der DDR spricht: "Es gibt so geschichtliche Momente, die man nicht wieder einfangen kann."[28]

Auf Sarah Kirschs in der DDR entstandene Werke sei in diesem spezifischen Kontext nur ganz kurz eingegangen. Als damaliges SED-Mitglied war sie mit Begeisterung an der Lyrikbewegung der sechziger Jahre beteiligt. An zweifelnden, zwiespältigen Reflexionen über sich selbst, über die DDR und die Welt schlechthin fehlt es allerdings nicht in ihrer Dichtung, und wegen des ostentativen Hervortretens des Ich, der betonten Subjektivität, wurden ihre Gedichte Ende der sechziger Jahre "privatisierend" gescholten. Aber unter dem Druck des Spannungsverhältnisses von Individuum und Gesellschaft sind andererseits poetische Loyalitätsbekenntnisse zur DDR entstanden, die sich durch karge Schönheit und Klarheit der Dazugehörigkeit auszeichnen. Man erinnere sich u.a. an das Gedicht "Fahrt II," in dem eine Reise "durch mein kleines wärmendes Land"[29] gestaltet wird; an das Gedicht "Angeln,"

---

[28] Michael Rehsche, "Momente, die nicht wiederkommen . . . ."

[29] Sarah Kirsch, "Fahrt II," in dies., *Landaufenthalt* (Ebenhausen bei München: Langewiesche-Brandt, 1977), S. 6.

wo alles "nützlich" wurde "vom Augenblick als ich / tätig war;"[30] an das Vertrautsein mit ihrem Land in dem Fünfzeiler "Haarewaschen auf dem Land,"[31] und, letztlich, an das berühmte doppelbödige Gedicht "Grünes Land" aus den *Zaubersprüchen*, dessen entzaubernde Bilddissonanzen mit der abschließenden Geste des Anpflanzens von "vierblättrige[m] Klee"[32] ein "Dennoch" etablieren, eine Geste der "Hoffnung" — wie Franz Fühmann es formulierte — die das "Unmögliche" birgt.[33]

Nach der Furore der politischen Ereignisse um Biermann und ihrer Einreise in den Westen schien die Dichterin den Wunsch nach Abgeschirmtsein zu haben. Sie wohnte vorübergehend in Westberlin, weilte ein Jahr lang in der Villa Massimo in Italien und zog sich schließlich in den Norden der BRD, in die Nähe der dänischen Grenze, zurück, ein Rückzug ins Private, der maximenhaft in den Anfangszeilen des Gedichtes "Zugeflogene Rose" eingefangen ist: "Ersprießlicher ist der Umgang mit Pflanzen" (*K*, S. 69). Und dabei bleibt es vorwiegend, was die Thematik anbetrifft. Die Dichterin, die in der restriktiven provinziellen Enge des "Ländchen[s]" ihrem "Wunsch nach Welt"[34] in einer berstenden Fülle von Metaphern des "Fliegens," des "Offenen," des "Kontaktaufnehmens" und des "Überschaubaren aus der Vogelperspektive" Ausdruck gegeben hatte, empfängt jetzt ironischerweise ihren kreativen Stimulus in einer Lebenssphäre, die noch enger und geschrumpfter ist als die vorige. "Komm / Ins Offene Freund und Leben rückwärts buchstabieren" heißt es im Rahmen einer fiktiven Reise in der Transkyrillischen Bahn in dem Gedicht "Eichen und Rosen" (*K*, S. 6). "Komm! ins Offene, Freund!" — diese Anfangszeile der Hölderlinschen Elegie "Der Gang aufs Land"[35] — ist ein Versatzstück von Aktualität. Man erinnere sich, daß auch Volker Braun das Hölderlinsche Postulat *verbaliter* in sein im selben Jahre, 1984, veröffentlichtes Gedicht

---

[30] Sarah Kirsch, "Angeln," in *Landaufenthalt*, S. 41.

[31] Sarah Kirsch, "Haarewaschen auf dem Land," in dies., *Rückenwind* (Ebenhausen bei München: Langewiesche-Brandt, 1977), S. 56.

[32] Sarah Kirsch, "Grünes Land," in *Zaubersprüche*, S. 53.

[33] Franz Fühmann, "Vademecum für Leser von Zaubersprüchen," *Sinn und Form*, 27, Nr. 2 (1975), 419.

[34] Ester und von Stekelenburg, "Gespräch mit Sarah Kirsch," S. 108.

[35] Friedrich Hölderlin, "Der Gang aufs Land," in *Hölderlin. Sämtliche Werke*, hrsg. von Friedrich Beißner (Frankfurt a.M.: Insel, 1965), S. 289.

"Das innerste Afrika"[36] montierte, wo es auf operative Sprengung "der Grenzen dieser Revolution"[37] weist. Bei Kirsch wird das "Offene" mit dem rückwärts buchstabierten Wort "Leben," d.h. "Nebel," verzahnt. Es nimmt folglich kaum wunder, daß ein Großteil der in den Bänden *Katzenleben* und *Irrstern* veröffentlichten Gedichte vom Motivbereich des Winters, des Regens und des Nebels durchdrungen ist. Konturlosigkeit führt zu Undurchschaubarkeit; eine verschwimmende Welt (z.B. in "Amphibischer Tag," *I*, S. 46) manifestiert sich als "zusammengeschrumpft" ("Gasthaus," *K*, S. 35), als "gestautes Nichts" ("Vergangenheit," *I*, S. 24).

In der Vielfalt der Stimmungsschwankungen überwiegt das Resignative, gekoppelt mit Mattigkeit, Trägheit, einem Gefühl von Eintönigkeit und oft Langeweile. Dieser Gestus sei in meinem Interpretationsansatz nicht künstlich überstrapaziert. Es gibt gelöstere Gedichte Sarah Kirschs. Variationen des Themas von Monotonie spürt man jedoch durchweg, vielleicht am einprägsamsten eingefangen in dem Kurzprosatext "Schwarzer Vogel":

> Wenn ich . . . dieses Haus vor mir sehe die
> altmodischen Rosen an den Spalieren die
> tanzenden kurzen Gardinen die goldenen
> Klingelschilder und Katzen hinter den
> Scheiben würde ich sagen wenn ich nicht
> wüßte daß es um meins sich handelt hier
> müssen glückliche Leute wohnen. . . . Gegen
> Langeweile kann ich Länder verwechseln
> ein geringes Anwesen haben darauf Leben
> zu spielen ich schüttele mich vor Lachen
> weil alles so gut gelungen erscheint. . . .
> (*I*, S. 37)

Ironischerweise klingen — wenn auch nur *en passant*— entgegengesetzte Emotionen von Begeisterung und Vitalität in einem Kontext erinnerter DDR-Erlebnisse an. In dem Text "Mondnacht" reflektiert die Künstlerin über einen im Ausland erworbenen Hirtenmantel: "Als ich ihn in einer Steppe erwarb

---

[36] Volker Braun, "Das innerste Afrika," in *Luchterhand Jahrbuch der Lyrik 1984*, hrsg. von Christoph Buchwald und Gregor Laschen (Darmstadt/Neuwied: Luchterhand, 1984), S. 27.

[37] Volker Braun, "Geschichtsloser Raum," in ders., *Es genügt nicht die einfache Wahrheit. Notate* (Frankfurt a.M.: Suhrkamp, 1976), S. 38.

damit das Ländchen betrat aussem Ausland ach wassen Vergnügen so macht hier kein Ding mehr Furore" (*I*, S. 31).

Man vergleiche diese poetische Aussage wieder mit Statements aus Interviews, in denen Kirsch die erinnerten "hellen" Seiten hervorhebt. Damit schließt sich der Kreis, und ich befinde mich wieder am Ausgangspunkt meiner Ausführungen über widersprüchliche DDR-Reminiszenzen im Werke Sarah Kirschs. In dem "Gespräch mit Schülern" gab Kirsch einerseits ihrem Ärger und ihrer Frustration über die DDR Ausdruck; andererseits stellte die Künstlerin dem Materialismus einer übersättigten Konsumentengesellschaft im bundesdeutschen Kulturbetrieb einen "sinnvolleren" DDR-Kulturbereich gegenüber, in dem sie die hochgesteckte Erwartung vom Gebrauchtwerden der Dichter temporär erfüllt sah: "Es war eigentlich alles sehr sinnvoll. Es gab in Zeitschriften Diskussionen noch und noch über Lyrik zum Beispiel, die mit einer Vehemenz ausgetragen wurden, wie man sie sich hier gar nicht vorstellen kann."[38] Sie bekräftigte den erinnerten Enthusiasmus der frühen Jahre: "Die Lyrik-Begeisterung verbreitete sich über die ganze Republik, wir . . . [hatten] gar nicht so rasch neue Gedichte zur Hand . . . , wie wir sie lesen sollten."[39] Und letztlich noch einmal die bereits erwähnte Bilanz: "Ich möchte wirklich nicht woanders aufgewachsen sein."[40]

Kirschs westliche Dichtungen im Schatten des "verdunkelten Stern[s] de[s] gehaßten geliebten"[41] werfen die Frage auf, ob ein DDR-geprägter Staatsbürger-Dichter endgültig zum bundesdeutschen bzw. gesamtdeutschen Dichter werden kann. Die Antwort auf diese Frage hängt von der Interpretationsweise des Betrachters ab, bleibt also in der Schwebe. Die Dichterin, die bisher konsequent auf das Etikett "deutschsprachige[r] Schriftsteller, weiter nichts"[42] gepocht hat, scheint in dem Rollengedicht "Die Verdammung" (*K*, S. 75) nun eigenartigerweise einen ganz anderen Schlüssel zu diesem Problem zu liefern. Sie bemüht in diesem Gedicht den Prometheus-Mythos und mißt dem folternden Adler verfremdend die Macht fortwährender Einflußnahme zu, eine Funktion, die ihm im Mythos gar nicht zukommt. Sieht man inner-

---

[38] Kirsch, "Ein Gespräch mit Schülern," S. 43.

[39] Ester und von Stekelenburg, "Gespräch mit Sarah Kirsch," S. 105.

[40] Rehsche, "Momente, die nicht wiederkommen . . . ."

[41] Kirsch, "An Rylejew," in *Erdreich*, S. 36.

[42] Ester und von Stekelenburg, "Gespräch mit Sarah Kirsch," S. 107.

halb der Vielschichtigkeit dieses Gedichtes den Adler als Symbol für das Auf-Sich-Nehmen von Härten und Leiden in unvergeßlichen historischen Momenten, so wirkt der vom lyrischen Ich erlebte Erfahrungsbereich unabänderlich fort. Lassen wir Sarah Kirsch sprechen:

> Weil ihm zu sterben verwehrt war
> Angekettet dem heimischen Felsen der Blick
> Auf die ziehenden Wolken gerichtet und immer
> Allein die Bilder im Kopf stimmlos
> Vom Rufen Anrufen Verdammen
> Das Leben fristen war nicht zu bedenken
> Göttliche Hinterlist nährte ihn so gewöhnte
> Er sich langsam ins Schicksal nach Jahren
> Sah er den Adler gern wenn er nahte und sprach
> Stotternd mit ihm bei der Verrichtung
>
> Oder mit entzündeten Augen verrenktem Hals
> Weil der Flügelschlag ausblieb die niederen Wälder
> Aufschub ihm angedeihn ließen um Tage
> Harrte er des einzigen Wesens und glaubte
> In der Leere des Winds der glühenden Sonne
> Wenn der Fittiche Dunkel fürn Augenblick
> Erquickung schenkte geborgen zu sein
> Liebte den Folterer dichtete Tugend ihm an
>
> Als die Ketten zerfielen der Gott
> Müde geworden an ihn noch zu denken
> Der Adler weiterhin flog weil kein
> Auftrag ihn innezuhalten erreichte
> Gelang es ihm nicht sich erheben den
> Furchtbaren Ort für immer verlassen
> In alle Ewigkeit hält er am Mittag
> Ausschau nach seinem Beschatter.

Neue Lyrik in der DDR:
Überlegungen zum Gegen- und Nebeneinander der Generationen

Wolfgang Ertl

Der 1985 von Sascha Anderson und Elke Erb in der BRD herausgegebene Band *Berührung ist nur eine Randerscheinung*[1] ist angelegt als repräsentative Sammlung neuer Literatur aus der DDR, als Dokument eines gewandelten Selbstverständnisses der Jüngsten. Viele der hier abgedruckten neuen Texte scheinen im Fahrwasser allzu spät entdeckter avantgardistischer Literaturbewegungen zu schwimmen und in unfreiwilliger Nachahmung der Kunstmittel des Dadaismus, Surrealismus oder der konkreten Poesie unterzugehen. Dabei ist allerdings hervorzuheben, daß einerseits unter den besonderen Bedingungen der Literaturentwicklung in der DDR nicht unbedingt eine intensive textorientierte Beschäftigung mit diesen vermuteten modernistischen Vorlagen anzunehmen ist und andererseits ein Anknüpfen an eine wie auch immer geartete Tradition zunächst kaum der gelegentlich anzutreffenden Unkenntnis oder dem Mißtrauen entspricht, das viele dieser Jüngsten dem sprachlich Vorgeprägten gegenüber hegen.[2] Ein neuer Aufguß von Altbekanntem ist schwerlich ihre Absicht. Die Gleichartigkeit mit früheren, anderswo längst vermarkteten vorkämpferischen Kunstpositionen bleibt aber ein bemerkenswertes Kuriosum.

---

[1] *Berührung ist nur eine Randerscheinung. Neue Literatur aus der DDR*, hrsg. v. Sascha Anderson und Elke Erb (Köln: Kiepenheuer & Witsch, 1985). Seitenangaben im Text beziehen sich auf dieses Buch. Zu erwähnen wäre auch der von Dorothea von Törne herausgegebene Band *Vogelbühne. Gedichte im Dialog* (Berlin: Verlag der Nation, 1983).

[2] So berichtet Elke Erb zum Beispiel, daß Bert Papenfuß-Gorek, befragt, "ob er sich Jandl zum Vorbild nehme," Jandl gar nicht kannte (*Berührung ist nur eine Randerscheinung*, S. 14).

Zufällig ist die Übereinstimmung des sich als Neues Behauptenden mit der alten "Avantgarde" wohl sicher nicht. Vielmehr wiederholt sich ein Sich-Abstoßen von einer gesellschaftlichen Wirklichkeit, die nicht als Eigenes erfahren wird, sondern als individueller Entfaltung hinderlich.[3] Als Beispiel sei ein Gedicht des 1951 in Dresden geborenen Michael Wüstefeld zitiert, das im Titel Uwe Kolbe gewidmet ist und dessen Metapher vom Hineingeborensein in die sozialistische Gesellschaft aufgreift und in gleichklingenden, aber antithetischen Wortpaaren weiterspinnt:

> Hineingeboren wie hineingeborgt
> Eingenommen wie gefangengenommen
>
> Festgehalten nicht fester Halt
> Aushalten nicht Anhalt
>
> Ankommen wie wegkommen
> Ankunft wie Wegkunft
>
> Hierbleiben nicht dableiben
> Ausreisen nicht ausreißen
>
> Lachen wie Masken
> Maskieren wie Weinen
>
> Verrecken nicht um Ecken
> Umrunden nicht im Kreis
>
> Loseisen wie festrosten
> Geborensein wie totleben   (S. 82)

Mit plakativ-positiven Bedeutungen belegte Begriffe werden gleichgesetzt mit negativen Erfahrungsinhalten. Die Zeile "Festgehalten nicht fester Halt" verdeutlicht besonders eindrücklich die sprach- und ideologiekritische Einstellung des Autors. Die Gegebenheiten des realen Sozialismus haben das Individuum fest im Griff, ohne ihm festen Halt zu geben. Der Wunsch auszureisen hat nicht unbedingt etwas mit "ausreißen," d.h. der Bedeutung "das Land verlassen," "abhauen," zu tun.

---

[3] Vgl. hierzu besonders Anneli Hartmanns Studie "Schreiben in der Tradition der Avantgarde: Neue Lyrik in der DDR," die in dem geplanten Band *DDR-Lyrik im Kontext*, hrsg. v. Christine Cosentino, Wolfgang Ertl und Gerd Labroisse (Amsterdam: Rodopi) erscheinen wird.

Neben dem freien oder frechen Verfügen über überlieferte Formen und Inhalte ist hier und anderswo in dieser Sammlung durchaus diverser Stimmen ein ausgeprägter Stilwille auffällig, ein Vertrauen in das sprachliche und auch graphische Ordnungsgefüge. Bei Sascha Anderson und anderen zeigt es sich zum Beispiel in der säuberlichen Beschneidung des rechten Randes, die zum Wortenjambement führt. Oft wird das Zerreißen der Wörter nicht einfach dem Zufall überlassen, sondern bewußt manipuliert, indem die einzelnen Gedichtzeilen verschiedene Längen bekommen. Hier ein kurzer Auszug aus einem Text von Anderson:

> welche sprachen spr
> ichst du
> außer der die
> du behe
> rrscht
> denn sie sprechen mit d
> ir
> & dein ohr ist ein offener wi
> ndfang   (S. 94)

Das ungewohnte Zerbrechen der Worteinheit zerstört dann nicht nur Leseerwartungen, es erweitert hier und da auch den Spielraum der Bedeutungen. "Es bedeutet ja eigentlich eine Normalisierung," schreibt Elke Erb in ihrem Vorwort, "wenn sie [die jungen Autoren] die Vielschichtigkeit, die ein Text im gewohnten Sprachgebrauch hintersinnig . . . aufbaut, im Textvordergrund selbst 'Zur Sprache bringen', also Hinter- und Untergründiges veröffentlichen" (S. 13-14).

In diesem Sinne ist dann auch das sich oft trotzig dem Politischen verweigernde neueste Gedicht wieder ein Politikum. Genregeschichtlich ist in dieser Sammlung kaum eine "Revolution der Lyrik" festzustellen, im Kontext der literarhistorischen Entwicklung der DDR ergibt sich jedoch ein neuartiges verwirrendes Nebeneinander der Formen, eine Freude am Entlarven einer "Metasprache," die sich nicht einfach im Sprachspiel verselbständigt, sondern einen Ausweg sucht aus dem konventionellen Sprachgebrauch, der als verlogen erfahren wird. Uwe Kolbe bemerkt, daß er sich "in einer Grammatik" bewegt, "die eigentlich Metasprache *zitiert*" (S. 40). Mit "Metasprache" meint er die "Sprache der Sprachregelung, die Kollektivlüge der herrschenden Sprache" (S. 41). Indem er sie bewußt zitiert, rückt er sie in den Kontext der veränderten Grammatik seines Denkens und behauptet diese so, wie er sagt, "als zweite Naivität: ich — als autonomer Mensch — mit allen Sinnen — und wieder in der Lage, Baum zu sagen" (S. 41).

Elke Erb weist darauf hin, daß die Sammlung "kein Buch über die DDR, sondern ein Buch aus der DDR" ist und meint, es trete "gerade mit den vielstimmigen Positionen zu den über alle Grenzen der zivilisierten Welt reichenden Themen so real und leibhaftig auch über die deutsche Grenze, daß es die nebulöse Vorstellung von der DDR als einer terra incognita" zerstreue (S. 16). DDR-Spezifisches ist zwar keineswegs aus den Gedichten gänzlich verschwunden, es wird nur nicht mehr so prononciert dargestellt. Viele Gedichte beginnen mit ganz alltäglichen Situationen: "ES WAR EIN RUHIGER TAG / an dem ich dir vorschlug / in einer Parterrewohnung zu übernachten" (Andreas Röhler, S. 19); "Im Jahr einundsechzig / in der vierten Klasse der Schulzeit / ging meine Leistung bergab" (Rüdiger Rosenthal, S. 61); "Ich bin der Handlanger // hole den Hammer den dickeren Bohrer / die Schrauben M6" (Christa Moog, S. 65); "AN MANCHEN ABENDEN / setzen sich alle meine freunde / in einen kreis / trinken roten wein / und reden wesentliches" (Fritz-Hendrick Melle, S. 143).

Vom erlebten Alltag gehen sie aus und schreiben, wie es ein Gedichttitel Uwe Kolbes sagt, "Ein Gedicht, worum es mir geht" (S. 41). Um nicht im Alltag zu ersticken, rücken sie ihm zu Leibe, rufen sie auf zur Befreiung aus seinen Zwängen. So zum Beispiel Bert Papenfuß-Gorek: "schrei gegen die wand / schreib es an die wand / schreite durch die wand" (S. 156). Dieser Aufschrei ist nicht mehr der marktschreierische des frühen Volker Braun, von dem sich neben Uwe Kolbe besonders Fritz-Hendrick Melle abgrenzt: "Volker Braun? — Da kann ich nur sagen, der Junge quält sich. Dazu habe ich keine Beziehung mehr. Ich bin schon in einer frustrierten Gesellschaft aufgewachsen. Diese Enttäuschung ist für mich kein Erlebnis mehr, sondern eine Voraussetzung" (S. 147). Das Schreiben an die Wand, um die Metapher aufzugreifen, ähnelt bei vielen dieser jungen Autoren eher den respektlosen Graffiti aus der versteckten Sprühdose als der aufklärerischen Geste des Öffentlichkeit suchenden Mahners.

Bei Melle selbst allerdings finden wir im Gedicht "Novalis der 8.8." Anspielungen an Novalis' *Heinrich von Ofterdingen* und Gustav Mahlers *Kindertotenlieder*, sowie Reflexionen über Traum und Zeit. Melles Gedicht "Kleines Lied" zitiert konventionelle romantische Poesie, ohne sich offenkundig von ihr zu distanzieren:

> durch nächte geht ein sichelmond
> der wohnt in blauen räumen
> schneid't mit seinem weißen licht
> das blühen von den bäumen
> schneidet mir die träume weg
> ich wage nicht zu klagen
> durch nächte geht ein sichelmond
> und ich stell keine fragen   (S. 144-45)

Der im Band *Berührung ist nur eine Randerscheinung*[4] abgedruckte Ausschnitt aus einem Gespräch mit dem Autor enthält neben der Absage an Braun auch folgende bezeichnende Antwort auf die Frage, was dem Autor Melle Geschichte bedeutet: "Sprache ist für mich ein permanentes Präsens" (S. 147). Auch hier also die Pose oder Position der Verweigerung.

Die Distanzierung der in diesem Buch versammelten Jüngsten von der "mittleren Generation," d.h. der großen Gruppe der in den dreißiger Jahren und Anfang der vierziger Geborenen, von denen Volker Braun auch nur eine, wenn auch sehr profilierte, bei aller Gruppensolidarität individuelle poetische Stimme ist, überrascht zunächst. Es sind ja durchaus Autoren, die der Subjektivität in der Dichtung seit Mitte der sechziger Jahre zu einem neuen Durchbruch verhalfen. Ihre erhöhte subjektive Sensibilität schloß allerdings ein intensives Geschichtsbewußtsein ebensowenig aus wie DDR-spezifische Gesellschaftskritik und den weitergespannten internationalen Kontext. Unter dem Titel "Material II: Brennende Fragen" finden wir bei Volker Braun folgende Passage:

> Überhaupt Worte (Reizwörter, Sprach-
> Regelungen, Memoranden zwischen den Zeilen
> Zu entziffern) haben mehr Wirkung
> Als die Dinge
>   warum? weil sie verdecken
> Verallgemeinern, vervielfältigen
>   weil sie verdecken was fehlt[5]

---

[4] Der Titel ist übrigens eine Zeile von Melles Gedicht "GLAUBE NICHT ICH WILL MICH ENTSCHULDIGEN" (S. 143).

[5] Volker Braun, "Material II: Brennende Fragen," in ders., *Training des aufrechten Gangs* (Halle/Leipzig: Mitteldeutscher Verlag, 1979), S. 48.

Vielleicht nehmen die Jüngsten die neueren Texte Brauns — dieser ist 1979 erschienen — aus Aversion gegen den frühen Braun einfach nicht mehr zur Kenntnis. Oder haben sie es satt, sich an einer Weltanschauung zu reiben? Es stimmt schon, der Dichter Braun "quält sich," aber sicher nicht, weil er sich aus seiner anfänglichen Umarmung eines obligaten Optimismus nicht zu lösen vermag und, wie Uwe Kolbe impliziert, einer fixen "Grammatik des Denkens" (S. 40) verhaftet bleibt, sondern, weil er — im Unterschied zu manchen der Jüngeren — nicht aufhört, ein kommunistisches Denkmodell als Maßstab zu bemühen. Dies befähigt ihn unter anderem zu einer neuen satirischen Sicht auf den realen Sozialismus in der DDR.[6] Seine neuesten Gedichte lösen sich auf in Zitatmontagen, präsentieren sich als zerrissene Materialsammlungen, liefern keine Antworten, sondern provozieren immer wieder Fragen. Seltsam, daß sich von hier aus keine "Berührungen" ergeben.[7] Sicher aber kommt den verstreuten Bemerkungen, mit Volker Braun habe man nichts mehr zu tun, über das einzelne private Bekenntnis hinaus nicht allzu viel verallgemeinerungswürdige Gültigkeit zu.

Werfen wir nun einen Blick auf die Stellungnahme der älteren Generation zu dem neuen Selbstverständnis der Jungen und Jüngsten. Stephan Hermlin, geboren 1915, hat selbst seit Ende der fünfziger Jahre keine Gedichte mehr veröffentlicht. Anfang der sechziger Jahre setzte er sich für die damals jüngste Generation ein, unter anderen für Volker Braun und Wolf Biermann, was ihm scharfe Kritik eintrug und woraufhin er seine Stelle als Sekretär der Sektion Dichtkunst und Sprachpflege der Akademie der Künste verlor. Er habe Gedichte verbreitet, "die vom Geist des Pessimismus, der unwissenden Krittelei und der Feindschaft gegenüber der Partei durchdrungen waren," so Kurt Hager.[8] Walter Ulbricht sprach von "Bemühungen, mit Hilfe einiger Gedichte die Jugendlichen gegen die Alten zu hetzen."[9]

---

[6] Siehe Volker Braun, *Hinze-Kunze-Roman* (Halle/Leipzig: Mitteldeutscher Verlag, 1985).

[7] Vgl. Christine Cosentino, "Volker Brauns Essay 'Rimbaud. Ein Psalm der Aktualität' im Kontext seiner Lyrik," in *Studies in GDR Culture and Society 7*, hrsg. v. Margy Gerber u.a. (Lanham/New York/London: University Press of America, 1987), 171-84.

[8] Zitiert nach Lothar von Balluseck, *Literatur und Ideologie 1963: Zu den literar-politischen Auseinandersetzungen seit dem 6. Parteitag der SED* (Bad Godesberg: Hohwacht, 1963), S. 18.

[9] Zitiert nach Lothar von Balluseck, ebenda, S. 18.

In einem Interview mit Silvia Schlenstedt von 1983 gesteht Hermlin, daß er "nicht das gleiche Verhältnis . . . zu der inzwischen herangewachsenen jungen Generation" habe: "Im Moment sehe ich unter den ganz Jungen . . . kaum etwas, was mir ähnlich bedeutend scheint."[10] Außer Uwe Kolbe habe er niemanden bemerkt, der ihn "im gleichen Maße" interessiere (S. 24). Hermlin fährt fort:

> Ja, das Brechen der Tradition, die Unkenntnis alles dessen, was geleistet worden ist, einschließlich der Unkenntnis selbst des Sprachexperimentellen, das ja in Deutschland auch eine große Rolle gespielt hat, vor langer Zeit, in der Zeit des Expressionismus bis zu Stramm hin. Ich wiederhole — das kann auch an mir liegen zu einem großen Teil, denn man wird ja älter und man schließt sich ab von den Dingen, und da muß ich mit einkalkulieren, daß ich auch bestimmte Mängel und Vorurteile zeige —, aber ich kann es nicht anders sagen als mit den Worten: das, was gegenwärtig geschieht, findet nicht mein Interesse.
>
> (S. 25)

1949 schrieb Hermlin das Gedicht "Die einen und die anderen," in dem die Fronten noch klar waren: Auf der einen Seite standen die nationalsozialistischen Henker, auf der anderen ihre Opfer, die antifaschistischen Widerstandskämpfer. Zur "Forderung des Tages" gehörten für den sensiblen Kenner der lyrischen Moderne jetzt, da er zum ersten Mal die Möglichkeit eines direkten gesellschaftlichen Mitwirkens am Aufbau des Sozialismus auf deutschem Boden durch das dichterische Wort zu sehen glaubte, auch die emblematische Verkürzung und plakative Kontrastierung:

> Sie sind immer da, wie der harte
> Blick des Himmels ist da,
> Wie das Rauschen der Stille, das in
> Blut und Muschel geschah.
>
> Woher sie auch immer kommen,
> Wohin sie auch immer gehn:

---

[10] Silvia Schlenstedt, *Stephan Hermlin* (Berlin: Volk und Wissen, 1985), S. 24.

Sie sind da, bis die einen erliegen
Und die andern im Lichte stehn.[11]

In Volker Brauns 1979 erschienenem Gedichtband *Training des aufrechten Gangs* finden wir das Sonett "Zu Hermlin, Die einen und die anderen":

Er hat sie genannt. Und kein Wind
Wird diesen Steckbrief aus der Brust reißen.
Wir wissen nun, wie die und jene heißen.
Und wer die einen und die andern sind.

Und sind gewarnt. Denn in den andern Zeiten
Wenn so viel anders wird, bleibt eines gleich
Wir werden vergehn vor unserm Fleisch
Wenn wir uns nicht bei jedem Schlag entscheiden

Wenn wir uns immer nicht zu andern machen
Und wieder andern, die das andre wollen
Als was die einen sehn, die andre waren

Zu ihrer Zeit, die aber ist im Rollen.
Und wieder hören wir die Türen krachen.
Und durch die Wände brechen andre Scharen.[12]

Eine solche Auseinandersetzung mit der literarischen Tradition aus dem eigenen Lager, auch wenn sie das klassenkämpferische Modell umfunktioniert in den Aufruf zur Veränderung dessen, was die früheren "Anderen" erreicht haben, findet Hermlin "außerordentlich schön" und bedauert, daß sie "sehr selten" stattfindet.[13]

Der historische Blick, die ideologische Auseinandersetzung fehlt in manchem Gedicht der neuen Sammlung *Berührung ist nur eine Randerscheinung*. So wird der Generationskonflikt in dem Gedicht "Wos'n Vater?" von Christa Moog (1952 in Eisenach geboren) nur auf der Ebene banaler Alltagserfahrung sichtbar:

Im Keller, hackt Holz.
Im Keller, legt die Lichtleitung neu.
Im Keller, repariert die Waschmaschine.

---

[11] Stephan Hermlin, *Dichtungen* (Berlin: Aufbau, 1956), S. 84.

[12] Volker Braun, *Training des aufrechten Gangs*, S. 22.

[13] Schlenstedt, *Stephan Hermlin*, S. 24.

Im Keller, streicht Fenstergitter.
Im Keller, hörst du nicht die Kreissäge.
Im Keller, was weiß ich, was er da unten macht.
(S. 66)

Traditionelle rhetorische Mittel, hier die anaphorischen Vers-
ansätze, werden eingesetzt, um die Monotonie der Beschäf-
tigungen des Vaters wiederzugeben.

Der 1922 geborene Franz Fühmann — auch er gab nach
1958 das Gedichteschreiben auf[14] — hat sich wie Hermlin
sehr um die Förderung jüngerer Talente von Sarah Kirsch
über Wolfgang Hilbig bis zu Uwe Kolbe verdient gemacht. Im
Unterschied zu Hermlin rät er allerdings anläßlich seiner
Würdigung der Gedichte Uwe Kolbes den Jungen, "nicht so
viel auf uns zu schauen; wir sind kein besonders gutes Vorbild,
und ein Modell können wir schon gar nicht sein."[15] Fühmann
erklärt weiter: "Und sosehr ich die Generation Uwes verstehe,
wenn sie die meine ob Erfahrungsquantitäten beneidet, sosehr beneide ich auch die seine: um eine Qualität, die mir
versagt bleibt, um ihre Homogenität." Fühmann sagt dies angesichts des Kreuzes, das seine Generation zu bewältigen hat:
"Durch unser Leben geht ein Riß" (S. 427). Ob das unsichere
Suchen vieler der Jüngsten nach einem Halt in einem Alltag,
der keineswegs zur Feier einlädt, tatsächlich ein Lebensgefühl
offenbart, das als homogen bezeichnet werden könnte, sei
dahingestellt. In einem Gespräch mit Margarete Hannsmann
von 1980 versucht Fühmann kurz den "Differenzierungs-
prozeß" zu umreißen, der sich in der Geschichte der DDR-
Literatur vollzog:

Jetzt nur soviel, daß in diesen Differen-
zierungsprozeß ein neues Moment durch
jene kam, die unsern Bruch, unsre crux,
nicht kennen, die in der DDR aufgewachsen, in sie hineingeboren sind, im Sinn von
etwas Schicksalhaftem. Wir hatten die
Möglichkeit der Wahl; ich glaube, daß Jeder

---

[14] "Das hing eben damit zusammen, daß gewisse, in der Mitte der fünfziger
Jahre aufgeblühte Hoffnungen einfroren und abstarben, und da starb dann
auch die Poesie ab, die sich aus diesen Hoffnungen speiste," erklärt Franz
Fühmann in seinem "Gespräch mit Horst Simon," in Fühmann, *Essays,
Gespräche, Aufsätze 1964-1981* (Rostock: Hinstorff, 1986), S. 478-79.
[15] Franz Fühmann, "Anläßlich der Gedichte Uwe Kolbes," in *Essays, Gespräche, Aufsätze 1964-1981*, S. 427.

all der Jahrgänge bis zu den heute Vierzigjährigen die Möglichkeit hatte und noch hat, frei zu entscheiden, wo er leben und wirken will. Die "Hineingeborenen" haben diese Wahl nicht; und bei dieser Generation ist nun alles da, was eben von menschlicher Anlage her in der Dichtung — ich möchte fast sagen: "naturgemäß" — da ist, nicht eine Selektion wie bis in die sechziger Jahre bei uns.[16]

Fühmann versäumt auch nicht, auf die Probleme hinzuweisen, die sich im Rahmen kulturpolitischer Restriktionen und überhaupt des Literaturbetriebs in der DDR ergeben:

Und daß diese junge Generation ihre spezifischen Probleme und viel zuwenig Gelegenheit hat, sie artikulieren zu können, das ist eine der Fragen, mit der unsre Gesellschaft nicht und nicht und nicht fertig wird; für mich eine der quälendsten Fragen. . . . Und nun kommt als doppeltes Nachholebedürfnis diese Vielfalt der Ismen hoch, und da sie für die meisten nicht als Möglichkeit kommt, die Wahl ihrer Lektüre frei zu treffen, fließt auf die ärgerlichste Weise ein Schwall von Zweit- und Drittrangigem ein, das der Zufall halt irgendwie vermittelt, das aber als erstrangig angestaunt und nachgemacht wird — man kennt halt nichts Andres.[17]

So bedauerlich der mangelnde Zugang zu allem "Erstrangigen" in der literarischen Tradition, besonders der Tradition der Moderne sein mag, was zählt, bleibt das mehr oder wenig zufällig Rezipierte, von dem sich schon immer jede Generation, jedes Individuum, anregen ließ im Sinne einer Wiederaufnahme oder des Sich-Abstoßens. So prägt sich zum Beispiel Rüdiger Rosenthal, 1952 geboren, die Zeile "Wie leben die Menschen ohne Poesie?" aus einem Gedicht des Griechen Jannis Ritsos ein. In dem in *Berührung ist nur eine Randerscheinung* abgedruckten Gespräch mit Elke Erb erzählt

---

[16] Franz Fühmann, "Miteinander reden. Gespräch mit Margarete Hannsmann," in *Essays, Gespräche, Aufsätze 1964-1981*, S. 449.
[17] Ebenda.

Rosenthal, wie er sich vor langer Zeit, d.h. 1976, 1977, der Deutschen "Brecht, Braun und Kirsch usw." (S. 63) überdrüssig, in der Weltliteratur umschaute: "ich wollte aus den Sprachgrenzen der DDR. Whitman, Vincente Aleixandre. Ich habe gemerkt, daß ich da wieder eine Heimat gefunden habe, mehr, als ich jetzt hier in der DDR hatte" (S. 64). Der Physiker und "Rationalist" von Hause aus, wie er sich beschreibt, begann sich mit "Gedanken jenseits der Rationalität" (S. 64) zu beschäftigen. Nun scheut er sich nicht, das Wort "Poesie" ohne ironischen Unterton an markanter Stelle in seinen Gedichten zu verwenden. In der "Bollersdorfer Elegie" steht es am Ende einer Reflexion über den Alltag, die übergeht in poesievolle Klischees:

> Manche Menschen lieben Autos
> oder zählen Fotos nach dem Urlaub
> Andre haben Gott als Vorgesetzten
> und verweigern den Befehl
> Ein Mann und eine Frau
> haben ein Kind gemeinsam
> Zwei Feldsteingiebel stehen ohne Haus
> einander einsam gegenüber
> Eine Spinne schleppt ihr gelbes Ei durchs Gras
> Die Haut der Mädchen ist die Haut
> frühreifer Kirschen
>
> Die Bienen saugen Nektar aus den Blumen
> Ich sauge aus den Tagen POESIE. (S. 62)

In dem Gedicht "Absprung" schwebt das lyrische Ich von einem Kometen "mit dem Fallschirm der *Poesie* auf dem Rücken" zur Erde, um im Gefängnis zu landen. "Jetzt kann ich dir meine Einsamkeit zeigen" lautet die letzte Zeile (S. 63). Seltsame Gedichte, vergleicht man sie mit den experimentellen Texten von Rainer Schedlinski oder Tohm di Roes in derselben Sammlung. Die Herausgeberin Elke Erb denkt jedenfalls ganz ernsthaft darüber, "wie sich das Schreiben zum Leben verhält; ob das Wort Poesie in deinen [Rosenthals] beiden Texten selbst poetisch wird, wenn man sich deutlich genug vorstellt, was es für dich bedeutet" (S. 64). Was dem Literarhistoriker als Regression in abgegriffene Poetisierung erscheinen mag, präsentiert sich als Ausbruch "aus den Sprachgrenzen der DDR" (S. 64).

Die sprachkritische Haltung vieler dieser Jüngsten richtet sich nicht gegen die literarische Tradition – welche auch immer, sei es die deutsche Romantik oder die internationale Avantgarde vom Anfang des Jahrhunderts, nicht gegen die Dichtung früherer Generationen schlechthin, sondern gegen jegliches Inbeschlagnehmen von Kunst für didaktische Zwecke. Das "operative Gedicht," so gesellschaftskritisch es sich auch gebärden mag, hat für manche Vertreter der "Hineingeborenen" an Anziehungskraft verloren, weil sich ihre Alltagserfahrungen nicht mehr einbetten lassen in weltanschauliche Konzepte. Es gibt zu viel Näherliegendes, mit dem man sich plagt, so daß selbst der utopische Entwurf einer besseren Gesellschaft kaum mehr Anreiz zum Schreiben gibt. Der lyrische Eklektizismus verrät dabei wohl auch eine große Verunsicherung.

Zu den Alltagserfahrungen dieser Schriftsteller aus der DDR gehört die Bedrohung der natürlichen Umwelt durch industriellen Raubbau und das atomare Waffenarsenal. Es ist verständlich, daß sich die unterschiedlichsten künstlerischen Temperamente aller Generationen der Gestaltung eines Themas nicht verschließen, das keine Grenzen kennt, auch keine ideologischen. Der 1960 in Gera geborene Tohm di Roes zum Beispiel gibt seiner großangelegten apokalyptischen Assoziationskette von Satzfetzen, Wortreihungen und Lauten ("ICHs / APOKALYPTUS / eine autobiographische Weltgeschichte") folgenden Vorspann:

AUFGRUNDEINESMEHRHEITSBESCHLUSSESDERERDBEVÖLKERUNG
    WURDE
ENTSCHIEDENDIESENPLANETENVOLLSTÄNDIGZUVERNICHTENUM
    SCHLIMMERES ZU
        VERHINDERN
DIEAKTIONHATLÄNGSTBEGONNENUNDWIRDSYSTEMATISCHZU
    ENDEGEFÜHRT   (S. 209)

Im letzten Gedicht "Dies schwierige Thema" ihres Buches *Sturzacker* stellt sich Gabriele Eckart, geboren 1954, diese Frage: "Nachdem ich mir aufgezählt hatte was auf der Erde mich zornig macht / Ob sie nicht verdient vielleicht habe die Apokalypse."[18] Es folgt eine Aufzählung, um welche Dinge es doch schade wäre, nämlich "[u]m alles was jemals mich freute und freuen noch wird." Die letzten Zeilen des Gedichtes lauten:

---

[18] Gabriele Eckart, *Sturzacker: Gedichte 1980-1984* (Berlin: Der Morgen, 1985), S. 84.

Es wäre doch schade darum
Um die Vögel und fahrenden Sänger
Um jedes Blatt eines Baums der noch grünt
Um jede Seite eines Tagebuchs voll eines Herzens
                  wechselnder Gezeiten
Um den Anblick der Dämmerung wenn sie langsam die
                  Zöpfe löst
Um jedes Fragment auf Papyros das wir rauskratzten
                  mühsam aus der Geschichte Geröll
Um die bogige Spur die das Leben zurückläßt in der
                  Erinnerung
Und um jedes Gedicht das noch einer zu schreiben Mut
hat über den Frieden dies schwierige Thema. (S. 84-85)

Bei den Autoren der mittleren Generation, bei Sarah Kirsch,
Heinz Czechowski, Volker Braun, Axel Schulze u.a., ist inzwischen die ökologische Problematik im weitesten Sinne zu
einem immer wieder aufgegriffenen Thema der Gedichte geworden.[19]

Zu den Vertretern der älteren Generation, die von Anfang
an an der Entwicklung der DDR-Literatur teilhatten und
weiterhin auch Gedichte schreiben, gehören Hanns Cibulka
(geboren 1920) und Walter Werner (geboren 1922), auch
wenn sie kaum jemals im Rampenlicht größerer öffentlicher
Diskussionen standen. Cibulkas 1982 erschienenes Tagebuch
Swantow, das sich intensiv mit Erscheinungsformen der Umweltzerstörung und Verarmung des Lebens beschäftigt, ist
hier eine Ausnahme. Man denkt an Rüdiger Rosenthals Hin-
wendung zur "Poesie," wenn man den Anfang von Cibulkas
Gedicht "Lagebericht" — eine Art Kernstück des Tagebuches —
liest: "Nicht musisch / lebt heute der Mensch, / berechnend /
geht er durchs Leben."[20]

Freilich sind die neuen Texte dieser Dichter noch wesentlich stärker als selbst die der mittleren Generation geprägt
von einer langen, auf andere Art schwierigen Entwicklung.
Angesichts der aktuellen Umweltbedrohungen fühlen sie sich
eher bestätigt in ihrem Traditionsbewußtsein und ihrer Na-

---

[19] Vergl. hierzu meine Studie "Ökolyrik in der DDR: Eine Beispielreihe," in
Studies in GDR Culture and Society 5, hrsg. v. Margy Gerber u.a. (Lanham/
New York/London: University Press of America, 1985), S. 221-35, die auch
weitere Literaturangaben enthält.
[20] Hanns Cibulka, *Swantow: Die Aufzeichnungen des Andreas Flemming*
(Halle/Leipzig: Mitteldeutscher Verlag, 1982), S. 36-37.

turnähe. Sie bewahren auch in ihren neuesten Gedichten das poetische (Natur-)Bild, entfalten es unentwegt, lassen es, wie Walter Werner in dem Gedicht "Umwelt" aus seinem letzten Lyrikband *Der Baum wächst durchs Gebirge* sich spielerisch verselbständigen:

> Das All friert ins Gehölz.
> Der Apfel fällt und fault.
> Die Erde ist auf der Flucht,
> die Bäume treten aus ihrem Kreis,
> schütteln sich in ihren Mänteln,
> kommen von den Wurzeln und fliegen.[21]

In der 1985 erschienenen Ausgabe von Miniaturen und Gedichten einer Schriftstellerin, die bisher nur als Autorin unzähliger Prosawerke bekannt war, findet sich unter dem Titel "Aufbruch" eine kleine Parabel über einen alten Eichenwald, der gefällt werden sollte und sich daher entschloß, "an einem lichten Nachmittag auszuwandern":

> Ast in Ast geflochten, eine grüne Wucht aus Hunderten von Stämmen, begann er mit seinen Wurzelfüßen, das Erdreich aufzubrechen. Und zog und zerrte heraus, was sich ziehen ließ. Was riß, blieb.
> Und der Eichenwald wanderte stämmig stampfend, zügig voran, hügelab, hügelan.
> Da griff ihm der Abendwind unter sein Laub und hob ihn mit starken Schultern. Ich sah ihn durch den blassen Himmel dahinschleifen, rauschend im Gegenzug, grün mit schwarzen hängenden Elefantenbeinen, urzeitliches Käferwesen, ein Hunderttausendzentnergewicht. So flog der Eichenwald dahin, hoch über mich ins Abendrot.[22]

Axel Schulze, 1943 geboren, bemerkt zu diesem Text: "Ihre [der Autorin] nachdenkliche Verbundenheit mit allem Lebenden macht sie ebenso gefeit vor platter Proklamation wie vor süßlicher Naturschwärmerei. Solche 'ur-eigenen Mit-

---

[21] Walter Werner, *Der Baum wächst durchs Gebirge: Gedichte* (Halle/Leipzig: Mitteldeutscher Verlag, 1982), S. 31.

[22] Marianne Bruns, *Luftschaukel: Miniaturen und Gedichte* (Halle/Leipzig: Mitteldeutscher Verlag, 1985), S. 63.

teilungen' gehen mich jedenfalls an."[23] Die Verfasserin des Textes "Aufbruch," Marianne Bruns, feiert übrigens dieses Jahr ihren neunzigsten Geburtstag. Es bleibt zu hoffen, daß diese sich thematisch berührenden lyrischen Stimmen verschiedener Generationen keine Randerscheinung bleiben.

---

[23] Axel Schulze, "Eine Bietung. Marianne Bruns: 'Luftschaukel'," *Neue Deutsche Literatur*, 34, Nr. 11 (1986), 133.

Rock Music and Everyday Culture in the GDR

Peter Wicke

It is always the workaday routine of everyday life in which a society must prove its social and political effectiveness. Only those things which reach into the subtle ramifications of everyday life become social qualities, i.e., something which influences people's relationships and behavior and thus can become a catalyst for the development of their creativity and other capabilities. These interdependent connections far exceed the institutionalized forms of the social, political, and economic organization of society; and, although they are transmitted by society and shaped thereby, they are by no means reducible to this process.

Everyday life is made up of a large variety of moments — fixed activities within social institutions such as job, school, family, etc., but also casual and fleeting experiences such as dreams, desires, and hopes which reach beyond purposeful actions within a social framework. These disparate moments are not isolated events; they are embedded in a cultural pattern in which they are related to each other, where they crystallize into values and value concepts and thus continue the complex dynamics of life, the individual appropriation of social conditions. This cultural experiencing of everyday life is informed not only by socially different living conditions and by forms of appropriation specific to certain classes and groups, but by a complex network of cultural symbols, the so-called popular arts — music, film, literature, art — as well. By means of mass cultural communication the popular arts penetrate all aspects of everyday life, introducing sensual forms and value structures and at the same time allowing certain correlations and value conceptions to be pinned to themselves and thus passed on.

This brings me to my topic: rock music as an essential part of everyday life for the young generation in the GDR. In order to understand the functioning and modes of this music in socialist culture, its importance within a socialist concept of culture, and — finally — socialist cultural policy vis-à-vis rock music, it is essential to bear in mind the basic interrelationships outlined above. Rock music is a catalyst for very complex cultural connections within the everyday activities of young people — and this is precisely *der springende Punkt* if one wants to describe the special features, the social content, and cultural significance of this musical practice under the social, economic, and political conditions of socialist society.[1]

This is not to deny the significance of the modes of performance and stylistic concepts developed in the United States and Great Britain. Socialist culture develops neither independent of nor isolated from the processes of cultural internationalization associated with the audio-visual mass media. And, although we do criticize the fact that the concrete economic and political structure of these media is dominated by a small number of — essentially U.S.-based — companies which use them as a sort of cultural "one-way street," we do not attempt to set up cultural alternatives or ban those popular art forms, such as rock music — for the sole reason that these processes are developing in patterns which can be neither defined in nor limited to national dimensions.[2]

This does not mean that we have dispensed with the concept of the autonomous development of those forms of artistic practice that are tied to modern means of mass communication. On the contrary, this is a proving ground for the concept of socialist culture — and not only because the confrontation of the different social systems increasingly is being determined by who is able to win the masses over to his side, but especially because socialist culture, in its self-understanding, is a culture of the working masses, and one prerequisite for its being a mass culture is cultural mass communication and the resulting artistic processes. The central issue here is the form of culture in the everyday life of a socialist society; this is the

---

[1] For a more in-depth discussion see Peter Wicke, *Zur Ästhetik und Soziologie eines Massenmediums* (Leipzig: Phillip Reclam jun., 1987). English edition forthcoming: Cambridge University Press.

[2] Cf. Werner Rackwitz, "Wie steht es mit unserer Tanzmusik? Referat des Stellvertreters des Ministers für Kultur, Dr. Werner Rackwitz, anläßlich der Tanzmusikkonferenz am 24. und 25. April 1972 in Berlin (Berlin: Ministerium für Kultur, 1972).

test for the development of art forms that involve and attract the masses.

One cannot reduce popular music to a mere means of transporting verbal ideological messages. A rock song is not an ideological pill sugar-coated with modern sounds, no matter whether it is a song by Bruce Springsteen or by the Puhdys, a GDR rock group. This is the wrong way to try to come to terms with this kind of music. The fact that VEB Deutsche Schallplatte, the state-owned record company in the GDR, in 1987 released Bruce Springsteen's hit album "Born in the USA" in a licensed edition on its AMIGA label — productions of Michael Jackson, Tina Turner, the Rolling Stones, Pink Floyd, and others have also been issued — does not represent the importation of bourgeois ideology — neither does it mean that the fans of Bruce Springsteen in the GDR would prefer to have been born in the USA, as the lyrics of the title track might suggest. Nor does this mean that we regard Bruce Springsteen as an advocate of socialist ideology. And least of all should it be seen as an indication of a pragmatic surrender of socialist views.

The ideological efficacy of rock music derives from the fact that it provides a cultural form for communicating everyday experience. And this cultural form is highly effective in ideological terms because it has to do with sense structures and value patterns, with a world outlook, and the emotional perception of social reality. The verbal message of the lyrics can support this, or the lyrics can simply act as a sound form. In other words, even a song by Bruce Springsteen, Tina Turner, Michael Jackson, or the Rolling Stones, as a musical medium, is capable of having an ideological impact by fostering cultural connections between disparate events of social reality within a socialist society; still, it has this impact solely in regard to this experience. This is all the more true since the rhythm patterns and sound structures of rock music reflect a sensuousness, a sensuous relation to reality, which, irrespective of all commercial filters, has its social roots in the working-class youth of the capitalist countries and is therefore by no means alien to us. All other interpretations, particularly those which reduce the question of ideological efficacy to the content of the lyrics, represent an oversimplification of the problem — as occurred in the political-cultural discussion in the GDR.[3] It

---

[3] See Heinz Peter Hoffmann, *Beat, Rock, Rhythm & Blues, Soul* (Berlin: Lied der Zeit, 1973).

goes without saying, however, that discussion about the nature of rock music and its development becomes increasingly difficult when the central issue is not the commercial but the cultural value of a rock song.

This is of decisive importance for understanding GDR rock music inasmuch as this music does not owe its originality and autonomy to formalistic speculations about how socialist rock 'n' roll is supposed to sound nor to the content of its German lyrics. One can truthfully say that this music has been formed by the cultural correlations within the everyday lives of young people in which it is embedded. And since this everyday life is not determined by the escapism of exaggerated individualism or by class barriers specific to a certain age group, or by sexist publicity images — I don't mean to indicate that the GDR is paradise on earth, but we don't have these problems — it has found a highly audible expression in the sensuous sound forms of rock music produced in the GDR.

The essential issue here is the social form of communication which takes place under socialist conditions. It is after all by means of this process that music praxis such as rock music is brought into association with the subtle and differentiated aspects of everyday cultural experiences of young people. The assumption that this is being done by administrative decree is simply absurd. Culture cannot be prescribed; popularity cannot be dictated. It is, however, similarly absurd to presuppose the intact world of a village green where such communication happens spontaneously and to dismiss all forms of direction by government authorities and centralized production as undemocratic.

Because of the industrialized processes involved and the dependence on the mass media, the production and distribution of rock music are highly socialized and thus reliant on a complex network of institutions which cannot be modeled along the lines of a spontaneous "basic democracy." The historic challenge for a socialist cultural model is to provide a social form for those processes of cultural development which are becoming increasingly socialized and thus centralized: a form which allows their inherent contradictions to become a productive force rather than a fetter. And this is the reason why a production process organized along commercial lines is not acceptable. Not only because the implied private ownership of the means of production is contradictory to the socioeconomic basis of socialist society, but also because this would be tantamount to a *simple* cultural reproduction of social aspects, i.e., formal innovation along with the reproduction of ever the same cultural forms of activity.[4]

Socialism, however, as the first stage of an evolving social structure, constantly requires the *extended* reproduction of its characteristic bases, and this not only in the economic but also in the cultural sphere. This can become reality only if the conveyance process assumes a *political* form, i.e., when it is organized along lines which link the development of rock music — its production as well as its cultural use by young people — with the essential social and political issues of society, with the internal dynamics of society's development. Only then does the cultural form of everyday experience mentioned at the beginning of this paper become more than a mere preserving and harmonizing wrapper which detaches everyday life from the basic processes of social development, thereby contributing to the substantiation of the individual in his privacy rather than his sociality. This presupposes that rock music, instead of existing in the niches of youth sub-cultures or as a lucrative marketing fetish, be transformed into a relevant means of communication in the socio-political sphere, that it be taken seriously in political terms. This does not happen spontaneously, however; nor can it be decreed.

A structure for encouraging this process has been developed in the GDR; it enlists all relevant social forces, such as the FDJ and the labor union, in the promotion of rock music. The FDJ, for example, organizes "workship weeks" for amateur rock bands once every two years; the FDGB, in its function of fostering the cultural interests of working-class youth, runs non-professional talent contests and talent shows. These activities are carried out on all administrative levels, i.e., district, county, and national, with the best bands being delegated to the next highest level. Rock music and some 3,500 non-professional rock bands occupy a firm place in the cultural work of these organizations and receive encouragement and support all along the line. Song contests and talent shows are likewise held — again at all levels — in the professional sector, which includes some 150 rock bands, among them such successful groups as Karat, the Puhdys, Silly, Pankow, City, and Enno, to name only some of the best known.

---

[4] See Lothar Kühne, *Gegenstand und Raum. Über die Historizität des Ästhetischen* (Dresden: Verlag der Kunst, 1981), pp. 174ff.

The Committee for the Entertaining Arts (Komitee für Unterhaltungskunst), an umbrella organization attached to the Council of Ministers, coordinates all activities and maintains contact with the official agency, VEB Konzert- und Gastspiel-direktion, and with the GDR's artist agency responsible for guest performances abroad. The purview of the Committee, as evident from its name (here one must know that the some-what clumsy designation "entertaining arts" has a tradition of its own in the GDR),[5] includes not only rock music but all other popular forms of music, from chansons to jazz, as well as circus entertainment, i.e., artistic mass culture in all its forms. The Committee for the Entertaining Arts comprises senior representatives of all relevant cultural institutions and elected representatives from among the artists themselves. The special feature of the Committee is that it allows the artists to administer their affairs themselves. President of the Commit-tee is Gisela Steineckert, a poet and author of a number of popular lyrics; among the vice-presidents are such popular artists as Frank Schöbel; among its members are musicians from rock bands like the Puhdys, City, electra, and Dialog. The members are elected in their specific sections, which provide an association-like organization for the approximately 9,000 freelance artists in the GDR, i.e., musicians, artistes, disc jockeys, cabaret performers, etc. A number of advisory boards attached to the Committee provide a forum for critics and scholars working in the respective fields.

I will skip the details of this complex organizational mech-anism. The outcome of its work, with regard to our subject, is that rock music has been assigned a socio-political value which makes its further development an important aspect of both cultural and youth policy. Rock music is being taken seriously in political terms, and this not only by the authorities but by the musicians themselves and their young audiences as well. Rock music in the GDR is of course fun, entertainment, a sensual pleasure, a collective experience, yet it is at the same time a political medium which articulates social experience, reflects social consciousness, and clashes with social reality. Its special feature is that these processes are carried out by means of verbal and cultural symbols as opposed to direct argument. This is not always the easiest way, since the music has something to do with argument, with friction and the lack

---

[5] The term "Unterhaltungskunst" was coined in the 1950s as a way of signal-ing that so-called "lower" or popular culture should be treated seriously, i.e., as art.

of friction, but it offers the possibility of being socially effective, a quality which this music has not always had. The building in which the national parliament is housed, the Palast der Republik in Berlin, is the setting for the annual GDR rock festival "Rock für den Frieden" ("Rock for Peace"). This shows the value placed on rock music in the GDR.

Critics of our model maintain that such an organizational structure detracts from the spontaneity and immediacy of rock music and has transformed what should be a medium of expression for young people into representative "state art" — whatever this may be — and made it the object of a vast cultural bureaucracy.[6] The production of rock music is no more bureaucratically organized in the GDR than in comparably complex production units in the West such as EMI or CBS, which I had the opportunity to visit in 1987. To what extent this organizational structure provides young people with a say in the cultural mass media, giving them not only a voice that can be heard — which is undoubtedly the case — but actually passing this means of expression on to them so that they can communicate the way they see themselves and the world, their priorities, and their value concepts through music — this is obviously a decisive criterion for evaluating the social quality of socialist culture.

The assumption that commercial criteria are ignored so that this music can be "administered" from the top down without economic considerations misses the point. The product/money ratio is a factor in the production and distribution of rock music in the GDR, too — although not a decisive one; it has detached itself from the give-and-take of the market place and is subordinate to the premises of socialist culture and youth policies. The development of rock music in the GDR is thus not confined to expression that is in strong financial demand.

This of course raises the question: what does influence the development of rock music in the GDR? Why do bands make music if not for commercial reasons? Let me say that the motivation does not stem from the Party or state leadership; these bodies merely give the motivating factors their socially binding force and thus their necessary political weight. The development of rock music in the GDR is the result of a per-

---

[6] See for example Olaf Leitner, *Rockszene DDR. Aspekte einer Massenkultur im Sozialismus* (Reinbek: Rowohlt, 1983).

manent and public debate about its value standards and prospects. The talent contests, workshops, and competitions mentioned above play a decisive role since these activities provide a forum for the discussion of criteria, contents, and values. No matter what form such activities take, they have one thing in common: the performances of the bands are publicly discussed and evaluated by a panel of experts — musicians, text writers, journalists, media representatives, producers, musicologists — together with the performing bands themselves.

These heated discussions result in the formulation of standards which, due to the prestige associated with the winning of prizes, the active encouragement of bands by means of recommendations, and the media coverage, have a signal function for the overall process of rock development. During such discussions the work of a given rock band is evaluated without regard for the number of albums it has sold. It is precisely this feature which produces the motivation for music making, which is not the result of moral appeals or decrees: the challenge to contribute something to the social consciousness, something useful for the furthering of society, something which sparks new activities or ways of thinking.

I don't mean to imply that our model for the development of this kind of music is perfect. It represents an attempt to provide rock music with a social form that brings to bear the social, economic, and political foundations of socialist society. Above all, it strives to realize the musical, aesthetic, and cultural potential of this music by freeing it from the constraints of commercialization and instead fostering a social and sociopolitical effectiveness that is adequate to and expressive of the intensity and commitment with which young people deal with this music.[7]

---

[7] Additional works on GDR rock music: Jürgen Balitzki, *Rock aus erster Hand* (Berlin: Lied der Zeit, 1985); Stefan Lasch, *PS: Rockmusik* (Berlin: Tribüne, 1980); and Peter Wicke, *Anatomie des Rock* (Leipzig: Deutscher Verlag für Musik, 1987).

Alltag, Apathy, Anarchy:
GDR Everyday Life as a Provocation in
Christoph Hein's Novella *Der fremde Freund*

Phillip S. McKnight

Christoph Hein's reputation as a writer has grown substantially since 1982, when Peter Hacks publicly recognized his potential as a master of the German language at the presentation to Hein of the Heinrich Mann Prize for literature.[1] Hein is no ordinary talent; in just a few short years he has established himself in the GDR as one of the most respected intellectuals of the generation following Christa Wolf and Heiner Müller. His comedy *Die wahre Geschichte des Ah Q* has played in many locations throughout Europe, and 1987 marked its fifth season at the Deutsches Theater in Berlin. In the fall of 1987 a new play, *Passage*, premiered in Dresden, Essen, and Zurich; and at the same time an earlier play, *Lasalle fragt Herrn Herbert nach Sonja. Die Szene ein Salon*, opened for the first time in the GDR in Erfurt. After a long delay due to the controversial depictions of a party functionary and of problems related to Stalinism in the 1950s, Hein's first novel, *Horns Ende*, appeared in 1985.[2] Although reviews and commentary on this novel were apparently suppressed for two years, public discussion of *Horns Ende* was finally initiated in the GDR in the spring of 1987.[3] The work which created the greatest sensation throughout the GDR and Western Europe, however, was his long novella *Der fremde Freund* (*Drachen-*

---

[1] Peter Hacks, "Heinrich-Mann-Preis 1982," *Neue Deutsche Literatur*, 30, No. 6 (1982), 159-63.

[2] Christoph Hein, *Horns Ende* (Berlin/Weimar: Aufbau, 1985; Darmstadt/Neuwied: Luchterhand, 1985). Page citings in the following are to the Luchterhand edition.

[3] Cf. Phil McKnight, "Ein Mosaik zu Christoph Heins Roman 'Horns Ende,'" *Sinn und Form*, 39, No. 2 (1987), 415-25; and Klaus Hammer, "Christoph Hein: Horns Ende," *Weimarer Beiträge*, 33, No. 8 (1987), 1358-69.

blut is the title in the West), which, first published in 1982, has enjoyed numerous printings in both East and West.[4]

Hein began writing *Der fremde Freund* with the intention of telling the story of a man he had known who died as a result of irresponsible actions related to a trivial set of circumstances. Dissatisfied with the story's potential, Hein came upon the idea of portraying the man through the "spectacles" of a second party, a woman.[5] The woman, Claudia, quickly evolved into the central figure of the novella. Her subjective description of Henry, the "fremder Freund," was extended to other characters and events as well, so that the narrative is related exclusively from Claudia's perspective. She ultimately tells us a good deal more about herself than about other people.

Hein's protagonist Claudia resists any sort of meaningful participation in either the public or the private sphere; she ultimately prevents her own "humanization" by not allowing her relationship with Henry, or with anyone else, to go too deep. She covers up reality with colorful, loud, forgettable, but salubrious "transfer stencils," her "alltägliche Abziehbilder" (p. 6). These metaphorical stencils, or stickers, take the form of routine, everyday aspects of what has become for her an ordered, humdrum, and reliable existence. The security derived from predictability functions to mask her "Berührungsangst" (p. 38), to suppress any potential misadventure leading into unknown realms, and to prevent any penetration into sensitive and possibly unstable regions of her psychic constitution.

Claudia considers herself invulnerable: "Ich habe mich in Drachenblut gebadet, und kein Lindenblatt ließ mich irgendwo schutzlos" (p. 154). She doesn't realize or refuses to ac-

---

[4] Christoph Hein, *Der fremde Freund* (Berlin/Weimar: Aufbau, 1982); *Drachenblut* (Darmstadt/Neuwied: Luchterhand, 1983). In 1987 the GDR edition was in its fifth printing. In the following I will be quoting from the sixth hardcover edition of *Drachenblut* (1984); page references will appear parenthetically in the text.

[5] This summarizes Hein's answer to a question regarding his choice of a female as the central figure of the novella given at a workshop conducted during his stay at the University of Kentucky in April 1987. Providing a different answer to the same question for an interview given at UCLA, Hein said, "Das ist die Frage, die ich am häufigsten gehört habe. Um nicht immer das gleiche zu sagen, habe ich verschiedene Antworten gefunden, die alle gültig sind" (Janice Murray and Mary-Elizabeth O'Brian, "Interview mit Christoph Hein," *New German Review*, 3 [1987], 57).

knowledge that a figurative linden leaf covered a spot on her, too, as she "bathed in dragon blood," i.e., that she is innately sensitive. She differs from the robot-like runners in the opening dream (pp. 5-6), who trot steadily and sure-footedly across the bridge with no awareness of the abyss below. Unable to ignore the danger, Claudia and her companion cling anxiously to each other, trying desperately to inch their way across. Terrified, Claudia thinks: "er soll mich loslassen. Jeder für sich" (p. 5). Claudia's dream — or "fernes Erinnern" (p. 6) — ends before she makes it across and with the feeling that it is futile to try to cross over.

Claudia's attitude —"Jeder für sich" — is not only an antagonistic position with respect to socialist political ideology; it is also symptomatic of her self-imposed alienation and resulting aloofness.[6] This latter is, to a large extent, based on her feeling that the suppression of disturbing events functions as a "heilsamer, natürlicher Mechanismus" (p. 85) which enables the human being to exist. Claudia uses the word "healing" to describe the function of the various "Abziehbilder" in her life (p. 6). She rejects the maxim of her grandparents, "Wenn man einem Übel ins Gesicht sieht, hört es auf, ein Übel zu sein" (p. 85), because she has "andere Erfahrungen. Was man fürchtet, bringt einen um, wozu sich also damit beschäftigen" (p. 85). When faced with stress or fear, Claudia prescribes sedatives for herself and seems to imagine — to follow the dream metaphor — that she made it across the abyss of her fears (p. 53). The tablets, in reality, help cover the unsettling truth and thus enable her to maintain the image of herself she prefers.

This procedure is also illustrated by Claudia's encounter with a woman for whom she eventually prescribes placebos in order to accommodate the latter's insistence that the heart trouble she thinks she has has nothing to do with her failed marriage and her alienation at work (p. 89). Claudia sees others refusing to accept a correct diagnosis, but she refuses to

---

[6] Claudia's aloofness is conveyed in the narration by Hein's use of staccato sentence structure and indirect discourse when Claudia describes other people's sensitive areas, and by his technique of creating an unwritten sub-text where one thing may be said while implying something else: "Wenn die Person sagt, sie sei zufrieden und ihr gehe es gut," according to Hein, "wird eigentlich immer etwas anderes, nicht das Gegenteil, aber etwas anderes noch erzählt" (Hein, "Die Intelligenz hat angefangen zu verwalten und aufgehört zu arbeiten. Ein Gespräch," in his Öffentlich arbeiten. Essais und Gespräche [Berlin/Weimar: Aufbau, 1987], p. 158. First published in Deutsche Volkszeitung – Die Tat, Frankfurt/M., No. 10, 1984).

diagnose herself correctly. In the case of the woman patient, as well as in her own, pills become a dangerous remedy: a prescription for apathy.

Although the primary meaning of *Der fremde Freund* does not necessarily depend on the fact that it is a work of GDR literature set in the GDR, the peculiarities of its *Alltag*, including perceptions of GDR history, nevertheless anchor the novella in GDR culture and society. For the GDR reader, Claudia's suppressed problems raise "die bange oder mißtrauische Frage, ob dies die Beschreibung eines allgemeinen Zustands 'unserer Gesellschaft' sein solle," as Hans Kaufmann puts it.[7] The individualization of the Claudia-character is based on socio-political issues to be found in the GDR, as opposed to the West. The Western reader, for example, is not likely to have a collectively applied concept of an enlightened and humane society of the future, a concept which was an integral part of Claudia's education and of Hein's contemporary readers in the GDR. Even more importantly, her personality was influenced by occurrences in GDR everyday life: forces which negatively affected the development of her personality and her assumption of social and political responsibilities.

The turning point of Claudia's life, setting in motion the defense mechanisms which brought about her indifference, took place when she was twelve, not too long after the stationing of a Soviet tank in the center of her town as a consequence of the strikes of June 17, 1953. Hein enables the reader to calculate the dates of the story by having Claudia mention the introduction of daylight-saving time, which occurred in the GDR in 1981. Since she is currently forty years old, she was twelve years old in 1953. During this time of collectivization in the GDR the churches were singled out for discrimination because of what was described as their lack of solidarity with the revolutionary mandates of the GDR leadership. Hence Claudia was pressured by her parents, teachers, and classmates to dissolve her relationship with her best friend, Katharina, with whom she had sworn eternal friendship and loyalty, because of the religious orientation of Katharina and her family.

---

[7] Hans Kaufmann, "Christoph Hein in der Debatte," in his *Über DDR-Literatur. Beiträge aus fünfundzwanzig Jahren* (Berlin/Weimar: Aufbau, 1986), p. 235. See also the essays by various critics included in "Für und Wider: 'Der fremde Freund' von Christoph Hein," *Weimarer Beiträge*, 29, No. 9 (1983), 1635-55.

When Katharina refused to join the youth organization and, as a result, the whole class was kept after school to discuss the political repercussions of her decision, Claudia denounced Katharina,[8] making a joke about the "christlich-abergläubischen Ansichten einer gewissen Mitschülerin" (p. 112). Claudia and her classmates were irritated at being held after class because of Katharina's "stubbornness," i.e., refusal to compromise her values. They "hörten uninteressiert und mürrisch den bekannten Phrasen zu" (p. 112) as the teacher equated Katharina's decision with "Kriegshetze." The class was not interested in the central issues, although they represented a key dialectic and existential problem. It was not a matter of denouncing one of the brightest students in the class in order to subjugate her to the political collective; they wanted to go home and not have to listen to the teacher's harangues. Here Claudia displaced political and ethical issues with the trivia of *Alltag* for the first time.

On the psychological level, Claudia was not only under pressure from peers and authorities. The situation was exacerbated by problems which are fairly universal to puberty and the fragility of friendships in the eighth grade: Katharina had became interested in the precenter's son, a development which left her with less time for Claudia. Claudia felt a strange alienation when Katharina talked about her boyfriend; "argwöhnische Eifersucht" (p. 111) disrupted her feelings for Katharina. Shortly before she denounced Katharina, Claudia let a piece of petty gossip told to Katharina about her by another girl go uncorrected — a piece of trivia stenciled in over the jealousy issue, with which she was unable to cope.

Claudia repressed the trauma of having denounced the friend she loved "so rückhaltlos . . . wie ich nie wieder einen Menschen sollte lieben können" (p. 113). The psychological mechanism she found for neutralizing her trauma — her escape into daily routine — carried over into her adult life, where she masks her private feelings in a similar way. One example of this is to be found in the first chapter of the novella when Claudia reduces the issues involved in the decision whether or not she should attend Henry's funeral to the superficial question whether or not she would wear her dark blue coat, which could pass for black. Thus she diverts her attention away from her emotions, avoiding the risk of going out

---

[8] Denunciation, an extremely emotional issue, is explored at length by Hein in *Horns Ende* and, to a lesser extent, in *Die wahre Geschichte des Ah Q*.

on the precipice where she could experience herself intensely and possibly have a new opportunity to develop and grow.

A second part of the turning point in Claudia's life took place shortly after the ostracism of Katharina when she discovered that her own uncle Gerhard, a grandfather figure for her, stood accused of having denounced his colleagues in the Social Democratic Party during the war (p. 114). Claudia felt that she, as the niece of a "Nazi criminal," had lost the right to be shocked or indignant about the injustice of the Nazi regime or to feel sympathy for its victims. Her self-righteous denunciation of Katharina became for her an act of hypocrisy. After this she disclaimed any further political responsibility, a step which culminated in her alienation and her aloof contemptuousness toward both the public and private spheres of society, an attitude which characterizes her adult life.

The fictional Claudia raises questions about the degree to which, as stated in a recent GDR *Diplomarbeit* on Hein, "Verhalten, Fühlen, Denken der Menschen selbst" can become an "Ursache individueller und gesellschaftlicher Stagnation."[9] Social progress does not necessarily foster individual emancipation. Conversely, the resulting impoverishment of Claudia's personality, the alienation predominant in everyday communication "gefährden überhaupt die gesellschaftliche Emanzipation."[10] The result is a catch-22 dilemma in modern society, a vicious circle: the individual is harmful to social progress and social progress is harmful to the individual.

Although many of the problems depicted in the figure of Claudia are clearly rooted in GDR history and consequently a part of the GDR *Alltag*, this is not to say that the Claudia-personality doesn't exist elsewhere. In fact, the events portrayed in *Der fremde Freund* imply the GDR, in spite of its reeducation program and its efforts to isolate itself from Western influences during its early history, is linked to the larger family of industrialized nations. Hein hints perhaps that the GDR, too, has "bathed in dragon blood" and gained a false sense of security.

A passage from Hein's "Worüber man nicht reden kann, davon kann die Kunst ein Lied singen" indicates that Hein may

---

[9] Mathias Pfennig, "Untersuchungen zum literarischen Werk Christoph Heins," *Diplomarbeit*, Karl-Marx-Universität Leipzig, 1985, p. 73.

[10] Pfennig, p. 73.

see Claudia as a representation of twentieth-century tendencies unrelated to national boundaries, as a person responding to stress, trauma, and *Alltag*:

> Zum Selbsterhaltungstrieb des Menschen, einer bewußt-unbewußten natürlichen Regung, die ihm hilft, die tödliche Gefahr zu vermeiden, zu umgehen, sich gegen sie zu wehren, gehört auch die Fähigkeit, die unerträgliche Wahrheit nicht wahrzunehmen, die Augen vor ihr zu verschließen. Unsere Welt, unser Jahrhundert ist uns unerträglich geworden. . . . Wäre die Welt beständig vor unserem Auge, wir wären nicht fähig, ein Gedicht zu lesen oder auch nur gelassen einen Kaffee zu trinken. Der Selbsterhaltungstrieb bewahrt uns davor, diese Welt wirklich aushalten zu müssen, indem er unsere Sinne mit einem dicken Fell versieht. Eine nützliche zweite Haut, die uns vor dem schützt, was uns zu diesem Leben unfähig machen würde, und ein gefährliches Fell, denn es erlaubt uns, Unerträglichkeiten zu ertragen und damit das Leben insgesamt zu gefährden.[11]

The dangerous side of "invulnerability" has gained the upper hand in Claudia's life, the insensitivity that is detrimental to the development of society toward a more humane form. The narrow span between having too thick a skin and being too sensitive has become precarious and fragile in the twentieth century, and Claudia is not able to find an effective balance between the two.

Claudia, like other characters in Hein's works, conforms to the expectations of society — albeit passively and apathetically. The roots of this behavior lie in the public reaction to the political events associated with the 17th of June: at school nobody spoke about the presence of the Soviet tank in town and her father urged her to avoid the subject. Claudia couldn't understand why the issue was suppressed, but since the adults were resolutely silent, she realized "daß auch ein Gespräch

---

[11] Christoph Hein, "Worüber man nicht reden kann, davon kann die Kunst ein Lied singen," in his *Schlötel, oder Was solls. Stücke und Essays* (Darmstadt/Neuwied: Luchterhand, 1986), pp. 13-14.

etwas Bedrohliches sein konnte. . . . Ich lernte zu schweigen" (p. 108). Here the public reflex mechanism to suppress rather than to confront was ultimately internalized into her private personality.

There is evidence however that Claudia, despite the incidents which took place when she was twelve, was not always a conformist. In the young couple pictured in the wedding photograph of herself and her ex-husband Hinner, Claudia discovers "ratlose, verschüchterte Umstürzler" (p. 74) with the "Hoffnung aller Anarchie" (p. 75) to destroy and improve the conditions represented by the other people in the photograph. They were enemies of "Ordnung" (p. 75). What caused her transition from anarchy to apathy is not made clear, [12] but it may well have occurred as part of her reaction to her two abortions, which will be discussed below. In any case, as she matures Claudia's anarchistic tendencies are reduced and transformed into contempt.

As a risk-taking pseudo-anarchist, spontaneous and indifferent, her friend Henry represents a person who might be able to rekindle the anarchy that has lain dormant in Claudia. Claudia's encounter with Henry is a chance to overcome her apathy and indifference. GDR commentary has appropriately concentrated on the events immediately following Henry's reckless driving and his run-in with the farmer whose life he had endangered.[13] Brigitte Böttcher argues that the poetic turning point of the novella takes place in the forest when Claudia learns that Henry is married. After this Claudia begins searching for the "Wurzeln ihrer problematischen Existenz,"[14] a search which leads her back to her childhood and her denunciation of Katharina. Claudia learns the truth about Henry immediately following the only situation in the entire narrative in which normal human reactions and feelings begin to awaken in her. The sequence of events which follow her

[12] By comparison, the change from radical socialist to anarchist and, finally, to conformist without personal conviction form the subject matter of Hein's short story "Der Sohn" in his *Einladung zum Lever Bourgeois* (Berlin/Weimar: Aufbau, 1980), pp. 61-70.

[13] Bernd Schick points out parallels between Henry and Jack Kerouac's hero Dean Moriarty (*On the Road*); certain passages, such as Henry's reckless driving and the incident with the farmer on the tractor, are also reminiscent of Kerouac's novel ("Für und Wider. 'Der fremde Freund' von Christoph Hein," p. 1650).

[14] Brigitte Böttcher, "Diagnose eines unheilbaren Zustands. Christoph Hein: 'Der fremde Freund,'"*Neue Deutsche Literatur*, 31, No. 6 (1983), 147.

climbing up to a precarious position on the wall of some ruins to get a better angle to take pictures is, according to one commentator, the literal enactment of the dream which opens the book.[15] Since she neither plunges into the "abyss" nor makes it safely across when the opportunity presents itself, her situation remains unchanged.

Claudia's attitude toward photography is revealing. She never takes pictures of people, only of landscapes, because — as she says — landscapes always change (p. 133), while people appear awkward and unnatural in photographs (p. 75). Walter Benjamin's views regarding photography provide a key to interpreting Claudia's position.[16] It may be the aura of portraits, their "Kultwert," that makes Claudia uneasy. Benjamin points out that the "Kultwert" of portrait photography is connected to memory and remembrance.[17] Here one is reminded of Claudia's dream or "fernes Erinnern," which she describes as a "Bild, mir unerreichbar, letztlich unverständlich" (p. 6). According to Benjamin, photography can also capture the aura of landscapes. Asking "Was ist eigentlich Aura?" Benjamin gives as an answer:

> Ein sonderbares Gespinst von Raum und Zeit: einmalige Erscheinung einer Ferne, so nah sie sein mag. An einem Sommermittag ruhend einem Gebirgszug am Horizont oder einem Zweig folgen, der seinen Schatten auf den Betrachter wirft, bis der Augenblick oder die Stunde Teil an ihrer Erscheinung

---

[15] Gabriele Lindner, "Für und Wider: 'Der fremde Freund' von Christoph Hein," p. 1646.

[16] Hein is greatly interested in Benjamin. Cf. his new play, *Passage*, in *Theater der Zeit*, 42, No. 5 (1987), 54-64. One of the characters, Dr. Hugo Frankfurther, bears a close resemblance to Benjamin. Hein addresses Benjamin's *Das Kunstwerk im Zeitalter seiner technischen Reproduzierbarkeit* in his recent essay "Maelzel's Chess Player Goes to Hollywood. Das Verschwinden des künstlerischen Produzenten im Zeitalter der technischen Reproduzierbarkeit," in his *Öffentlich arbeiten. Essais und Gespräche*, pp. 165-94. This essay, originally written in March 1986 for the 1986 Kentucky Foreign Language Conference and read there in absentia, was also published as "Das Verschwinden des künstlerischen Produzenten im Zeitalter der Reproduzierbarkeit" in *Freibeuter. Vierteljahresschrift für Kultur und Politik*, Nos. 31 and 32 (1987), pp. 63-71, 11-19.

[17] Walter Benjamin, "Das Kunstwerk im Zeitalter seiner technischen Reproduzierbarkeit," in his *Das Kunstwerk im Zeitalter seiner technischen Reproduzierbarkeit. Drei Studien zur Kunstsoziologie* (Frankfurt/M.: Suhrkamp, 1977), p. 21.

hat — das heißt die Aura dieser Berge, dieses Zweiges atmen.[18]

On this day, climbing up the wall of the ruins, Claudia subconsciously senses the aura, and this moment triggers her anxiety, her sudden fear of falling. Climbing down to Henry, the aura is preserved for her as they walk through the forest, that is, until his unexpected revelation about his estranged wife. At this moment she seals herself off for the last time against intimate relationships: "Ich war gegen mich gewappnet" (p. 51). The description of the forced sex in the forest immediately thereafter combines associations with the vulnerable spot left by the linden leaf on Siegfried's back and her negative reaction to aura. Claudia observes a branch overhead which casts its shadow on her, evoking the "Gefühl endgültiger Einsamkeit" (p. 52). At this crucial moment, expressed in language reminiscent of Benjamin, the loss of aura becomes final:

> Vor meinen Augen tanzte ein Zweig mit stumpfen, glanzlosen Blättern. Ich spürte, wie Tränen mir ins Ohr liefen. Und immerzu dieser Zweig, ein fahles Blattgrün, durchsetzt von Lichtern und den bräunlichen Schatten des Waldes. Schatten und Licht, Hell Dunkel, Vordergrund Hintergrund, die Kühle der Erde, die Baumwurzel, die meinen Rücken wund rieb. (p. 52)

Later, after Henry's burial, she begins to be afraid of her photos. She had filled her drawers and closets with her prints of trees, scenery, grass, country lanes, and deadwood, "eine entseelte Natur, die ich erschuf" (p. 155). The fact that her diversion, or hobby, is a compensation for her fear of creative spontaneity is illustrated by her fascination with photographs as they develop on paper in the darkroom, "ein Keimen, das ich bewirke, steure, das ich unterbrechen kann" (p. 76). By comparison, she had undergone two abortions while still married to Hinner because, as she says, her pregnancies were a spontaneous creative process over which she had no control: "Ein monströser Eingriff, der meine ganze Zukunft bestimmen sollte, ein Eingriff in meine Freiheit" (p. 77). The disappearance of spontaneous interaction between Claudia and others

---

[18] Walter Benjamin, "Kleine Geschichte der Photographie," in his *Das Kunstwerk im Zeitalter seiner technischen Reproduzierbarkeit*, p. 57.

enables her to remain free, unattached, and private, covering her vulnerability with everyday trivia, secure in the unvarying, fixational quality of life. Her attempt to escape dependency on other people and things in order to determine her own needs and follow her own interests without external direction or guidance ends on a fatally discordant note, as Frank Hörnigk has pointed out: "Nicht Selbstbefreiung, sondern Selbstisolation ist das Ergebnis."[19]

In summary, one can say that the historical circumstances that triggered the changes in Claudia are clearly part of the GDR, while the fragile psychological constitution that was disrupted is universal. As Hein stated at the workshop at the University of Kentucky in 1987, Claudia's experience was similar to that of thousands of GDR citizens, most of whom did not, however, turn out like Claudia when they became adults. The incident provides a penetrating glimpse into the nature of an earlier *Alltag* to which most GDR citizens over forty can relate; it represents an important dimension of GDR social experience and contradiction.

In his essay "Öffentlich arbeiten" Hein maintains that literature consists of reports by individuals about what affects individuals, what causes them to be stricken or afflicted: literature as autobiography, personal but not private, "keine repräsentative, aber doch gesellschaftliche Autobiographie."[20] In "Worüber man nicht reden kann, davon kann die Kunst ein Lied singen," Hein indicates that literature functions as a "Lagebericht" which, although it is "machtlos," is by no means "ohnmächtig."[21] Reality itself, "die Lage, der Zustand, das Geschehen" may be generally known and accepted by the public; however, the simple description — be it literary, journalistic, or visual — has historically drawn a great deal more attention than the event itself: "das Benennen jedoch, die einfache, literarische oder nichtliterarische Beschreibung . . . führte zu

---

[19] Frank Hörnigk, "Christoph Hein," in *Literatur der Deutschen Demokratischen Republik. Einzeldarstellungen*, ed. Hans Jürgen Geerdt and Hannelore Prosche, III (Berlin: Volk und Wissen, 1987), p. 112.

[20] Christoph Hein, "Öffentlich arbeiten," in his *Die wahre Geschichte des Ah Q. Stücke und Essays* (Darmstadt/Neuwied: Luchterhand, 1984), p. 161. "Öffentlich arbeiten" was originally a "Diskussionsbeitrag" given in Berlin on March 6, 1982 at a meeting of the Writers' Union of the GDR. The essay was also published in *Tintenfisch 24. Jahrbuch für Literatur* (1985), pp. 42-44, and in *Öffentlich arbeiten. Essais und Gespräche*, pp. 34-38.

[21] Christoph Hein, "Worüber man nicht reden kann, davon kann die Kunst ein Lied singen," p. 13.

einem Aufschrei der Freude oder des Schreckens und zu eingreifenden Maßnahmen."[22] Once issues, dilemmas, taboos are "named" the reader is virtually compelled to contribute directly to his own cultural emancipation by continuing with the fragmented "naming." "Sprich weiter!" is Hein's exhortation in *Horns Ende* (p. 99 and passim).[23]

The "naming" of the Claudia-character has evoked an overwhelming reaction from readers, who continue the discussion. Hein reported on the initial reception of the work:

> Es gab ein heftiges Dafür und ein heftiges Dagegen. Ich war als Autor glücklich. Es gab keine Gelassenheit, sondern man reagierte sehr persönlich. Ich habe es selten erlebt, daß Kritiker auf eine solch persönliche Art und Weise reagierten. Auf einmal fielen alle wissenschaftlichen Kriterien beiseite, und sie teilten im Grunde etwas über sich selber mit.[24]

Hein observed that readers tend not to speak about the book itself, "sondern über die Frage: 'Wie kann ich leben?'"[25] They thus continue the dialogue, fulfilling the goal of Hein's literary program, that is, "daß über unseren Stand der Zivilisation gesprochen wird . . . , über Kosten . . . , die dieses durch die Produktionsweise notwendige Leben uns erbracht hat."[26] The character of Claudia provokes a response, an evaluation, a diagnosis, a moral judgment, because for the reader one thing is sure: he does not want his life to be like Claudia's.

---

[22] Hein, "Worüber man nicht reden kann," p. 12.

[23] Cf. also *Die wahre Geschichte des Ah Q*, where Wang remarks about the au - dience: "sie sollen sich selber was denken" (p. 107).

[24] Murray and O'Brian, "Interview mit Christoph Hein," p. 56.

[25] Murray and O'Brian, p. 57.

[26] Christoph Hein, "Die Intelligenz hat angefangen zu verwalten und aufge - hört zu arbeiten," p. 155.

The Possibility of Possibility in Franz Fühmann's *Saiäns-Fiktschen*

Stephen Brockmann

In 1976 Franz Fühmann published a science-fiction story entitled "Die Ohnmacht" in *Sinn und Form*.[1] This story was to become the first in a series of stories eventually collected and published in book form as *Saiäns-Fiktschen* by Hinstorff in 1983. In 1985, the year after Fühmann's death, Reclam published this little book in a paperback edition, making it available to a wider audience.[2]

Saiäns-Fiktschen consists of seven interconnected short stories dealing with the characters Janno, Pavlo, and Jirro, three scientists working in the imaginary country of Uniterr around the year 3,483. The world has experienced two nuclear wars since the second millenium and is now divided into two rival power blocs, Janno-Pavlo-Jirro's Uniterr and the opposing world of Libroterr — a constellation reminiscent of the two opposing power blocs of the late twentieth century.

The three central stories of the book are "Die Ohnmacht," "Das Duell," and "Pavlos Papierbuch." The other four stories — "Der Haufen," "Das Denkmal," "Die Straße der Perversionen,"

[1] Franz Fühmann, "Die Ohnmacht," *Sinn und Form*, 28, No. 1 (1976), 86-108.

[2] Franz Fühmann, *Saiäns-Fiktschen* (Rostock: Hinstorff, 1983; Leipzig: Philipp Reclam jun., 1985). All subsequent page references will be to the Reclam edition. Fühmann spells the book's title in such a strange way in order to distinguish the book from ordinary science fiction and to fend off readers' complaints that his stories do not live up to the science-fiction tradition (p. 5). Very little has been published on *Saiäns-Fiktschen* in either the East or the West, as scholars have tended to focus on Fühmann's earlier and better-known works. Three exceptions will be mentioned below. Of the various eulogists on Fühmann after his death, the only one who explicitly mentions *Saiäns-Fiktschen* is Wieland Förster, Fühmann's close friend, in a *Sinn und Form* (37, No. 2 [1985], 287-97) interview with Peter Liebers, but only to express his dislike for the stories.

and "Bewußtseinserhebung" — flesh out the literary world with details, but the three central stories provide all the key elements of the book and form a consistent story by themselves.[3]

The protagonist of this series is Pavlo, an alcoholic scientist ("Diplomkausalitätler") at the Institut zur Erforschung von Zukunftsstrukturen (ZS for short). "Die Ohnmacht," which begins the book, actually shows Pavlo at the *end* of his career; his working area is located at the dead end of a long corridor in the red (for least secret) zone, where he has invented a machine that allows people to see brief episodes from their own immediate future. "Das Duell," in the center of the book, shows the beginning of Pavlo's career, when as a student of the "Kausalitätswissenschaften" he experiences a traumatic episode in the history of late medieval Europe by means of a device that allows people to look into the past. And the last story, "Pavlos Papierbuch," occupies the chronological middle of Pavlo's story, when for a brief period he stops drinking and begins to read "Papierbücher" from the distant past.

The central acts in the first two stories thus involve the film-like vision of the individual future and the social past, while the third story centers on the individual act of reading a book, an activity which has been virtually forgotten in Uniterr, where books have been replaced by computers and reading machines, and the act of reading has lost the sensory qualities associated with a book which one can pick up and hold in one's hands.

On the level of *erzählte Zeit*, the tripartite structure works from the end to the beginning to the middle: future-past-present. At the same time this structure reflects the content of the stories themselves: the first story relates the process of seeing into the future; the second, that of seeing into the past; and the third story concerns the continuous and active present of reading. Fühmann's book thus becomes at its deepest level a reflection on the meaning of time, both in form and in content. In this dystopia the questions of time and free will are inextricably intertwined. While the attempt to control the future, to pin it down to one series of outcomes, creates the

---

[3] "Das Denkmal" and "Die Straße der Perversionen" provide glimpses of the egotism and debauchery of Libroterr; "Der Haufen" is an exercise in Uniterran scholasticism as Jirro tries to define what a "Haufen" is by using Uniterr's great philosophers as authorities; and "Bewußtseinserhebung" is a nightmarish story about Janno's indoctrination.

"Ohnmacht" — impotence — of the first story, the search for the past almost becomes a liberating experience.

"Die Ohnmacht" provides the introduction to the problem of time and free will. At the end of his career, Pavlo, the down-and-out scientist of causality, has been reduced to a mere sideshow. The machine he has invented, which allows people to see a small portion of their future, works by means of what Janno, his higher-level colleague, calls the "AK Sog" — the anti-causation force. This reverses normal causality, so that the present causes the past, rather than vice versa. It is no longer the stamping of a foot which causes a noise; it is a noise which causes the stamping of the foot. In this anti-causal world time works backwards, just as Fühmann's book itself works backwards. Janno refers to this as anti-teleology: development away from, as opposed to towards, something.

Seeing into the future disrupts causality and at the same time negates the possibility of free will, which is the crux of the problem in "Die Ohnmacht." The subjects in Pavlo's lab are determined to prove their free will by doing the exact opposite of what they see themselves doing in the future: if they see themselves sitting, then they will stand, but if they see themselves standing, they will sit. Of course these attempts at free will fail, and in every instance the subjects are frustrated by the irrefutable proof of their own impotence: if they see themselves sitting, they sit; and if they see themselves standing, they stand. Their future is determined, at least to the extent that they have seen it. Causation works backwards, not forwards, so that human beings are completely determined by what has not yet occurred.

But another possibility exists. If the subject had not insisted on looking into his own future — if he had managed to resist the fascination and pull of the "AK-Sog," none of this would have happened and the future would have been different. The subject's desire to know the future actually changes the future, closes it down, removing even the possibility of free will. The "AK-Sog" is here not just a science-fiction wrinkle in space/time; it is also the strange attraction humans have to trying to find out what by definition is the very negation of their own free will: knowledge of the future. It is their perverse fascination with their own subjugation. It is no accident that the hallway leading to Pavlo's laboratory is decorated with a picture of "des großen Aufklärers Christian Wolff optimistisches Lächeln" (p. 14). Wolff is the epitome of the optimistic free-will spirit of the Enlightenment that "Die Ohn-macht" contradicts. Pavlo's experiment makes a mockery of Wolff, instead proving David Hume's denial of a necessary relationship between cause and effect, and thus discounting the value of everyday human experience and observation, which teach that causes must precede and determine their effects, and that the past is unalterable, while the future is open. In this world it is the future which is unalterable, and the past is shaky ground. This is not Leibniz's or Wolff's best of all possible worlds; it is the worst of all possible worlds, a world deprived of other possible worlds and completely closed. This is all there is, a prescribed future without free will. Here the individual is meaningless, lost in a merciless and uncaring determinism. This realization causes Pavlo to become a cynical alcoholic.

But if the future is so dreadful, what of the past? At one point Janno notes: "Das Knifflige ist die Vergangenheit; die Zukunft liegt doch offen da" (p. 16). At another point the past is again made to seem mysterious:

> "Und das Vergangene?" fragte der Gast. . . .
> "Verzeih," sagte Janno schließlich mühsam,
> "doch das fällt in unsere Geheimhaltungs-
> pflicht — die Institutionsordnung, du ver-
> stehst doch . . ." (p. 24)

Thus the great mystery is not the future; it is the past. If knowledge of the future evokes "Ohnmacht," then what does knowledge of the past cause? These questions lead directly to the center of the *Saiäns-Fiktschen* world, the story "Das Duell," which shows Pavlo as a young student, not yet an alcoholic, at the crucial turning point of his career: the point at which he decides to abandon the past and work only with the future, and the point at which he begins to drink and turn into the alcoholic scientist — the future which has already been glimpsed in "Die Ohnmacht."

The conceit of "Das Duell" is very similar to that of "Die Ohnmacht": the technology of the fourth millenium allows human beings to recapture light waves that escaped the earth many centuries ago, thus making it possible literally to look back into the past. This is not written history seen through the abstract filter of the historian; it is every historian's dream, the experiencing of history as it actually happened, in all its sensory immediacy: real and tangible, filled with the excitement of living possibility.[4]

For Pavlo, a young student of causation interested in history because he assumes "daß die Gesetze der Kausalität auch in der Geschichte der Menschheit hervortreten müßten" (p. 78), and for the rest of Uniterr's historians as well, this "ocular demonstration" is to supply visual evidence of the infallibility of Uniterr's historiography. It is intended to prove the causal chain of history which works backwards from Uniterr to more primitive forms of social organization. All of these earlier forms had their chief historical value in the fact that they were stepping stones on the long, inexorable road to Uniterr itself, which is the goal and end, the telos and the final cause of world history.

But something happens to Pavlo and the rest of the viewers in the lecture hall. Instead of absolute certainty, they experience a strange kind of excitement and curiosity ("dies untilgbare Menschenrecht," p. 82):

> Es war nicht die Erwartung des Vorhergewußten (mit der etwa ein Kind sein Märchen erwartet), sondern die eines gänzlich Neuen (wenn groteskerweise auch eines Vergangnen); eines Ungekannten also, das nicht Ungekanntes im Sinne eines für den Ereignisfall noch nicht Festgelegten aus einem Vorrat an Geläufigem war, sondern ein dem Betrachter absolut Unbekanntes oder, um es endlich exakt zu fassen: *die Möglichkeit solch eines Unbekannten.* Sie trat nicht als Begriff ins Bewußtsein: Sie war ja in einer Notwendigkeit, die sich als das notwendig Alternativlose dargab, etwas, das gar nicht gedacht werden konnte.[5]   (p. 85)

In Uniterr, a place absolutely devoid of possibilities and alternatives, a place where the role of science and scholarship is merely to prove what is already known, the possibility of the

---

[4] This is Ranke's history "wie es eigentlich gewesen," but it is also strangely subjective and entirely in keeping with Fühmann's emphasis on the personal.

[5] Emphasis mine.

unknown which the concrete past represents is so enticing that one dare hardly even think about it:

> es war die Möglichkeit jeden Geschehens, unbegrenzt, wie Sehnen wäre, wüchse es nicht in Verkümmerung auf. — Im Gefüge des wirklichen Nur-Einen *die Möglichkeit von Möglichkeiten als Möglichkeit eines Anderen*: Pavlo erfuhr sie zum ersten Mal, als Betroffensein von etwas Unfaßbarem, das, sich allen Worten entziehend, als Grauen wie Lust eines Ahnens aufdämmerte, sie könnte und könne, diese vollzogne Geschichte, sich in einer anderen Weise vollziehen, als Uniterrs Historologie sie festgelegt und man sie daher auch erwartet hat.[6]
>
> (p. 84)

The exciting thing here is the very possibility of possibility, the possibility that this is not the only possible world, that Leibniz and Wolff were right after all. But this possibility is not necessarily dependent on proof that Uniterr's historiography is false. The point is not the truth or falsity of particular historical conclusions; rather, it is the method by which one reaches those conclusions. With regard to the duel that Pavlo observes, Uniterr's historians have always contended that previous unenlightened historians in the service of the bourgeoisie sought to cover up the victory of the lower-class swineherd against his noble adversary. While pre-Uniterran historiography claims that the mighty count beat the lowly swineherd, Uniterran historians claim the opposite: that the battle ended in a victory for the oppressed over their oppressor, a crucial breakthrough of freedom on the road to Uniterr.

When the ocular demonstration is suddenly cut off at a command from on high, the naïve assumption is that the interruption comes because the actual history of the event contradicts Uniterr's historians. But in an ironic twist at the end of the story, it turns out that Uniterr's historians were right after all about the outcome of the duel: their postulate was correct. It is the *method* of the ocular demonstration that challenges Uniterr's historical method. And here Pavlo comes to the crux of the issue in his long interior monologue. For the third time he reflects on the formula "possibility of possibili-

---

[6] Emphasis mine.

ties," and he realizes that, no matter what the outcome of the duel, the sensual concreteness of the demonstration is the diametrical opposite of the abstract certainty that Uniterr stands for:

> In diese Erwartungslosigkeit abstrakter Ge-
> wißheit brach also das Unerwartete ein, das
> — um es ein drittes Mal zu sagen — *die*
> *Möglichkeit aller Möglichkeiten als Wirk-*
> *lichkeit des Anderen* war. Denn das Kon-
> krete ist schon dadurch, daß es konkret ist,
> das Andere zu einem Abstrakten, das An-
> schauliche das Andre zum Unanschaubaren,
> und wo Geschichte als ein Andres sich
> zeigt, wird sie schon in ihrer äußeren Er-
> scheinung das, was sie ihrem Wesen nach
> ist: die Daseinsform von Alternative.[7]
>
> (p. 86)

History thus becomes the most radical of all possible fields of study, and it is now clear why in the first story it is Janno's and not Pavlo's research that is top secret. The three-fold development in Pavlo's meditations runs from the recognition of the possibility of the unknown ("die Möglichkeit solch eines Unbekannten") through the recognition of the possibility of differentness ("die Möglichkeit von Möglichkeiten als Möglichkeit eines Anderen") to the recognition of the concrete revolutionary reality of otherness that the past brings: "die Möglichkeit aller Möglichkeiten als Wirklichkeit des Anderen." In history as it is experienced here there is concrete proof of the fact that reality is dynamic and changing, that it is possible for other kinds of personal and social formations to exist than those one is used to, and, ultimately, as Pavlo recognizes in a moment of electric excitement: "daß es möglich war, nicht Uniterr zu sein" (p. 86).

In spite of the fact that the demonstration does indeed prove the correctness of at least one of Uniterr's historical postulates, it nevertheless must be broken off because of the destructive, anti-social quality of the "Alternativsyndrom" (p. 87) that sensory experience of the past brings. In Fühmann's imaginary world, knowledge of the future brings slavery, but knowledge of the past brings a strange and frightening kind of freedom.

---

[7] Emphasis mine.

Pavlo is not strong enough for this freedom. Provoked by the past to an intense form of introspection, he suddenly thinks that by changing himself he will also be able to change Uniterr — although he has no idea of what changing himself would really mean:

> [Pavlo] glaubte . . . das Verändern seiner selbst als jähe Möglichkeit zu erkennen, auch Uniterr verändern zu können, und im festen Glauben, daß solches geschähe, sagte er in selig-bewußter Verträumtheit, er beantrage einen Wissenschaftlichen Disput.
>
> (p. 96)

The "Wissenschaftlicher Disput" ("WISDIS" for short) ends with a conclusion exactly opposite to Pavlo's experience of the ocular demonstration. Pavlo believes: "Wenn die Schau etwas demonstrieren konnte, dann den Widerspruch der Theorie der Wahrhaft Wahren Geschichte zu der Realität der Geschichte selbst" (p. 105). But Pavlo's professor shows the opposite with a perfect illustration of Uniterr's scholastic logic: the ocular demonstration

> sei als glänzendste Bestätigung Wahrhaft Wahrer Geschichtsbetrachtung von schier unermeßlicher Bedeutung: habe sie doch sinnenfällig, unwiderleglich und jedermann faßbar die vergangenen finsteren Zeiten, die in Uniterr endgültig überwunden, als wahrhaft finster und wahrhaft vergangen und somit endgültig überwunden gezeigt.
>
> (p. 106)

This is, of course, a contradiction in terms; it is precisely the sensuousness and tangibility of the ocular demonstration which makes it so concrete for Pavlo, showing him that in a strange way the past is *not* "endgültig überwunden" but lives on in the present as the possibility of alternatives.

Pavlo does not change Uniterr; rather, Uniterr changes Pavlo. In the face of immense pressure from his professors and the spectators at the WISDIS, Pavlo realizes that he has nothing to say. He has not thought carefully enough about what changing himself means, and he becomes a victim of his own foolish and immature hope. Rather than reflecting quietly upon what the ocular demonstration might really mean, Pavlo automatically assumes that it proves the opposite of what Uniterr's historians had thought, and thus he involves himself in empty negation which is easily refuted by his professor. He becomes a mere nay-sayer, no more free than history's yesmen.[8]

The third story, "Pavlos Papierbuch," begins where "Das Duell" left off, during the time between Pavlo's defeat in the duel with his professor and his final appearance in "Die Ohnmacht." This is a time of introspection and reflection, for here Pavlo is seen reading, and the emphasis is no longer on the almost film-like passive vision of the earlier stories; it is on the act of reading itself, which involves individual action. While reading, Pavlo has the chance to insert his own thoughts and predictions, and so "Pavlos Papierbuch" is, as the title implies, a combination of the book and Pavlo's reactions to it.

The year is 3,483, and the book Pavlo is reading dates all the way back to 1998. It is different from anything Pavlo has ever experienced before; reading Kafka's "In der Strafkolonie," Pavlo makes many predictions about what will happen, for he thinks he already knows the future of the book — as he knows the future of the experimental subject in the earlier — or later — story "Die Ohnmacht." He is nonplused when his predictions prove to be incorrect. Again he senses the kind of excitement he had felt during the ocular demonstration of the past: "diese Spannung! — wiewohl man doch das Ende wußte, aber ehe man dahin kam!" (p. 146).

However, Pavlo does *not* know what will happen. Instead of the morality tale he is expecting, he gets a riddle. The condemned man and the soldier do not rebel against the officer; rather, the officer condemns himself. Pavlo's disappointment is almost palpable: "Aber das war doch niemals ein Ende! Wo wurde denn erklärt, wer gut und wer schlecht war, wer recht und wer unrecht hatte, wem man nacheifern sollte und wen entlarven . . ." (p. 147).

---

[8] At the end of the story Pavlo sees a jelly fish, which he is trying to reach when the story breaks off. The amorphous jelly fish recalls Fühmann's note in the introduction that he had been fascinated by science-fiction stories on the "*Denkstruktur von Seesternwesen, die, ihrer radialen Anlage entsprechend, keine Entweder-Oder-Entscheidungen, sondern nur Positionsbestimmungen auf der Skala eines Kontinuums kennen*" (p. 5). (Italics are Fühmann's.) Pavlo is unable to achieve this rejection of either-or thinking.

Moreover, where was the happy ending? Where was the evidence that all was right with the world? Pavlo is not used to the freedom that this kind of story gives him. Accustomed to being told the meaning of everything, he becomes uncertain when he has to figure it out for himself. Reading this book has suddenly created a kind of open world for him, and the openness frightens him.

Pavlo's experience is repeated when he reads the other two stories. "Die Marter der Hoffnung" by Villiers de l'Isle-Adam tells of a condemned Jew who is toyed with by his Jesuit inquisitor, who intentionally leaves the Jew's prison cell unlocked so as to give him the false hope that he will be able to escape being burned to death. The third story, "Der Nasen-stüber," is the account of a brutalized concentration camp prisoner whose captors heighten his anticipation of punishment in order to destroy him morally. The prisoner is ultimately murdered and disposed of.

In a strange way Pavlo comes to identify with the prisoners' tragic fate, for the structure of the book he has just finished bears a remarkable resemblance to the story of his own life as reflected in *Saiäns-Fiktschen:* a tripartite structure beginning with the nightmare world of self-condemnation in "In der Strafkolonie," followed by the vision of imprisonment and dashed hope of gaining freedom in "Die Marter der Hoffnung," and then by the experience of a concentration camp in the Third Reich. The similarity can be carried even further: both "Die Ohnmacht" and Kafka's story deal with the machinery of destruction and self-destruction produced by personalities in thrall to authority. "Das Duell" and "Die Marter der Hoffnung" create visions of the past and a false hope that is quickly destroyed. "Pavlos Papierbuch," in its self-reflective description of the expectations generated by the reading process, raises questions about openness, closure, and sanity also touched on in the meting out or withholding of punishment in "Der Nasenstüber."

All three stories revolve around one central problem which is also Pavlo's problem: human subjectivity in its struggle with and obeisance to power. As Pavlo comes to the end of the last horrifying story he becomes painfully aware of his own present, and suddenly he remembers a line from the Kafka story that he had passed over earlier: ". . . es war armes, gedemü-tigtes Volk" (p. 157). These words become an eerie comment on the *Saiäns-Fiktschen* world itself, where an entire people has had its subjectivity brutalized and a cheap optimism is used to cover over the real horror of existence. Pavlo wants his happy ending not because it is true, but because he cannot face the truth; the openness that he experiences in the world of the stories is intolerable to him. The happy ending would make him feel better, just as alcohol does.

When Pavlo finishes his "Papierbuch" at the end of the third story, Fühmann's readers have likewise come to the end. Like Pavlo, they are forced by the author's artifice to reflect self-consciously on their reading and their own present. As the West German critic Lothar Köhn points out, the structure of the stories "leitet das Leserinteresse nicht ins Irreale, sondern zu sich selbst zurück."[9] Protagonist and reader form a system of reflecting literary mirrors.

Like Pavlo, the reader now finds himself back in his own real world, in this case the present-day reality of the German Democratic Republic, in which and for which Fühmann wrote his book. It would be easy to draw the conclusion that what the reader has read is nothing more than an allegory attacking present-day reality in the East and West; the connection between Uniterr and Libroterr and the East and West blocs is obvious. As Köhn maintains, "Hinter Uniterr und Libroterr sind unschwer die politischen Machtblöcke zu erkennen . . . (p. 183).

There are clear parallels with the GDR. The strong critique of a hermetic teleological historiography in "Das Duell" is, for example, an obvious allusion to GDR and Marxist historiography in general, which sees the past as the prelude to the inevitable triumph of the proletariat over the bourgeoisie and the subsequent end of history in an earthly paradise of genuine communism. It would be ingenuous to think that Fühmann did not intend this.

On the other hand, although perhaps not for the same reasons, one can agree with the GDR critic Dieter Schiller, who deemphasizes interpreting Uniterr as "das satirische Zerrbild unserer Gegenwart."[10] While Schiller's avoidance of the alle-

---

[9] Lothar Köhn, "Vergangenheitssprachen: Christa Wolfs 'Kassandra,' Franz Fühmann's 'Saiäns-Fiktschen,' und 'Der Sturz des Engels,'" *Michigan German Studies*, 8, Nos. 1-2 (1985), 183.

[10] Dieter Schiller, "Franz Fühmann: Saiäns-Fiktschen," *Weimarer Beiträge*, 29, No. 2 (1983), 352.

gorical East-West implications of the story may be careful diplomacy, it seems wrong to suggest that Fühmann intended a one-to-one allegorical correlation with present-day reality. As Heinz Entner indicates, allegory is "das Festgelegte, Nichtüberschreitbare, und ihr einziger Reiz besteht in der Mühe herauszubekommen, welcher 'Sinn' denn nun darin verkleidet ist."[11] Entner cites Jean Paul Sartre's equating of freedom and literature: "sie [eröffnet] dem Leser eine Unendlichkeit von Verstehenshorizonten, die nicht Sicht-Ender sind, sondern Grenzen, die überschritten sein *wollen*, die zum Überschreiten locken . . ." (p. 155). The central feature of Fühmann's book is the rejection of "Sicht-Ender" and insistence on a complex process of interpretation and self-questioning leading to the overcoming of boundaries.

In his introduction to *Saiäns-Fiktschen* Fühmann writes that the work is in no way a closed system, but rather intends to show the painful result of such closure and stagnation, while itself remaining open:

> *Sie sind, diese Geschichten, insgesamt Schlußpunkte, im Bereich gestockter Widersprüche, wo Stagnation als Triebkraft auftritt. — Entwicklung als Entwicklungslosigkeit. — Der Schlaf der Vernunft, sagt Goya, gebäre Ungeheuer; das Stocken des Widerspruchs treibt Monstren heraus. (p. 6)*

Fühmann stresses that he wrote the stories in order to overcome "eine existentielle Lähmung" (p. 5); he exorcised his fears by driving them to their bitterest extreme in an "irreale Endzeit, Summe und Konsequenz all des Negativen, das die sich bildende Menschheit entäußert" (p. 6). Fühmann describes his method as "fearing something through to the end," as opposed to "thinking something through to the end," and he notes that his fears "*zwar der Realität entstammen, sie doch, die Realität, wohl maßlos überschreiten*" (p. 5). *Saiäns-Fiktschen*, then, is not an allegory, though it certainly has elements of the allegory in it; rather, it is an exercise in the imagination of fear in order to overcome that fear. It is a nightmare about what happens when, in a world completely dominated by authority, possibility no longer exists.

---

[11] Heinz Entner, "Facetten des Phantastischen: Träume und Alpträume," *Neue Deutsche Literatur*, 30, No. 7 (1982), 155.

On the one hand, this authority is certainly the state, but Pavlo is partly to blame for his own subjugation; he bears the state within himself. Fühmann notes in the introduction that everything begins with the personal — not the political — realm (p. 6); and the emphasis throughout is on the subjective experience of the individual who desires, in spite of himself, to be controlled. Köhn correctly underscores the subjectivity of the stories, "den subjektiv-existentiellen Ausgangspunkt, der sich in Fühmanns Werk seit dem Judenauto (1962) zunehmend verschärft hat" (p. 181). The GDR critic Schiller, on the other hand, criticizes this subjective point of departure; he sees as "das eigentliche Problem der Geschichten" the fact "daß . . . der 'persönliche Bereich' es ist, wo 'alles anfängt'":

> so gerät der Autor in die Gefahr, das spontane Ausscheren seiner Figuren, ihren aus unbewußten Reaktionen gespeisten Widerstand gegen verinnerlichte Verhaltensnormen und klischierte ideologische Muster zum entschiedensten Moment individueller Selbstbestätigung und Selbstbehauptung werden zu lassen. (p. 352)

Schiller's dislike for Fühmann's subjectivity reflects official GDR literary criticism — views to which Fühmann clearly stands in opposition. If Fühmann's intention in writing the stories was to free himself from the paralysis and impotence of stagnation and lack of contradiction — to reject the situation of Pavlo — then this is the task of Fühmann's reader as well. The act of reading should become a declaration of spiritual independence.

Contributors to *Studies in GDR Culture and Society 8*

Authors

Lothar Bisky, Cultural Sociologist, *Rektor*, Hochschule für Film und Fernsehen der DDR "Konrad Wolf," Potsdam-Babelsberg.

Stephen Brockmann, Ph.D. candidate in German, University of Wisconsin, Madison.

Christine Cosentino, Germanist, Professor, Department of German, Rutgers University, Camden, New Jersey.

Wolfgang Ertl, Germanist, Associate Professor, Department of German, University of Iowa.

Gary Geipel, Ph.D. candidate in International Relations, Columbia University.

Irma Hanke, Political Scientist, *Privatdozentin*, Institut für Sozialwissenschaften, Technische Universität München.

Heinz Kersten, Film and theater critic, West Berlin.

Heinz Knobloch, Author and feuilletonist for the East Berlin *Wochenpost*.

Manfred Lötsch, Sociologist, Professor, Akademie für Gesellschaftswissenschaften beim ZK der SED.

Nancy Lukens, Germanist, Associate Professor, Department of German and Russian, University of New Hampshire.

Phillip S. McKnight, Germanist, Associate Professor, Department of Germanic Languages and Literatures, University of Kentucky.

Richard L. Merritt, Political Scientist, Professor, Department of Political Science and Institute of Communications Research, University of Illinois at Urbana-Champaign.

Magdalene Mueller, Germanist, Assistant Professor, Department of Germanic Languages, Columbia University.